And Still The Hour Shines ...

Verse By Verse Through The Sermon On The Mount

Stephen M. Crotts

CSS Publishing Company, Inc., Lima, Ohio

AND STILL THE HOUR SHINES ...

Copyright © 2009 by
CSS Publishing Company, Inc.
Lima, Ohio

All rights reserved. No part of this publication may be reproduced in any manner whatsoever without the prior permission of the publisher, except in the case of brief quotations embodied in critical articles and reviews. Inquiries should be addressed to: Permissions, CSS Publishing Company, Inc., 517 South Main Street, Lima, Ohio 45804.

Scripture quotations, unless otherwise marked, are from the Revised Standard Version of the Bible, copyrighted 1946, 1952 ©, 1971, 1973, by the Division of Christian Education of the National Council of the Churches of Christ in the USA. Used by permission.

Scripture quotations marked (NRSV) are from the New Revised Standard Version of the Bible, copyright 1989 by the Division of Christian Education of the National Council of the Churches of Christ in the USA. Used by permission.

Scripture quotations marked (NIV) are from the Holy Bible, New International Version. Copyright © 1973, 1978, 1984 International Bible Society. Used by permission of Zondervan Bible Publishers. All rights reserved.

Library of Congress Cataloging-in-Publication Data

Crotts, Stephen M.
   And still the hour shines— : verse by verse through the Sermon on the mount / Stephen M. Crotts.
   p. cm.
   ISBN 0-7880-2607-0 (perfect bound : alk. paper)
   1. Sermon on the mount—Meditations. I. Title.

BT380.3.C76 2009
226.9'07—dc22

2008050531

For more information about CSS Publishing Company resources, visit our website at www.csspub.com or email us at csr@csspub.com or call (800) 241-4056.

Cover design by Barbara Spencer
ISBN-13: 978-0-7880-2607-2
ISBN-10: 0-7880-2607-0

PRINTED IN USA

To Greg and Sue Taylor,
two who make it possible to stay in the ministry.
You opened your home and hearts to Christ.

Table Of Contents

Foreword	7
Tired, Old Religion	
You Guys Are Gonna Be Different!	9
Poverty Of Spirit	15
Blessed Are Those Who ... What?	21
The Beautiful Attitude Of Humility	29
Happy The Hungry Hearts	37
The Beautiful Attitude Of Mercy	43
The Bliss Of A Clean Heart	51
Peacemaking: The Seventh Beatitude	57
The Bliss Of A Martyr's Way	65
No Salt In The City?	73
Light! More Light!	81
From Legalism To Obedience	89
Do The Old Rules Still Apply?	99
Anger: The Misunderstood Emotion	107
Adultery: Saying No And Knowing Why!	115
Lust: The Fire Inside	123
Divorce: The Deadlock Of Wedlock	129
A Woman's Place	137

Don't Waste Your Breath!	145
You Guys Are Really Gonna Be Different!	151
How To Treat Your Enemies	159
Is Pacifism Biblical?	167
Confessions Of A Healed Perfectionist	173
The Fine Art Of Giving	181
Prayer: Moving The Hands That Move The World	187
It's Called Forgiveness ... And It's On Your Exam!	195
Are You Going To(o) Fast?	203
Is Your Reward Waiting?	209
What Does The Bible Say About Materialism?	217
Television: The Plug-In Drug	227
How To Worry Like A Christian!	235
Of Logs And Specks ...	241
Praying Through	249
The Most Famous Thing Jesus Ever Said!	259
Door Number One Or Door Number Two?	263
The Heart Of The Matter	267
The Measure Of Success	271
Afterword	281

Foreword

Tired, Old Religion

The world is growing tired of religion. I'm tired of it, too. And not just tired; I am becoming fretful, even fearful.

Hindu and Muslim are at each other's throats in Pakistan and India. And they both have fingers on nuclear triggers. Judaism and Islam fight a never-ending duel in Palestine. Crying, "God is great!" Muslim suicide bombers devastate mosques and shatter lives. Israel builds a wall to seal itself away. Christians too often act brutishly as self-righteous know-it-alls. One wag said, "God is not dead. He's just embarrassed that we keep quoting him."

I tremble when I see secular governments, like France, distancing themselves from historic moral-valued religion, declaring the nation a public religion-free zone and in its place offering a man-centered secular humanism.

The problem is not religion. The problem is bad religion.

Anthropologists studying humankind have never found a single civilization without religion. Theology is not going away. It's here for good or ill for the duration as a human need.

All people seek God.

Just as we have a passion for food or profit or sexual expression, so, too, we have a passion for meaning. Hence we have religion — right or wrong. We have worship, we seek the truth, and we go to temple.

Religious passion unbridled by love can turn nasty real fast. I've seen it slander, ostracize, and divide. Historically, it has caused wars, cut off heads, and burned people at the stake.

Ah, but religious passion shaped like Christ, softened by his Spirit, started Harvard University, built Presbyterian Hospital, opened Thornwell Orphanage, and helped the poor.

We must get swiftly back to faith-based godliness that is kind, that meets human needs, or it becomes irrelevant, hated, and feared.

To regain our credibility in today's world, the faith I know, Christianity, must return to being shaped like Christ's beatitudes. His opening words in Matthew 5 ...

- "Blessed are the poor in spirit" ... not the arrogant self-religious.
- "Blessed are the mournful" ... as opposed to those who tout their spirituality in celebration.
- "Blessed are the meek" ... the teachable, not the know-it-alls.
- "Blessed are the hungry" ... not the smug, the full, or the satisfied.
- "Blessed are the merciful, the pure, the peacemakers" ... those who like Christ become suffering servants in this brutish world.

This is the shape of faith for the twenty-first century.
We can do this.
God's Spirit is ready to help.
The world is watching.
This season of quiet reflection and penance, I remind you, we will become softened, shaped into love ... or become lost in the carnage of brutish religious passion that will reduce our world to rubble.

All of this brings us to the opening pages of the New Testament. After Malachi, the final book of the Old Covenant, there were 400 years of silence, an era we call the intertestamental period. During that time, Greeks gave us right thinking and a common language. Romans gave us good government and safe travel. Jews gave us good religion and spiritual hunger.

Into this "fullness of time" Jesus Christ was born. He matured for thirty years, then he put down his carpenter tools, called twelve disciples to himself atop a hill, and broke 400 years of God-silence by voicing the most amazing message in human literature — the Sermon on the Mount.

In this hillside treatise is the shape of our faith. And still the hour shines for us to hear it, to wrap our flesh around it, and to live it.

— Stephen M. Crotts

You Guys Are Gonna Be Different!

When Jesus saw the crowds, he went up the mountain; and after he sat down, his disciples came to him. Then he began to speak, and taught them, saying....
— Matthew 5:1

It's the most famous sermon Jesus ever preached — The Sermon on the Mount. However, just because it is well known does not mean it is well understood, much less well obeyed.

We begin a study of it in hopes that in the end we can each wrap our flesh around Christ's Sermon on the Mount and go live it in the world.

As we begin, it is vital to comprehend the context in which Christ preached his message. There are four points that must be understood.

Master

The first point is about how Christ chose God the Father.

We know precious little about the first thirty years of Jesus' life. We know he grew in wisdom and in stature and in favor with God and man. We know that by age twelve Christ understood the scriptures so well he was able to converse impressively with the elders in the temple at Jerusalem. We think his father, Joseph, died during his teenage years, leaving him the oldest son and, thus, the breadwinner for his mother, Mary, and several brothers and sisters. Until he was thirty, Christ dutifully ran the carpentry shop and provided for his family.

Then suddenly it was as if Christ Jesus knew the hour had struck. He put his younger brother, James, in charge of the shop and set out as an itinerant preacher.

His first stop was Gilgal on the west bank of the Jordan River. There John the Baptist was calling for Israel to repent. As a symbolic gesture, each who responded passed through the waters of the Jordan River. Jesus believed John's message and he was baptized. The question is "Why?" Was it for the washing away of his sins? No, for Christ was sinless.

The answer lies much deeper. Historically, when Joshua led Israel from Mount Nebo down into the Valley of Shittim, they crossed over the Jordan into the promised land at Gilgal. Thus the place was not unlike our Plymouth Rock. It was where Israel first came over and where they began as a nation.

Many of the ancient Jewish prophets often called Israel to return to Gilgal, contemplate their God and their behavior, and to renew their fidelity with the covenant.

By going to Gilgal and baptizing, John was saying the old Israel was dead, apostate. He preached for a new Israel to pass through the Jordan River and become a nation.

Methods

Now that Christ had chosen God the Father and his new Israel as the master, he next selected his methods of ministry. Matthew 4 fills in here with the temptation story.

The Spirit led Jesus into the wilderness where our Lord fasted for forty days. Then Satan, ever up to his old tricks, slithered up to try to entice Christ away from God the Father. Just as he did to Eve and Adam, so he did to Christ — he got him alone, twisted God's word, and even used food as a lure.

Satan sneered, "So you want to serve God? Fine! But look how hungry you are! Turn these stones into bread! That's the ticket! People love food! Feed their bellies and they'll follow you anywhere!" Jesus said, "Man shall not live by bread alone, but by every word that proceeds from the mouth of God."

Then Satan took Christ to the pinnacle of the temple. "Jump!" he urged. "Crowds like magic tricks! Surely angels will catch you! That'd really dazzle the crowds! Such showmanship will insure a huge following!" All Christ said was, "Thou shalt not tempt the Lord thy God!"

Finally, Satan took Jesus to a high mountain and in a moment of time showed him all the kingdoms of history — Rome, Greece, the czars, England, and the USA. "This is mine," Satan preened, "and I give it to whom I will. I'll give it to you if you bow to me!" And Jesus rebuked the devil, saying, "It is written, you shall worship the Lord and Him only shall you serve."

Christ rejected being a materialistic belly-god of bread, a lord of dazzling magic tricks, and of occult power. First John calls all that the lust of the eyes, the lust of the flesh, and the pride of life: pleasure, power, and prestige.

Instead, Christ chose the methods of love, of suffering servanthood, and of the cross.

The Men

Now that Jesus had selected his master and his methods, he set about choosing his men. Matthew 4:18 (and following) tells of our Lord's call to Peter, James, John, Matthew, and Simon the Zealot, twelve in all. None of these men were rich. None were all that educated or powerful. Mostly they were fishermen. A few were government bureaucrats and a wealthy banker or two. Yet, Christ selected twelve no-names.

If one looks closely, these twelve did have something going for them. They were available. The Bible says Christ called them and "they left their nets" to follow him. They were teachable. Unlike the pharisaical know-it-alls, these twelve hadn't made up their minds what they believed yet. They were faithful. They trusted Christ; Peter trusted enough to actually step out of the boat and walk on water. And they were responsible. Jesus sent them out in pairs to minister. Each of them was willing to assume such a ministry.

Over the next three years of Christ's ministry, these twelve men were to be the primary focus of his work. The multitudes, the lukewarm — they got some of Jesus' attention, but it was the crumbs mostly. For it was these twelve, these faithful, available, responsible, and teachable men, who got the bread.

Sadly, in many a minister's priority and scheduling, it's the lukewarm and the worldly who devour the most of our time, and this shouldn't be! We should have time for the multitudes in every week, but every single one of us should be devoted to mentoring a small group of friends, perhaps a spouse, and our children, if the good Lord so blesses us.

The Message

So, Jesus chose his master, his methods, and his men. Now he chose his message, the Sermon on the Mount.

It's probably a mistake to call Matthew 5-7 one sermon. Jesus was a better preacher than to over-dazzle an audience with so much light. What the scriptures record for us in these three chapters is most likely a condensation, a summation of all Jesus taught over a weekend retreat.

Matthew 5:1-12 tells us Christ avoided the crowds and went up in the mountains calling only the twelve to himself. Such behavior should quicken your pulse. For the Lord is God of the mountains — Mount Sinai, Mount Moriah, Mount Carmel, and Mount Calvary. When God moves upon a mountain, something significant is in the offing!

A cursory reading of Christ's message usually results in astonishment. Many react to the sermon by calling it unrealistic, idealistic, and unworkable in the real world.

I'm told of a wife who liked to rearrange the household furniture. Her husband came home after a long business trip and found a note on the door: "Warning: New traffic patterns ahead. Stay alert!" This is basically what our Lord says in the Sermon on the Mount. At least six times Jesus says, "You have heard it said, but I say unto you: Love your enemy; go to the second mile. When slapped, turn the cheek. Give your cloak to one who asks."

Many read such pronouncements and recoil. "That's insane! No one can live like that!"

But G. K. Chesterton wrote, "The Sermon on the Mount is not a crazy message which our sane world cannot reasonably accept; it is rather absolute sanity preached to a world of lunatics."

One might say it's Jesus' sermon on how to live right-side-up in an upside-down world.

Standing alone, the beatitudes do seem irrelevant and unrealistic. But contrast Christ's words with their opposites and suddenly the message becomes intensely relevant!

Blessed are the poor in spirit as opposed to the proud, arrogant, and self-centered.

Blessed are the mournful as opposed to the indifferent, loveless, and jovial.

Blessed are the meek as opposed to the abusive, cocky, and overconfident.

Blessed are the hungry and thirsty for righteousness as opposed to the self-satisfied, sneaky, and ruthless.

The merciful as opposed to the unkind, unforgiving, and harsh.

The pure in heart as contrasted with the guilt-ridden, impure, and manipulative.

The peacemakers as opposed to the warmongers, troublemakers, and argumentative.

The persecuted for righteousness' sake as opposed to the fence-sitters, cowards, and compromisers.

Be quick to notice that after all of this astonishingly peaceful talk, Jesus ends this sermon with a threat: the parable of the wise and the foolish builders. "Hear and do what I say and you build on the rock. Hear and not follow my words? You build on sand and the storm will come and wash your life away," Jesus said.

So Jesus chose his master, his methods, his men, and his message. And if he didn't say anything else in his Sermon on the Mount, he most certainly said this: You guys are going to be different! He said that in a world of pain we'd stick out, not like a sore thumb, but like a healed thumb! We'd be different in our hunger for what's right, in our generosity, in our humility, in our peacemaking, our prayers, and our enduring quality of life.

What God told Israel in Isaiah 60 he tells us in the Sermon on the Mount: "Arise, shine, for thy light has come and the glory of the Lord has risen upon you. Nations shall come to the brightness of your rising."

Conclusion

A few winters ago, I was driving home from the mountains and, along with 200 other cars, got stuck on a mile-long hill that was glazed with ice. We were helpless to move without sliding into a ditch or each other. Suddenly, an old, yellow dump truck came up behind us, passed, and began to spread grit and salt on the road. A cheer went up, and within minutes, 200 helpless motorists began to find their traction and head home.

"Lord," I prayed, "thank you for that driver in the dump truck. Make me a Christian like that, able to change the very climate of our slippery, dangerous, freezing, helpless world!"

Suggested Prayer
Jesus, I hear what you're saying. Help me to do it. Amen.

Poverty Of Spirit

Blessed are the poor in spirit, for theirs is the kingdom of heaven.   — Matthew 5:3

Possibly the worst criticism anyone can level at us Christians is to say, "I've watched your life and you're no different than the rest of the world! You're just as greedy, malicious, and full of lust as I am!"

Admittedly, sometimes coming to church is like tossing a pebble into a lake. The pebble gets nice and wet on the outside, but the water never penetrates to the inside. Similarly, it's easy to come to church and allow the externals of the gospel to wash over our outer lives — how we dress, the cut of our hair, our speech, and so forth. All the while our inner life remains locked up tightly against any penetration by the gospel. Our conscience, our spirit, our values, and our attitudes remain unfazed by truth! We have a religion of outward show, but it's not life-changing.

Nowhere is the gospel's lack of penetration more evident than in the Sermon on the Mount. Oliver Wendell Holmes wrote, "Most people are willing to take the Sermon on the Mount as a flag to sail under, but few will use it as a rudder by which to steer."

We come now to the Beatitudes of Jesus, the first words of his most famous sermon. There are eight beatitudes in all. The first four deal with one's relationship with God. The last four deal with one's relationship with people.

Let's immerse ourselves in the first of these eight pronouncements of Jesus. Let's open our inner attitudes to God's beatitudes and find fulfillment in him.

Blessed

First, it is imperative that we understand the formula in which Christ presented the Beatitudes. The traditional English Bible translation reads, "Blessed are the poor in spirit, for theirs is the kingdom of heaven!" (NRSV). There is no "are" in the Greek original. A better translation is: "O the blessedness of the poor in spirit, for theirs is the kingdom of heaven!" Thus the first beatitude is not a simple declarative sentence, but an exclamation. It is an exclamatory remark meant to be shouted with excitement! "O the blessedness of the poor in spirit...!"

The word "blessed" is the word *makarios* in the Greek. It's the same word used for the island of Cyprus in the Mediterranean. Cyprus is known as "the Happy Island." It had it all in Christ's day. The saying was that a person need not go beyond its coastline to find joy. A fair translation of the first beatitude might be: "O the happiness of the poor in spirit, for theirs is the kingdom of heaven!"

To us moderns, happiness means feeling fine. "The wife and I are getting along. The children are behaving. My investments hit 12% last year. And it looks like I'll get that promotion at work!" Do you see how we base our happiness on our circumstances? The trouble with such happiness is that it is so fragile. Ninety percent of my life can be going just fine, but 10% going poorly can destroy my mood.

This is not the sort of happiness Christ is talking about. The Lord's blessedness or happiness is not what you feel but what is. Not what is temporary, but what is eternal. Not what you think of your circumstances, but what God thinks.

The Hebrew word for "blessed" has a word picture behind it — that of a kneeling camel. The idea is that a camel kneels so it can be loaded with silks, spices, treasure, and such, then gets up and joins a caravan taking its cargo to distant lands.

This is the picture in Psalm 68:19. "Blessed be the Lord who daily bears us up...."

The idea is that a camel is made to be "a ship of the desert." To be blessed, then, is to be like a camel, to be doing that which God put us here to do.

Back to the first beatitude. "O the blessedness of the happy islanders, O the loaded camels carrying treasure, O those happily fulfilled of God...." Thus our happiness in God is not a feeling but an abiding fulfillment, not what we think of our circumstances, but what God thinks.

That is the formula in which Jesus presented his beatitudes: the first fulfilling attitude.

Poor In Spirit

"O the blessedness of the poor in spirit, for theirs is the kingdom of heaven!"

Remember that the first four beatitudes have to do with one's relationship with God. Thus, having an attitude of spiritual poverty is the first principle Christ urges upon his disciples.

This has confused many Christians. Is Christ glorifying poverty? Yes, he is. But it is not physical poverty — lack of food and shelter. Rather, it is spiritual poverty — "poorness in spirit" that Christ is singling out.

In the Greek, "poor in spirit" means abject poverty, without resources, literally beaten to your knees — being so poor one can only look to God for solace. Thus, a literal translation of the first beatitude reads, "O the happiness of the person who realizes his complete spiritual poverty and puts all his trust in God, for his is the kingdom of heaven."

In Luke 18:9 (and following), Jesus told the parable of two men who went into the temple to pray. The first man was rich, proud, and self-righteous. He was a Pharisee. He stood in the most prominent place in the temple and preened like a peacock! Jesus said he "prayed thus with himself." He was not talking to God, but indulging in a kind of inner dialogue of self-congratulation. "I thank thee, Lord of heaven, that I am not like other men — adulterers, liars, and thieves. I pray five times a day, fast, and tithe."

The second man, a socially despised tax collector, hid in the shadows of the temple. He wouldn't even lift up his eyes to heaven! Rather he beat his breast and anguished in prayer, "Lord, have mercy on me, a sinner!"

I like to say the first man had one eye on himself, one eye on his neighbor, and no eye on God. The second man, however, had one eye on himself and one eye on God. And in comparing his character with the nature of God, he came away feeling poor and humble.

Jesus said the poor man went down to his house "justified," while the proud man went away "unjustified."

We've a saying here in North Carolina — "high and dry." It translates into this spiritual truth: high in ego, dry spiritually; high in pride, low (dry) with God; high in self, shriveled and dry in spirit and soul.

Do you want an example of this? Revelation 3:17 (and following) describes the church at Laodicia as very wealthy in education, material things, and social status, but very impoverished in the things of the Spirit: "For you say, I am rich; I have prospered and I need nothing; not knowing that you are wretched, pitiable, poor, blind, and naked." There you have it. High and dry. The more self-righteous we are, the less God-conscious we are.

One way we can tell we're growing spiritually is when we get more Calvinistic. By that I mean when we have a higher view of God and a lower view of self; a higher sense of God's sovereignty and a lower sense of our own plans. God's glory becomes everything. Our own glory becomes marginal. We become more concerned with being faithful than with being fruitful. Or, in short, I become convinced of my own utter poverty and yet become aware of God's incredible riches.

In the hymn, "Rock Of Ages, Cleft For Me," Augustus Toplady wrote, "Nothing in my hand I bring, simply to the cross I cling."

Jesus is saying that the disciples' relationship with God begins with a realization that there isn't one. And it continues from there with an ever-deepening understanding that only God is great. I am nothing. God is rich. I am poor.

It is helpful to study the apostle Paul here. When we first meet him in scripture he is a religious Pharisee strutting and preening himself in public, crowing self-righteously. Then he meets Jesus and quickly becomes singularly unimpressed with himself, while becoming overwhelmed with God's glory.

In 58 AD, he writes, "Paul an apostle — not from men nor through man, but through Jesus Christ" (Galatians 1:1).

In 63 AD, he writes, "The saying is sure, and worthy of full acceptance, that Christ Jesus came into the world to save sinners. And I am the chief of sinners." Note Paul did not say, "I *was* the chief of sinners." Poor in spirit, Paul says, "I *am* the chief of sinners."

The closer we get to God the more amazing his grace is. The more we realize all he is, the more we recognize all we are not.

"Nothing in my hand I bring, simply to the cross I cling!" Oh, Lord, it all depends on you!

Conclusion

Perhaps there is one of you reading this who has not known such truth. You have tried to establish your relationship with God by your own works. You've become devoutly religious. In the observance of rules you think you will earn your way back to God. Now you think you are better than others. Yet really on the inside you are tired, hard, and joyless.

You have one eye on yourself, one eye on your neighbor, and no eye on God. You are unjustified.

Good news! "O the blessedness of those who realize their complete spiritual poverty with God, theirs is the kingdom of God!"

Perhaps today you would look into the splendor of God and find your own raggedness. And kneeling like a camel, you'd ask God to load you with his rich grace.

Suggested Prayer

Lord, have mercy on me, a sinner. For Jesus' sake. Amen.

Blessed Are Those Who ... What?

Blessed are those who mourn, for they shall be comforted. — Matthew 5:4

I remember New Year's Day. The sadness. A gnawing ache. A restlessness. A deep sense of dissatisfaction. "Maybe you're just tired," I said to myself. "A touch depressed. Why don't you get some extra sleep, go see a funny movie, call an old friend, or get lost in a book?"

After all, I've been there before. I know what to do! When feeling depressed, if all else fails, read a good biography. You'll find out others had lives that weren't all that easy. John Wesley struggled in a difficult marriage. Robert Frost was past age forty when his first poem was published. George Fredrik Handel went bankrupt twice. This is life! This is the way living really is! It was then, is now, and ever shall be until Jesus comes!

Another ploy I use when down is to count my blessings. Let's see, 35 years of marriage to Kathryn. She's not only my best friend, but I get to take a long walk with her almost every day. We have three growing, healthy children, all Christians. I have good health. I don't think I missed a single day of work last year. I've been given the opportunity to preach on college campuses and impact a future generation. I've had four days of scenery and snow skiing in New Hampshire like you wouldn't believe! I have had a book accepted by a publisher, a chance to write for three national magazines, and enjoyed being part of a fine, local church with all her love and joy and challenge. I've enjoyed fixing up an old, stone house to live in. I was able to sit at the controls of an F-16 fighter jet, as well as piloting over the Grand Canyon. I've had the adventure of exploring and preaching across Bermuda. I've enjoyed driving around in an old, but restored, 1968 Mustang (even though the heater does not work!).

I said to myself, "Shouldn't that be about enough?" Still I wasn't perking up. I quoted Shakespeare to myself, the old priest's advice to Juliet, "A pack of blessings rests on your head, but thou, like a sullen and pouting wench, frowneth upon thy fortune!"

"Maybe you're just greedy," I mused. "You expect too much. You're just another overly ambitious preacher!"

"Or maybe," I feared, "it's repetition depression." You know. Last year was so wonderful, but can I do it again next year? Will there be more joy, more love, more faithfulness?

Still my spirits were low. So I sat down and seriously asked myself, "Just what is it you want, Stephen?" A new car? No. Another house? No. A boat? No. A fancy trip? No. A job that's different? No. New friends? No.

What I want is God. I don't want to sin anymore. I want the bridegroom to come. I don't want to have to look on human wreckage anymore. I want God's kingdom to come. I want to go to heaven. I want to look upon the face of Jesus.

No. I'm not suicidal. It's just a yearning, an unfulfilled longing, a grieving in my soul.

I'm not the only one who feels this way. I was having lunch with a businessman. He is one of those humans who has it all together — faith, spouse, children, career, looks, health, and income. We had a deep, brooding conversation for 45 minutes, and he confessed quite honestly, "I wonder what it'd be like to be really happy for ten minutes."

Jesus had a word about all this in his Sermon on the Mount. "Blessed are those who mourn, for they shall be comforted." The notion of mourning in this beatitude means grief or weeping or sadness. But it means more than crying over the death of a loved one. It also includes mourning over sinfulness, grief over loss of innocence, the sorrow of repentance. It is to feel the hurt God feels when he looks out over a sinful world.

The best translation of this passage is: "O the fulfillment of the unfulfilled. O the happiness of the unhappy." In the English language we recognize such a statement as oxymoronic. That's like "pretty ugly" or "rush hour" or "tax simplification" — two notions that don't belong together. Still Jesus utters his second beatitude: "O the blessedness of those who let God break their hearts with the things that break his heart. O the happiness of them that care, that feel, that cry over sin. They shall be comforted."

Some think the Christian life is all smiles and that we should try to be bubbly in the Spirit every moment of every day. But such an attitude flies in the face of Christ's second beatitude. It is more in keeping with the world's character than it is with God.

The world says, "Blessed are those who don't care, who don't get involved, the partygoers, the flippant, the high, those who insulate themselves, who live life in the fast lane, who go where the good is."

Jesus said, "O the fulfillment, the blessedness, the joy of those who care, who mourn, because God is going to bring in the day of comfort."

Did it ever occur to you that it is a sin to get too comfortable in this sinful, rebellious, and hurting world?

In Ezekiel 9, the Lord observed the wickedness of his people. He commanded his angels, "Go through the land ... and put a mark on the foreheads of all those who sigh and groan over sin. Then draw your sword and kill the rest! And begin at the temple!" (Ezekiel 9:4-6 cf).

Christ knew how to sigh and groan. He wept at John's funeral. He lamented Lazarus' passing. He cried over Jerusalem.

The psalmist wrote, "My eyes shed streams of tears, because men do not keep thy law" (Psalm 119:136).

In Philippians 3:18, Paul confessed, "For many, of whom I have often told you and now tell you even with tears, live as enemies of the cross of Christ."

Where is it one finds this sort of authentic sin-grief in our world today? In Durham, North Carolina, a jury was gathered to hear a case involving a brutal murder. A female juror, hearing the horrid details of drugs, rape, and homicide, was so overcome with the pain of it all she began to weep. She finally had to be dismissed.

I like that. For we today are far too calloused when we can look upon drunkenness, divorce, abuse, murder, lying, greed, sabbath breaking, and theft and never once feel so much as a twinge of heartache.

I see this beautiful attitude in the life and art of Vincent van Gogh, a turn-of-the-twentieth-century Dutch impressionist painter. As a young Christian, van Gogh sought ordination to the ministry. Since his education was inadequate, the only license to preach he could obtain was through a missionary society that sent him into the Belgian coal fields. Here were the poorest of the poor and van Gogh lived among them. He ate their food, shared their clothing, and preached his heart out.

The missions society, upon checking on him, found him to have become as starved, dirty, and ragged as his miners. He was fired for being an unfit reflection on the society.

Van Gogh began to paint out his grief. He used his canvas to show the world the face of coal miners and their abused plight. Over the next twenty years he finished 2,000 pictures.

Not one sold during his lifetime. Lonely, overlooked, unloved, some say van Gogh went insane. He shot himself and died two days later in a rented flat above a pool hall in France. His body was placed on a pool table. Many of his paintings were hung on the walls of the hall. He was laid to rest in obscurity.

My favorite van Gogh painting is titled *Starry Night Over The Rhone*. The viewer is on the shore of a lake. It is night and across the water is a town, the lights of a party, reveling happy couples making merry. Yet there is a cold, dark gulf separating the viewer from the fun. A feeling of isolation sweeps over you. But in the sky! Oh the sky! The stars burn brightly, like torches, lending a sense of hope from above.

Folk singer, Don McClean, wrote a song about van Gogh in which he laments: "For they could not love you, but still your love was true. And when no hope was left inside on that starry, starry night, you took your life as lovers often do. But I could have told you, Vincent, this world was never meant for one as beautiful as you."

I also see this godly grief in my friend, Jim. He and his wife were unable to have children of their own, so they adopted. A three-week-old baby girl was placed in their loving arms. They named her Joy. And together they set out to make a happy life. As the child grew, it became apparent something was seriously wrong. Her short attention span, volatile emotions, learning disabilities — all were symptoms of fetal alcohol syndrome. Evidently Joy's mom had drunk way too much alcohol during pregnancy and damaged the child. Joy will always struggle. She'll never have the life she should have. And Jim mourns.

A juror at a murder trial, a Dutch impressionist painter, an adoptive parent — they all teach us that some things in life are so awful that the only way we can handle them is by weeping. And when we weep, we find God with us.

Isaiah 53:3 describes Jesus as "a man of sorrows, and acquainted with grief."

There is a legend in Jewish folklore about "Lamed-Van-Tzaddkim." He is one of the ten righteous men by whose merit God allows the world to continue.

Recall Genesis 18:16-33. The two angels have set out to destroy Sodom and Gomorrah. Abraham greets them and invites them in for a meal, and learning of their mission pleads, "If you find ten righteous men in the city, will you show mercy?" (Genesis 18:32 cf). The Lord agreed.

According to rabbinical legend there was but one righteous man in Sodom. For many years he'd lived, taught, prayed, and encouraged his city to God. His labors were met only with scorn.

Still he begged his listeners to turn to God.

One day as he walked the streets of Sodom a child asked, "Poor stranger, why do you live here weeping and teaching us? You spend yourself body and soul, but can't you see it's hopeless?"

To which the righteous man replied, "When I first came here I thought I could change people. Now I know I can't. But if I keep crying and caring and praying I can at least keep them from changing me."

"O the happiness of the unhappy. O the fulfillment of the unfulfilled. O the blessedness of those who mourn, who let God break their hearts with what breaks his. O the joy of those who care, who weep, who can still feel. They shall be comforted, soothed, healed, and quieted."

I point out that there are large groups of Christians who promise to remove your grief. Some charismatics pledge to you a prosperity, an overflowing, so that you'll always live life on the peak.

Then there are some fundamentalists who look at mourning and say, "Buck it up! Pray harder. Do right. Open your Bible! There's no use feeling sad!"

There's the self-help book shelf at the Christian bookstore. Just fix yourself with a good read like *You Can Be Joyous Everyday*! Or *Blow Away the Dark Clouds of Depression Forever*! But I don't want my grief removed by anyone but Jesus!

Soon. So soon, my sisters and brothers! In that great getting up morning, fare thee well, fare thee well!

No more obesity! No more unemployment. No more scorn. No more cancer. No more alcoholism.

Arthritis? Gone forever! Loneliness? Vanquished! Old age? No more! Sin? History! Pain? A bygone! Rejection? A thing of the past! Death? Swallowed up in life!

What will it be like, then, to wake from sleep refreshed and find life an endless, pristine, celestial morning? What will it be like to raise an arm and find it strong, youthful, and new again? What will it be like on that distant shore to look into a mirror and see one's own face without wrinkles, fatigue, worry, or the ravages of time? What will it be like to look into the face of an old friend and see perfect companionship? What will it be like to stand and look on the face of Jesus, to be cuddled in his arms and have him wipe away every teardrop? What will it be like when we're comforted and can sing new songs of Zion without distraction, without hypocrisy, without the static of our feeble flesh?

I hear the voice of God say, "Behold, the dwelling of God is with men ... death shall be no more, neither shall there be mourning nor crying nor pain ... I make all things new!" (Revelation 21:3-5).

And the church says, "Even so, Lord, come!"

All of this God has taught me since New Year's Day. It's okay to feel sadness, to have unfulfilled longings, to grieve.

To do so is normal in a world like ours. It might not change anything, but it will surely keep the world from changing you.

"O the blessed fulfillment of those who mourn. They shall be comforted."

Suggested Prayer

Lord, let me feel as you feel, care as you care, mourn as you mourn. And on that day may I receive your comfort. Amen.

The Beautiful Attitude Of Humility

Blessed are the meek, for they shall inherit the earth.
— Matthew 5:5

The way of God's kingdom is opposite our modern way. We say, "Blessed are the self-righteous, those who don't lean on God, those who have it all together." Jesus says, "Blessed are the poor in spirit, those who realize their absolute spiritual poverty."

We say, "Blessed are those who laugh it up, who party down, who don't care, who won't be bothered." Jesus says, "Happy are the unhappy, who let God break their hearts with what breaks his."

The world says, "Blessed are the tough, overbearing intimidators who know how to get their way, the arrogant, the proud." Christ intones, "Blessed are the meek, for they shall inherit the earth."

Of all Jesus' beatitudes this one is the most antithetical, the most absurd, the hardest to swallow. "Aw, come on, Jesus! The wimps shall inherit the earth? Me be a doormat? Me let people ride roughshod over me? You've got to be kidding! What is this? Is this some sort of invitation to become a weakling, to be ignored?"

Years ago I was digging in my garden and accumulated a wheelbarrow fill of extra dirt. "What am I going to do with all this earth?" I wondered. My child said, "Dad, why don't we give it to the meek?"

Comedian Jerry Clower played football for Mississippi State University. Their opening game was with Baylor, a Baptist college. To get ready for the contest, Clower jogged, practiced, and didn't miss prayer meeting for six weeks. On the game day, in the first play from scrimmage, Clower got walloped. His helmet flew off and he hit the dirt face-first. He jumped up sputtering and complaining to his opponent, "I thought you were supposed to be a Christian, and see what you did to me?!" The lineman smiled and said, "Sure, I'm a Christian. The Bible says, 'The meek shall inherit the earth,' and I was just helping you get your share."

Then there's the one about the man who died and went to heaven. Standing in front of the pearly gates, he noticed two signs.

The first one read, "All men who were henpecked by their wives stand in this line." To no one's amazement, the line had 234 men in it. The second sign read, "All men who weren't henpecked stand in this line." One man waited there. Now Peter came out, looked at the first line, smiled knowingly, then did a double take at the solitary man in line two. "Excuse me, did you read that sign?" "Yes." "You mean to tell me you weren't henpecked?" "Oh, my wife told me to stand in this line!"

Meekness. We've turned it into a joke.

We have more in common with former Soviet Premier, Nikita Khrushchev, who on a 1950s visit to a French cathedral said, "There is much in Christ that is in common with us communists, but I cannot agree with him when he says, 'When you are hit on the right cheek, turn the left cheek.' I believe in another principle. If I am hit on the left cheek, I hit back on the right cheek so hard the head might fall off!" To which we all say a hearty "Amen!"

Let us study the third of Christ's beautiful attitudes. The three points we'll look at are: meekness, how meekness is applied to our relationship with God, and how meekness is applied to our relationship with people.

What It Means

"Blessed are the meek." The original Greek word for "meek" is *praus*. It translates as "gentle, humble, considerate, and courteous."

Meekness does not mean weak-willed, wimpy, or devoid of courage. Rather, it means self-controlled. In Canada, they have huge Clydesdale horses that can be hitched up to pull great logs out of the forest for timber companies. These horses are strong, yet so gentle that little children can crawl all over them and play about their hooves without injury. This is a picture of meekness, of tamed strength. It is mayhem and manners in perfect control.

In Matthew 11:29, Jesus described himself as "gentle and lowly in heart." It is the same word: *praus*. God in human flesh: tamed strength able to heal blindness, coddle little children, raise the dead, wear a crown of thorns, feed 5,000, hang upon a cross, and slay the wicked with the breath of his mouth.

In 2 Corinthians, the apostle Paul refers to both Jesus and himself as meek. You will understand that the Corinthian church was a mess. They didn't respect their elders. The authority of scripture was rejected. Anarchy reigned supreme. Paul visited them, but he came meekly. He wrote, "By the meekness and gentleness of Christ, I appeal to you — I who am timid when face to face with you, but bold when away" (2 Corinthians 10:1 cf).

The best understood translation of the third beatitude? "O the blessedness, O the happy fulfillment of the gentle, the humble, the considerate, the courteous! O the blessed meek, those of tamed strength, they shall inherit the earth."

The question arises: How does one develop this attitude in his life? I mean, humility is a hard quality! As soon as you say you've got it, you've lost it. "Don't you people understand just what an all-around good fellow of absolute humility I am?" "Perhaps you've read my book, *Humility and How I Attained It*, $39.95 at your local bookstore." "Last year the deacons gave me the humility award badge but they had to take it back because I kept wearing it." See what I mean?

How does humility come? Just bow your head and grunt prayerfully, "I will be humble. I will be humble. I will be humble!"?

Look at the logical progression of the beatitudes. "Blessed are the poor in spirit." My relationship with God begins by recognizing I am bankrupt morally and spiritually. I am totally dependent upon God's mercy.

The second attitude is mourning. I am spiritually impoverished and I care. I cry over it. I can feel God's hurt over this writhing, sinful world.

Third comes meekness. Because of my poverty and grief, I've no room for pride, for arrogance, and a sense of having arrived.

So how do I become humble? First, I gain a true estimate of who God is. Second, I gain a true estimate of who I am by comparison. When I do that I don't have any trouble being humble.

Meekness With God

That is something of what it means to be meek. Now consider: meekness in our relationship with God.

Five hundred years ago Martin Luther observed, "God created the world out of nothing. As long as you're not yet anything, God cannot make something out of you."

As a Christian I must recognize God as eternal, almighty, holy, and loving.

I also recognize God as my creator. I am dust. My life span is but a few years and I shall return to dust. I am neither very strong nor intelligent. There is sin in my life. I don't love very well. So I am poor in spirit and I mourn.

This keeps me humble. It kills pride.

All this, yet it is so easy to lose sight of these things and become impressed with myself. With some good looks, a career, money, a new car, and a few accolades, I can become so impressed with myself that I forget God.

A case in point is 2 Chronicles 26. King Uzziah's life is spread out before us there. God blessed Uzziah with a godly, two-parent home. His father was a king who "did what was right in the eyes of the Lord" (2 Corinthians 26:4). He was crowned at age sixteen. The nation unified behind him. He enjoyed excellent health. Zechariah the prophet guided him. He was a builder. He won his battles. His standing army was huge and well-trained. His fame and power grew. He ruled 52 years. But in verse 16 it says, "After Uzziah became powerful his pride led to his downfall" (NIV).

Did you hear about the woodpecker pecking on a tree when a lightning bolt struck? He got up and congratulated himself, saying, "Boy, I didn't know I had it in me!"

Uzziah's name means, "God is my help." He forgot that and became vain. And the Bible says one day he strolled into the temple, picked up a censer, and prepared to make an offering. Eighty-one priests opposed him. That was their job. God had strictly prescribed how he was to be worshiped. And Levite priests were to handle the liturgy. But Uzziah swept them aside. "I'll do it myself," he said.

Uzziah was sort of like Michael Jordan who conquered basketball and then went after baseball. Uzziah had conquered armies, built cities, and marshaled the masses. He now thinks he can do anything, even come to God on his own terms.

There he stood in the temple, censer in hand, raging at the 81 priests who opposed him, when, suddenly, leprosy broke out on his forehead. The Bible says the priests didn't have to show Uzziah the door for "he himself was eager to leave because the Lord had afflicted him" (2 Chronicles 26:20 NIV).

Uzziah spent the rest of his life as a leper remembering that only God is great.

Scripture is full of swell-heads who think they are something, but learn the hard way that God is God and we are not.

Acts 12:21-23 tells of King Herod accepting worship from his subjects. An angel smote him, his guts spilt and worms ate him.

Daniel 4:30 tells of Nebuchadnezzar, whom God made great. Walking on his palace roof he surveyed his realm and said, "Is this not the great Babylon I have built ... by my mighty power and for the glory of my majesty?" (NIV). He was smitten with madness and lived like a wild dog for many months.

I remind you that it's not just ancient history in which God opposes the proud. It still occurs in modern times. For years the Soviet Union said, "There is no God!" Even Russian cosmonauts sneered, "I went into the heavens and I didn't see God there." Finally, when God had enough, he said, "There is no Soviet Union!"

Lord Byron's poem, "The Destruction of Sennacherib," has this in it. Second Kings 18-19 tells of the Assyrian king Sennacherib of Nineveh. He wrote boastfully of himself that he was "king of the universe." But when he attacked Israel and mocked God, an angel unsheathed his sword and in one night slew 185,000 Assyrian soldiers. Sennacherib retreated to Nineveh and was himself assassinated by his two sons. Lord Byron tells the story.

The Assyrians came down like the wolf on the fold.
And his cohorts were gleaming in purple and gold;
And the sheen of their spears was like stars on the sea.
When the blue wave rolls nightly on deep Galilee.
For the angel of death spread his wings on the blast.
And breathed in the face of the foe as he passed.
And the eyes of the sleepers waxed deadly; and chill,
And their hearts but once heaved, and forever grew still.
And there lay the steed with his nostril all wide,

> *But through it there rolled not the breath of his pride:*
> *And the foam of his gasping lay white on the turf*
> *And cold as the spray of the rock-beating surf*
> *And there lay the rider distorted and pale,*
> *And with the dew on his brow and the rust on his mail.*
> *And the tents were all silent, the banners alone,*
> *The lances unlifted, the trumpet unblown.*
> *And the widows of Ashur are loud in their wail,*
> *And the idols are broke in the temple of Baal:*
> *And the might of the Gentiles, unsmote by the sword,*
> *Hath melted like snow in the glance of the Lord.*[1]

"Blessed are the meek, for they shall inherit the earth." Is it beginning to make sense?

So far we have sought to uncover the meaning of meekness and study it in one's relation to God.

Meekness With People

Numbers, chapter 12, tells of Moses leading Israel out of Egyptian slavery into the wilderness. Miriam wanted some of the glory. Being a hard-driving, high-achieving woman, she opposed Moses. "Does God speak only through Moses?" Rather than backhanding her, verse 3 says, "Now Moses was a very humble man, more humble than anyone on the face of the earth" (NIV). He invited Miriam to the tent of meeting to lay her case before the Lord. There God came in a pillar of fire, reaffirmed Moses' leadership, and Miriam was suddenly afflicted with leprosy! What does Moses do? What would you have done? "Ha, ha! You had it coming! That'll teach you to oppose me!" No, Moses would have none of this. He simply prayed for Miriam's healing and it was so. That's meekness — tamed strength.

I know of a meek grandmother. Her daughter-in-law is a feminist, humanist, egotistical know-it-all. When she visits with her husband and two children she is totally domineering, arrogant, and disruptive.

It would be easy to use your power to mash her, to drive her away in the heat of well-deserved righteous indignation. But if you're a Christian woman wanting to see your son, your grandchildren, and daughter-in-law ever again, meekness is your only recourse. This grandmother practices humility, servanthood, and lets her life speak for twelve years now. The impact is amazing. Over the years, the daughter-in-law is mellowing. She's going back to church. She doesn't have all the answers. What's more, she's still coming for visits.

Remember when the New Testament was being written? Nero was emperor of Rome. He was rich, iron-fisted, and cruel. He burned the slums of Rome to build it better. He blamed the fire on Christians, then severely persecuted them.

The apostle Paul was preaching at the same time. He was poor, rejected by his own people, meekly trying to sort out the problems of the Corinthian church. Paul was arrested and eventually beheaded by Nero. Two thousand years later we call our sons "Paul" and our dogs "Nero." Indeed! The meek do inherit the earth.

Visit the Vatican in Rome. The baptistry rests upon a beautiful slab of red jasper. It's Emperor Trajan's coffin lid. Trajan was one of the worst persecutors of the early church. He died and was buried along with his empire. Yet the church of Jesus lives on! The Vatican has dumped Trajan's body and commandeered his rich casket lid. New converts stand atop the grave of the proud as they are baptized into the faith.

In 1985, the church sent me to South Texas to do a Fellowship of Christian Athletes youth retreat — the junior high variety. Everyone should spend a week at a junior high retreat. The hysterics, the energy, the noise — who says there is no purgatory?

A junior high student's idea of fun is picking on other people. Bruce was their focus for the week. Bruce had cerebral palsy. He walked with jerks and spoke awkwardly. You guessed it — the kids spent their week imitating Bruce's awkwardness and mimicking his speech.

I was angry. I taught on self-esteem and on the goodness of God's creation. I talked to the leaders personally, trying to get them to desist.

You can imagine my anger when I found out the students had asked Bruce to give the devotional in our last assembly. Bruce jerked his way to the podium and it took him five minutes to speak nine words. "I love ... Jesus ... Christ ... and ... Jesus ... Christ ... loves ... me!" When he finished there was dead silence except for the wind blowing across the prairie and into the chapel filled with 400 kids. Then someone started to cry and revival broke out. Until way past midnight kids were coming to the open mike to repent, to ask forgiveness, and to give their hearts to Jesus.

I still walk into Christian Athletes conferences and campus meetings and nearly grown men say, "Remember me? I was at the South Texas camp with you and Bruce. That's when I gave my heart to the Lord!"

I tell you, it wasn't good preaching or music or discipline that won those kids over. It was Bruce's meekness.

"O the happy fulfillment of the meek, they shall inherit the earth."

In the south of Egypt half-buried in the sand is a broken statue of a sneering pharaoh. Carved into the base is the inscription, "My name is Ozymandias, king of kings: Look on my works, ye mighty and despair." Nothing else remains except a trackless desert waste.

My friend, only God is great! Remember this and be meek.

Suggested Prayer

Hide me, O my Jesus, in the shadow of your wing, for I know my place. Amen.

---

1. Lord Byron, "The Destruction of Sennacherib," 1815. In the public domain.

Happy The Hungry Hearts

Blessed are those who hunger and thirst for righteousness, for they shall be satisfied. — Matthew 5:6

Search as you might, you will not find the word "beatitude" in the scriptures. It is rather a word theologians assign to eight sayings of Jesus, the first eight sentences of the Sermon on the Mount. "Beatitude" means "a state of utmost bliss, the highest fulfillment."

We all want this bliss. Witness how we strive for it materially — clothes, cars, trips, looks, job, a house. Bliss comes in the next purchase! That's the problem with materialistic bliss. As a local farmer put it, "Worldly riches are like nuts. Many a clothes torn in gathering them. Many a tooth broken in breaking them. But never a belly full in eating them."

In their quest for bliss, others turn to the irrational — alcohol or drugs. This is a quick fix, a chemically induced euphoria.

Then there are those who seek refuge in fantasy. Take for example the romance novel. Before the American Civil War, Robert E. Lee was an Army officer on post out west. He wrote his wife with concerns about his children's education, giving detailed instructions. "Let them never touch a novel. They print beauty more charming than nature, and describe happiness that never exists. They will teach him to sigh after that which has no reality, to despise the little good that is granted us in this world and to expect more than is given."

So it is in one's quest for fulfillment we stretch our hands out for things, for some narcotic, or we might yearn through romance novels. All this, and we're still unfulfilled.

In the beatitudes, Jesus gives us the aim and the proper attitudes that bring ultimate bliss. In the first three beatitudes, we are told being poor in spirit, mourning, and meekness start us off in our relationship with God. In the fourth beatitude, Jesus says, "Blessed are those who hunger and thirst for righteousness, for they shall be satisfied."

What It Means

Words never exist in isolation. They have context on the printed page as well as in history. When Jesus discussed "hunger and thirst" he did so in a day when there was no corner grocery store, no faucet to twist to draw water, nor any refrigerator in which to store food. By far, the major portion of the population earned low wages, barely enough for daily food needs. It was what we call today a "hand-to-mouth existence." With no stockpiles of food, a famine or theft could lead quickly to starvation.

I've read stories of travelers by camel caravan who were trapped in a sandstorm. Unable to see, they hunkered down in the desert, wrapped themselves in their cloaks, and waited it out. Some storms lasted for days! The travelers ran out of food and water, and when the storm ended, the group crawled out of the desert, more dead than alive.

Such people had only two things on their minds: Food! Water!

When Jesus said, "Blessed are those who hunger and thirst," he was not describing a genteel hunger, a mere urge to nibble, a craving for a snack. He was describing the hunger of a starving man, the thirst of a desperate man.

Thus, this fourth beatitude asks the questions, "How much do you want God? Is there an intense desperation in your appetite for Christ? Do you only nibble at Jesus or is it your only desire to gulp him all down?"

There is, furthermore, in this beatitude an oddity in the Greek grammar. The sentence doesn't just read, "O the happy fulfillment of the man who is ravenously hungry and thirsty for righteousness." It says more.

I may say, "I want a piece of bread and a sip of that drink." Or I may explain, "I'm so hungry I want the whole pitcher and the entire loaf of bread!" The latter is what Jesus said in the beatitude. There is in the phraseology a sense of craving the entirety. "Blessed is the man with an overpowering hunger and thirst for all of God's righteousness."

Contrast such a mindset with today's lukewarm attitude toward God.

When Andrew Young's daughter graduated from college she decided to live in Africa as a missionary. Her daddy hugged her good-bye and complained, "Baby, I just wanted you to have enough religion to be respectable, not enough to go to the poorest continent and be a missionary."

If we're honest, most of us would pray, "Dear God, I'd like to buy a $2 bag of Jesus. Just enough to be saved, but not enough to make me stand out in a crowd. Enough to go to heaven, but not enough to get really involved, if you know what I mean. I just want $2 worth. Enough to make me a Christian: loved, respected, well-treated, and comfortable. This small bag full, please, so I can keep it in my pocket and have a little taste when I please."

Yet this fourth beatitude will have none of that! It insists on the prayer, "God, I want all of you! Now! I'm desperate! Please!"

So, how does one best translate the fourth beatitude? "O the blessedness, O the happy fulfillment of those who are ravenously hungry, who'll just die unless they're fed the whole of God's righteousness. They shall be satisfied!"

Logical Progression

In the first four beatitudes, one finds a sort of logical progression.

The first one teaches that a disciple's relationship with God begins with poverty, a sense of one's lack of everything that pleases God.

There are some who recognize this about themselves but fail to care. I've had hard-bitten businessmen say to me, "Stephen, I don't know a thing about religion, God, or the Bible. And I don't care! I have more important things to pursue!"

The disciple, however, recognizes his spiritual poverty and mourns over it. He cares. He learns to feel as God feels.

This leads to the third beatitude — meekness. The disciple is not proud, but teachable, humble, willing to be helped.

We come to the fourth beautiful attitude — that of spiritual questing. The disciple sees God's offer of imputed righteousness and hungers and thirsts after the whole of it.

These four attitudes are like an avalanche. A small piece of snow and ice breaks off a mountaintop and begins to tumble downward, gathering momentum as it goes until there is a veritable crescendo of thundering snow sweeping away all in its path. Likewise, poorness tumbles into mourning, which tumbles into meekness and soon one has an irresistible hunger and thirst for Jesus consuming his life and sweeping away all obstacles to the knowledge of God.

What It Looks Like

In Psalm 42, the poet prays, "As a deer pants for the water, so my soul longs after you, O God. My soul thirsts for God, for the living God. Where can I go and meet with God?" (vv. 1-2 NRSV). The Hebrew word for "pant" is *awrag*, meaning "to breathe heavily after." It did not escape the notice of the ancients that when a man and woman fell in love and embraced, they began to pant, to breathe deeply. Hence, their word for love and pant were much the same. So, "as a deer loves the waters, or breathes heavily after the waters, so my soul pants after thee, O God!"

Hunters used to take advantage of this situation and lie in wait for deer at watering holes. A deer's single-mindedness for water coupled with its heavy breathing made him less vigilant. He'd walk right into danger just to get water.

This has the gospel in it. John 3:16 says, "God so loved the world (God breathed so heavily after us) that he gave his only Son." He didn't even see the danger of the cross, he wanted us so!

And, as God loves us he asks that we love him in return.

Certainly there is not much panting after God in our society today. Oh, we breathe heavily after sex or money or fun or more, bigger, newer things. But when it comes to Jesus, our culture suffers what Robert Louis Stevenson called "the malady of not wanting."

Thankfully, I have seen such hunger and thirst for God from time to time.

I remember Beverly. She was nineteen, unmarried, and pregnant. Her boyfriend was insanely jealous and abusive. Beverly came to the church to talk over what choices she still had, became a

Christian, and for months afterward just couldn't get enough of worship, scriptures, and fellowship. I well recall a cold, rainy winter Sunday when attendance was low. There Beverly sat in the front row and she was soaking wet! It seems her car wouldn't start so she'd wrapped her baby in her raincoat and walked one-and-a-half miles to church!

When I first moved to Burlington I sat down with the elders and the people and we debated when we as a church were going to meet and why. The issue of a Sunday night Bible study came up. It would mean more work, more time, and more energy. It was pointed out that most churches had long ago quit their Sunday evening meetings. Yet someone pointed out if we had a night Bible study we could all grow twice as fast in our understanding of scripture. We called the meeting. For fifteen years I've watched many in that crowd come regularly, bringing their Bibles, pens and paper, and hungry minds. This when they could be out boating or watching television!

Some years ago, I preached during spiritual emphasis week at Messiah College in Pennsylvania. Young students came to Messiah from all across the nation and even some foreign countries. A young man from the rural poverty of Bolivia was there. Carlos was his name. I watched him the first time he walked into the library. An expression of awe filled his face. "You mean I can read all these books for free?" The librarian assured Carlos it was so. Carlos immediately sat down and said eagerly, "Well, I'm ready! Please bring me the first one!"

These are just a few pictures of true hungering and thirsting after righteousness I've seen over the years.

But what is "righteousness"? The Old Testament prophet, Hosea, best explains what it is. It seems Hosea was concerned about God's people. They'd lost their zeal for God and were panting like harlots after other idols, things, and themselves. The result was bad behavior.

Hosea diagnosed the problem as twofold. One: There was no knowledge of God among the people. Wise in worldly ways, they were ignorant of truth. "My people are destroyed for lack of knowledge" (Hosea 4:6 NRSV).

Two: Since there was no knowledge of God, there was no acknowledgment of God. What there was was bad behavior — lying, theft, adultery, greed, murder, idolatry, and so forth. "Their deeds do not permit them to return to their God. For the spirit of harlotry is within them, and they know not the Lord" (Hosea 5:4).

What is unrighteousness? Not knowing and not acknowledging God in one's behavior. What is righteousness? Knowing God and acknowledging him in one's behavior.

Conclusion

I have a friend who is a college president. He tells me that anyone who becomes a Christian and joins a good church and attends it with a hungry attitude for forty years will have gained the equivalent of ten college educations.

Think of it! If you are hungry for God just look at the banquet he has spread before you in his church! Within these walls are tapes, small groups, videos, fellowships, concerts, books, and worship events.

Here one may learn history, music, conflict resolution, loyalty, ethics, joy, sorrow, poetry, theology, but most of all — Jesus Christ! It's a never-ending adventure open to all who consider themselves as not yet having arrived.

Suggested Prayer

Jesus, you are God the Lord of me. Help me to stand up tall and straight for you this hour. Amen.

The Beautiful Attitude Of Mercy

Blessed are the merciful, for they shall obtain mercy.
— Matthew 5:7

General Omar Bradley, of World War II fame, lamented in his last speech at West Point, "This country has many men of science, too few men of God; it has grasped the mystery of the atom, but rejected the Sermon on the Mount."

Seeking to remedy this sad state of affairs, we've been working our way through the Sermon on the Mount, specifically the Beatitudes. It is God's desire to temper our lives by his Spirit and character as revealed in Christ's life and message.

We arrive now at the fifth beatitude. "Blessed are the merciful, for they shall obtain mercy."

What It Means

In Greek, "mercy" is *eleos*, meaning "compassion." The word is *chsedh* in Hebrew, meaning "to sympathize, to feel what others feel."

Mercy is not a wave of pity leading to "Aw, tough luck!" followed by a quick hug and the thought, "Whew! Thank God it's not me!"

When Queen Victoria's husband, Prince Albert, died she was left quite lonely. Her good friend, Mrs. Tulloch, lost her husband, also. The queen paid her a surprise visit, and when she was announced, she found Mrs. Tulloch resting on the sofa. The widow rose hastily to dress, but the queen insisted, "No, no! This is not a royal visit from the queen. It is a visit from one lady who has lost her husband to another." That's mercy. That is compassion, sympathy, and feeling the pain another feels. It is getting outside yourself, your plans and feelings, and experiencing the life of another.

Isn't this what God did in the incarnation? Job asks, "Hast thou eyes of flesh? Dost thou see as man sees?" (Job 10:4). In Jesus Christ the answer is a resounding "Yes!" Christ felt the hunger and fed the multitudes. He felt the leprosy and healed. He felt the grief of a widow now bereft of her son and raised the dead. He felt the lost's agony and sought them like a shepherd does his wayward sheep. He even encouraged us to do the same in his parable of the Good Samaritan.

Such sympathizing compassion is difficult to achieve, for we're each so absorbed with our own feelings, schedules, and personal problems, that it's very difficult to recognize there are, indeed, others around with needs. Consider Martha's story in Luke 10:38-42. Jesus is but a few days from his death and he knows it. The master retires to Bethany, the home of his good friends Lazarus, Mary, and Martha. He just wants to rest, to snare a few hours of peace from the hectic pace of ministry. Martha misreads Christ's needs, instead becoming overwhelmed in her own. The Lord is her houseguest. She must play the gracious host. She must live up to her reputation as a good cook. She must entertain!

All Jesus desired was a nap, peace and quiet, and listening ears. Yet he has to contend with Martha's hustle and bustle and complaints.

Still today, when one visits a sick friend in the hospital, it is easy to stay too long, to talk about one's own aches and pains, or to meet one's own needs while missing those of the ill friend.

I've a friend in ministry who lost his son in a car crash. "You'll never know," he says. "Fourteen years ago ... it still hurts so bad!" In his church last year another couple's son was killed in a car accident. The pastor visited. The father saw him coming and ran out the back door. The minister followed. The father, shedding hot tears of anger and grief, began to run. For over two hours in a cold, windy rain, the father walked and ran, the minister trailing him. Finally the dad stopped and allowed the minister to catch up. He had no words. The two simply embraced in the shivering cold and began to walk home together.

"Oh, the blessed fulfillment of the merciful, the compassionate, those who can feel the pain others have. They shall obtain mercy themselves."

That is something of what the fifth beatitude means.

The Mercy-To-Us, Mercy-From-Us Principle

The first four beatitudes prepare me for the fifth. I recognize my spiritual poverty and am poor. I mourn. And I'm meek. Thus, when God offers me his righteousness, I go after it with intense hunger.

Now, as a recipient of grace, I immediately run into other people. And guess what? They are sinners just like me. But will I give grace to them even as I've received it myself? The fifth beatitude teaches that one must be prepared to offer others the same mercy God has given them.

This "get/give mercy principle" is not isolated in Matthew 5:7. One finds it later in the Sermon on the Mount, specifically in the Lord's Prayer. "And forgive us our debts as we also have forgiven our debtors" (Matthew 6:12).

In Matthew 18:23-35, Jesus told a parable about what happens when we refuse to be merciful. A man who owed the king millions of dollars was told to settle his account. When the debtor begged for more time, the sovereign had mercy on him and forgave the debt. Whereupon the forgiven man went out, found a fellow who owed him a measly $20, seized him by the throat, and demanded payment. When the man couldn't pay he had him put in debtor's prison. Word of this reached the king and he got mad! He had the unforgiving man arrested and put in jail to be tortured. "I forgave you. Should you not yourself be forgiving?" The king asked. Jesus drove his point home: "So shall my heavenly father do to every one of you if you do not forgive your brother from your heart."

So there you have it! "The mercy-to-us/mercy-from us rule." Mercy in. Mercy out. Or we become clogged. We become a stagnant pool.

See this spiritual principle at work in King David's life. In middle age, a brooding, lonely David spied Bathsheba immodestly bathing atop her house. "Yes, here is a worthy conquest for a man of your talents!" Satan soothed. So David sent for her. She came. There was adultery.

When Bathsheba became pregnant, David panicked and had her husband slain. He married the woman and for a year went about his business as if he'd done nothing wrong.

Covetousness, adultery, murder, and lying — four of the Ten Commandments fell like dominoes. Then the prophet came. David did not once seek to justify himself. Psalm 51 is his prayer of penitence. God offered him mercy (2 Samuel 11-12).

Turn to 2 Samuel 9 and see how David, who knew how to receive mercy, also knew how to give mercy. One day, David recalled his friend, Jonathan, his loyalty, his servant's heart. David mourned Jonathan's death in battle. Wondering if any of his friend's family still survived, David investigated. Sure enough there was a son — Mephibosheth. He lived in hiding and, due to a terrible accident, was crippled in his feet.

Think of it! Mephibosheth, once a prince in line for the throne, was now hiding in fear of the new king. He was too crippled to work effectively. He had no pension, no hope. One might say Mephibosheth was in the same shape physically that David was in spiritually.

David offered him mercy. He called him out of hiding, gave him a place at his table, and treated him with dignity. You see, as David received mercy so he gave mercy.

This same principle must work in our lives as well. I must be meek because I am a sinner. But I must be merciful because others are sinners.

There is a wee poem I breathe daily. It goes:

> *I never go out to meet a new day,*
> *Without first asking God as I kneel down to pray,*
> *To give me the grace and tolerance to be,*
> *As patient of others as he is to me.*

Some Examples

What have we seen so far? We have seen that mercy is sympathetic compassion, the ability to feel what others feel and touch their need. We have seen that mercy received means we become a conduit of mercy to others.

In the early years of the twentieth century the German, Albert Schweitzer, was a world-class organist, the foremost interpreter of Bach. He was also a renowned theologian and author of the acclaimed *Quest for the Historical Jesus*. At age forty he was also a medical doctor. He left the comfort of Europe for the hurts of Africa, founding Lambrini, a Christian medical mission. There he treated the lame, the burned, the wounded, and the fevered. As his patients began to recover, Schweitzer would lean over their beds and whisper, "The reason you have no more pain is because the Lord Jesus Christ told the doctor and his wife to come to Africa to help you...."

Ernest Gordon fought in Burma during World War II. When the Japanese overran allied forces there, he, along with thousands of other soldiers, was put to forced labor on the Burma Road. The Japanese relished cruelty. As prisoners suffered hunger, fatigue, and jungle fever, many grew too weak to work. They were rifle-butted, even bayoneted, while the Japanese ate and drank in front of them.

Late in the war, however, the allies reversed the fortunes of war. Prisoners were released and put on trains for the coast. Japanese soldiers were captured and herded into prison camps. Gordon, in his book, *Through the Valley of the Kwai*, recounts how his train stopped to take on water and coal. Men got out to stretch their legs. There by the tracks, languishing in the tropical sun, was a group of wounded Japanese soldiers. A few of the GIs shared their water and food with them and began to treat the wounded.

Though the Japanese had not been merciful, a few GIs decided mercy had to start somewhere, and they'd be the ones to begin.

Then there is Martin Luther King Jr. At the height of his nonviolent 1960s civil rights campaign for black equality, it was brought to his attention that a trusted aide was embezzling funds. He wondered what he should do. If the press got wind of it, the scandal would injure his credibility. Other aides counseled harshness. "Expose the man and ruin him," they advised. King asked for a night to think it over and next day announced, "No. We're not going to ruin him. The world has enough examples of ruin. We shall give them an example of redemption." That aide went on to repent and prove his worth.

A few years ago, I was preaching in Camden, South Carolina. To clear my head I'd taken a walk through the village cemetery.

An odd grave marker caught my eye. It read, "Sergeant Richard Kirkland, the angel of Marye's Heights." It seems during the Civil War Battle of Fredericksburg, Virginia, that the rebels had hidden behind a stone wall and let the Yankees come to them. A huge massacre of bluecoats resulted, over 12,600 Northern casualties. The dead and wounded covered acres of ground in the chill of December. The killing fields writhed in agony, men calling for help, begging for water or for a blanket. No one moved to help, afraid of snipers. That's when a Southern soldier in his early twenties left his rifle pit and went to aid the wounded. From his selfless efforts he earned the sobriquet, "The angel of Marye's Heights." Sgt. Kirkland was later killed in action at the Battle of Chickamauga in Georgia.

In Bangladesh, some years ago, catastrophic floods swept away the lives and livelihoods of thousands. Christians moved in to help without regard to caste or religion. They provided food, shelter, and love. Today, as a direct result of such mercy, over 2,000 Hindu families are enrolled in a Bible course considering the claims of Jesus Christ.

At a church I once served in Virginia, some prison guards on a hot, summer day rested their work gang on the lawn in the shade. I invited the men to use the water fountain and restrooms inside. They took advantage of this hospitality for several weeks. However, at the next elders' meeting there was a complaint about how it looked for such criminals to be using church property. After ten minutes of intense debate, a wise elder put an end to the matter by quoting Jesus: "For as much as you have done it to the least of these, my brethren, you have done it unto me."

Conclusion

We are seven verses into the mere 107 verses of the Lord's Sermon on the Mount, and it is life changing! Church changing! City changing! Even world changing! For, indeed, nothing quite changes us like mercy.

At a local high school, Bruce, a seventeen-year-old, was asked as a part of a Fellowship of Christian Athletes Bible study to provide early morning transportation for a seven-year-old boy to and from a hospital for treatment. He didn't want to do it because it meant getting up at 6 a.m., picking the boy up at 7:00, and having them both back at school by 8:30. However, he'd agreed when the faculty adviser pointed out the family's lack of a car and the child's serious need of treatment.

Bleary-eyed from the early hour, he'd pulled in front of the boy's house, opened the door, and accepted the teary-eyed mother's thankfulness. With the child beside him, he'd pulled into traffic and sped toward the clinic. From the corner of his eye he could see the lad watching him intently. Finally the child asked, "Mister, do you work for God?" Bruce replied, "I'm afraid not, little fellow! Why do you ask?" The child explained that last night he'd heard his mother praying, asking God to send one of his workers to help him get to the doctor. "That's why I asked you if you worked for God."

Bruce hung his head. He held back the tears. And finally he said a prayer, "God, I haven't worked for you very much. But from now on I want to do so more and more!"

"O, the blessedness of the merciful, the sympathetic and compassionate. They shall receive mercy themselves."

Suggested Prayer

Give me mercy, Lord, that I may pass it on. In Christ's name. Amen.

The Bliss Of A Clean Heart

Blessed are the pure in heart, for they shall see God.
— Matthew 5:8

Oliver Wendell Holmes wrote, "Now and then men's minds and hearts are stretched by a new idea and never shrink back to their original dimensions." Certainly the Sermon on the Mount is such an idea. And certainly our lives are being stretched never to be the same again.

We come now to the sixth beatitude, "Blessed are the pure in heart, for they shall see God."

What It Means

The Greek word for "pure" is *katharos*. We get our name Kathryn from it. Besides being a wonderful name, *katharos* has several uses.

It can mean "clean," as in "Are the clothes clean?"

It can mean "sifted," as in "Has this wheat been sifted?"

It can even mean "purged," as in "Has this army unit been purged of all cowardly and ineffective soldiers?"

It can mean "unmixed," as in "This wine hasn't been watered down, has it?"

And, finally, *katharos* can also mean "unalloyed," as in "This ring is pure gold. It has not been alloyed with any other metal."

So, what does the sixth beatitude mean? "O the bliss, the blessed fulfillment of the pure, the clean of heart, those unalloyed...."

It is a fair question to ask what it means to be "pure of heart." The Greek word for "heart" is *kardia*, which means "the middle," or "the thoughts and feelings and will of a human." Simply put, the heart is the center of one's personality.

Hence, the purity Jesus is speaking of is not so much the outer cleanliness of a scrubbed face, clean hands, and clean feet. Rather, it is the inner cleanliness of thoughts, motives, and feelings.

As an example, consider the Pharisees of Jesus' day. They dressed with ceremonial appropriateness, ritually washed their faces and hands, and extraordinarily performed every religious rite —

fasting, tithing, praying, praising. Yet, in Luke 11:39, Jesus criticized these Pharisees harshly, "Now you Pharisees cleanse the outside of the cup and of the dish, but inside you are full of extortion and wickedness."

You see, it's rather easy to look religious by getting dressed up, taking a seat on a pew, being baptized, having your name on a church roll, and mouthing a hymn. But while one sits there looking pious, one can be brimming full of jealousy, lust, pride, and anger.

Martin Luther wrote, "Christ wants to have the heart pure, though outwardly the person may be a drudge in the kitchen, black, sooty, grimy, doing all sorts of dirty work."

"Blessed are the pure in heart ... fulfilled are the clean, the unalloyed, the sifted, the purged ... blessed are these pure, not just on the surface, but inside as well." That is something of what this beatitude means.

The Trouble With Purity

Sigmund Freud, the father of modern psychology, taught that there are only two motives: sex and money.

If in your busy week you will pause and inquire of yourself, "Why am I doing this?" you will surely find you have some hope for financial gain or you are flirting so as to be thought clever, attractive, and even desirable sexually. Truly these two motives lurk in the shadows of the human heart, motivating what we do. Oh, we may deceive ourselves, veneer our motives with pious talk, but as the prophet Jeremiah observed, "The heart is deceitful above all else, and desperately corrupt. Who can understand it?" (Jeremiah 17:9).

In 1971, I visited the Soviet Union. While in Leningrad I found an old Christian cathedral now housing a museum of atheism. Inside was chronicled every failure, every sham, every loveless deed of Christendom. I'll never forget holding a lovely crucifix, golden and bejeweled. The curator smiled and said, "Nice, isn't it? But push this button and see what happens!" I did and to my horror, a dagger blade shot forth from the bottom of the cross. Such is the human heart.

Several years ago, at the height of the televangelists' sex and money scandals, Skip Stogsdill and I interviewed Billy Graham at the Grove Park Inn in Asheville, North Carolina. "How do you stay pure, Mr. Graham?" we inquired. "I constantly run scared," the great evangelist confessed. "I can look in my life and see the depths of hell." So can we all, if we're honest. Ever since the fall, sin has reigned, bringing every sort of base motive, falsehood, and ravening wolflike desire within.

How To Achieve Purity Of Motives

A hard-bitten American businessman watched a young and pretty Christian nurse clean a man's gangrenous leg. The puss and odor were utterly revolting and the man exclaimed, "I wouldn't do that for a million dollars!" The nurse looked up, met his eye, and quietly spoke, "I wouldn't either. But I *will* do it for Jesus."

Obviously, there are other possible motives beside sex and money. True, the unregenerate may be pushed and pulled by a chaos of urges all cantering around money and sex. But for the regenerate, the born-again, the Spirit-filled Christian, there is the fact of a new heart and a new motivation.

I call it the most amazing picture of the twentieth century. It is the photograph of a man in a South African hospital. He is sitting up in bed, holding a jar in his hands, and looking at his own heart! The man had received a heart transplant so now he was examining his old, diseased one.

In the scriptures we are told our old *kardia* is sin diseased. There is no purity in it. It is turned to stone before God. Yet our Lord Jesus, the great physician, can perform spiritual surgery on us, take out our old heart, and give us a new one. In Ezekiel 11:19, God promises, "I will give them an undivided heart and put a new spirit in them; I will remove from them their heart of stone and give them a heart of flesh" (NIV).

Once any of us has received this spiritual transplant a whole new array of motives comes into play. One may observe this in 1 and 2 Corinthians. The apostle Paul had gone to Corinth to minister and found it one tough city! They criticized his preaching, did not respect his authority, and refused to pay him; infighting broke out among the congregation, and drunkenness and sexual immorality were apparent.

Any time you think your church has problems just go read Corinthians!

The question is, why would a man of Paul's caliber tough it out among the Corinthians? It certainly wasn't for sex or money! This is why it is so exciting to read the letters Paul wrote to the Corinthians. They are among his most intensely personal epistles. It is as if Paul takes the top off his head and lets you look inside. For there you can discern his motives.

In 1 Corinthians 15:11-21, Paul writes about the motivating power of love. "For the love of Christ constrains us." Elsewhere he mentions the motivating power of gratitude, duty, hope, beauty, reward, and faithfulness. Then in 2 Corinthians 5:11, he mentions fear as a motivation. "Therefore, knowing the fear of God, we persuade men."

There is fear that debilitates; these are your basic human phobias. There is fear that facilitates, the sort of fear related to awe, respect, and reverence. The facilitating fear is what Paul is talking about. It is the fear of the Lord!

I'll never forget taking my son, Bryan, with me to a university debate on abortion. I was representing the pro-life point of view while my worthy opponent took the pro-abortion position.

I was nervous. The feminist I was to debate was polished, intelligent, and wily.

I arrived three hours early, went over my reams of notes, prayed feverently, couldn't eat, and paced in a garden. All the while, my twelve-year-old son tagged along. Finally, Bryan looked me squarely in the eye and said, "You're scared, aren't you, Dad?" I told him I was. "But what are you scared of?" he pushed. I confessed I was scared I wouldn't do a good job. I was frightened my opponent would make me look silly.

"Then why didn't you just stay home?" he asked. And he reminded me that my favorite television show was airing at that very hour.

I grew quiet for some time. When I finally spoke again, I had the answer from my own heart, a new motivation Christ, himself, had put there. "I am afraid, son. Fearful of being unprepared, of being made to look silly in front of hundreds of students, but most of all I fear God. What will his judgment be for our nation when we sit back and allow over a million babies a year to be slaughtered by abortion?"

So you see, God can take away our impure motives and replace them with love, reverence, a sense of beauty, faithfulness, hope, and heavenly reward. As Jesus himself said, "Out of the heart flow streams of living water!"

Conclusion

You will notice in the sixth beatitude that the Lord offers a reward for the pure in heart. This is the case with every beatitude. For the poor in spirit there is the kingdom of heaven. For the mournful, comfort. For the meek, an inheritance of the earth. For the hungry and thirsty, satisfaction. For the merciful, mercy. But for the pure in heart, there is the most special gift of all! "They shall see God!"

Think of it! We shall behold the creator, the almighty God, ancient of days. The indescribable holy one in whose heart was born the divine redeeming strategy of the incarnation, the cross, the resurrection, and the indwelling fullness of his Spirt. We shall see him! And that will forever be enough!

Suggested Prayer

Lord, take my diseased heart and give me yours that my motives might be pure. For Christ's sake. Amen.

Peacemaking: The Seventh Beatitude

Blessed are the peacemakers, for they shall be called sons of God. — Matthew 5:9

In a Charles Schultz *Peanuts* comic strip, Lucy tells Charlie Brown, "If I were in charge of the world, I'd change everything.... And I'd start with you!" Isn't that just like us? But the beatitudes focus on one's own self. "Let's begin with you," God says.

So we move to the seventh beatitude of Jesus. "Blessed are the peacemakers, for they shall be called sons of God."

What It Means

In the Greek, "peacemaker" is *eirene*, which simply means "peacemaker." But in Hebrew, the root word for peacemaker is *shalom*, a word rich in meaning. Shalom-peace is never just negative, as in the absence of trouble or war. It is also the presence of everything that makes for someone's highest good.

A common misunderstanding of the seventh beatitude is the notion that it says, "Blessed are the peace-*lovers*...." There are some who love peace so much they go along to get along, refuse to make waves, settle for peace at any price, and evade the issues. To have peace they become appeasers. But Jesus warned, "Do not suppose that I have come to bring peace to the earth. I did not come to bring peace but a sword" (Matthew 10:34). So we are to be more than peace*lovers*. We're called to peace*making*.

As an example of peacemaking, consider a common pot of violets on your household windowsill. They are a bit parched, starting to brown, and they haven't bloomed in two years. So you determine to be a peacemaker for them.

First you have to take away harmful things. A dog chews on them. Children knock the pot off the sill. It's too cold or too hot where it sits. You remove these threats, but you still haven't created shalom.

You must add the presence of helpful things: sunlight in the correct amount, moisture, fertilizer, pruning. In four months the pot of violets is a verdant, blooming beauty. You were a successful peacemaker.

Saint Augustine defined peace as "the tranquility of divine order." It is the absence of things hurtful and the presence of things helpful. It is not something we only strive to do for houseplants, it is something we do for people.

Historically, this beatitude has been understood several ways.

The early fathers believed it meant making peace within their own souls. Each of us is a veritable civil war walking around battling within such foes as anger, bitterness, worry, jealousy, doubts, hate, and other unsettling passions. Being a peacemaker means starting with yourself. So many of our early fathers of the faith joined a monastery and in a life of quiet reflection-built peace. "The peace of God, which passes all understanding, will keep your hearts and your minds in Christ Jesus" (Philippians 4:7).

Others believe peacemaking is spiritual peace best achieved through evangelism. Romans 5:1 says, "Since we are justified by faith, we have peace with God through our Lord Jesus Christ."

C. S. Lewis observed, "Man is not only a sinner who needs to be saved, he is a rebel who needs to lay down his arms." You see, the entire human race is at war with God and we shall certainly be brought to bay and held accountable for our sinful deeds by an almighty, holy God.

Peacemaking then can be proclaiming the reconciliation and mercy God holds out in Jesus Christ. It is calling people to repentance and faith and a life of loving fellowship with God. This is spiritual peacemaking.

Still others understand being a peacemaker as creating sociological peace. It is working to make the world a better place, to establish justice, to cause quarreling to cease, to right wrongs, to establish right relationships with people.

During the Civil War, President Abraham Lincoln wrote, "Die when I may, I would like it said of me that I always pulled up a weed and planted a flower where I thought a flower would grow."

So will the real peacemaker please stand up? Is he spiritual? Is he sociological? Or is he psychological, sociological, political, or ecological? In 1 Thessalonians 5:23, Paul wrote, "May God himself, the God of peace, sanctify you through and through. May your whole spirit, soul and body be kept ..." (NIV). See here how God cares for the whole person?

You will pardon me if I tell an indelicate story, but it serves well to prove my point. I was traveling through eastern North Carolina to a remote college where I was to preach in chapel. I'd been on the road for three hours and needed to find a restroom. Mile after mile passed with nothing but swamps and fields, and I was getting desperate! You can imagine my relief when I rounded a curve and saw Piney Woods Baptist Church building with a "Visitors Welcome" sign out front. I pulled up and ran up to the door just as a deacon came out. "Please," I said, "may I use your bathroom?" He looked at me aggravatedly and said, "Well, I don't know! Are you a member here?" Without replying I pushed my way inside and found what I needed. As I left the old gentleman was still standing on the steps looking ill.

Shouldn't the church as peacemaker meet all of our needs? Bible study and friendship, emotional health and discipline, prayer and accountability, physical healing as well as missions?

Kodak Moments

That is something of what peacemaking means. Now this: Some examples of making peace. I call them "Kodak moments."

In the 1960s, civil rights activist, Dr. Martin Luther King Jr., encouraged blacks to put away violence as a tool to achieve goals. All the while, Black Panthers and Malcolm X were encouraging violence. King wrote, "The ultimate weakness of violence is that it is a descending spiral, begetting the very thing it seeks to destroy. Instead of diminishing evil, it multiplies it. Through violence you murder the hater, but you do not murder hate."

Dr. King tested his theory in his march on Selma, Alabama. He and his freedom marchers, hundreds of them, met the local sheriff at the Selma bridge. Told to disperse, King replied they had a valid permit. The sheriff sent in the dogs and billy-clubbing police. It was a very good place for a race war to begin. But King and his marchers simply absorbed the blows and did not resist. All the while the news cameras rolled. I watched it all on the evening news as a young teenager and understood even then who had won.

O the blessedness of the racial peacemakers, for they shall be called the sons of God!

In Rochester, Minnesota, a new church was struggling to be born. Over the years a fellowship of enough people to really begin to get things done came together. But there suddenly rose a divisive issue that split the church right down the middle. Tempers flared, there was nit-picking and ugliness. Finally one group left to form another church.

The remaining elders talked things over and decided no issue that divided them was all that important. The fight was mostly personality conflicts. So they all resigned and the remaining church went and joined the other group!

The other group was suspicious at first and didn't want to receive the second group. But with humility and acts of servanthood this group began to win their way.

Three years later, the new elders of the church told the former elders, "Now that we've been leaders for some time, we see how hard it must have been for you. Please forgive us for our surliness and division."

O the blessedness of peacemakers in the house of Jesus Christ, for they, indeed, shall be called children of God!

Go with me now to a US aircraft carrier in the Pacific. The time? World War II. Max was a young sailor caught up in war. One of the boys, he was out for a good time. In his berthing area was Henry, the only Christian in the squad. And Henry was the brunt of every joke. He was cursed, mocked, ignored, and just about anything else the enlistees could think of.

Every day, Max watched as Henry read his Bible and knelt to pray. The men threw their shoes at him. Henry quietly polished them. He was the only berth mate who did not gamble, read pornography, and constantly quarrel. If you asked Henry about his faith, he quietly and patiently explained things. Max watched Henry's life for six months and secretly admired him.

Then came a great naval battle and Japanese kamikaze pilots turned the US carrier into an inferno. The warship was barely afloat. Max fought fires for 48 hours nonstop. The dead were stacked in a hangar below deck. And the sailors finally took a break for food and rest. That's when Max noticed Henry was missing.

He searched for him among the living. He sought him among the dead. The next day he found Henry in the hangar under several corpses. Henry had been left for dead, horribly burned. He'd taken whole pages from his pocket Bible and torn them out, clutching them to his chest. Max tried to console him, gave him a sip of water, and just before he died, Henry told Max, "Tell my parents I fought the best I could, that I loved Christ to the end. And Max, tell my parents not to hate the Japanese."

For Max Scranton, that day started a search for the God who could help a man love like that. And it ended with faith in Jesus Christ, a call to the ministry, and Max's having no small impact on my own life.

O the blessedness of the peacemakers who lead others to know Jesus Christ!

Still another Kodak moment came in the mid-1970s with African-American tennis star Arthur Ashe. He was winning a match in a national tournament, but his opponent was being immature, abusive, and profane. Ashe, always well-mannered and cool, watched his losing opponent throw his racket down in unsportsmanlike conduct again. Ashe walked over to the referee and told him he was quitting the match before he lost his own temper.

The referee was stunned. It meant Ashe would forfeit the match even though he was winning! But Ashe did it anyhow.

Later, the US Tennis Association awarded Ashe the "win" and fined his opponent for his unsportsmanlike behavior. Such was the courage of Arthur Ashe to make peace and to be a positive role model for youth.

I could go on and tell you of parents peacemaking with their children, of divorcees learning to make peace with their ex-spouses, and of employees holding their corporation accountable. But you get the picture!

In 1938, Italy's dictator, Benito Mussolini, told his people, "War puts the stamp of nobility on a people who have the courage to meet it." How like us. But how unlike Christ.

Jesus said the outcome of his grace working within us is not hostility, jealousy, and injury. It is peacemaking. The stamp of divinity is to help bring the sinful chaos of life within and without into the tranquility of divine order.

My, but how the world tries to make peace! We've the League of Nations, the United Nations, treaties, and nonaggression pacts. It seems like there is always a peace conference going on. But two problems chronically arise: first, too much talk and too little action; and second, we leave God out of the peace. And it is forever true that we cannot achieve the brotherhood of man without the fatherhood of God.

Galatians 5:22 points out that peace is a fruit of God's indwelling Spirit. It is the result of following Christ. It is neither self-generated nor politically conjured.

In the early 1930s, a Protestant missionary to Japan wrote a terse letter to his church. In it he observed, "Japanese society is becoming militant by the day. Either send me 10,000 missionaries now to teach Christ's love or send me a million of your sons in ten years to fight them in war." To a world still so spiritually in arrears, his words still ring sorrowfully true.

Conclusion

As we conclude, be aware of the reward for peacemaking. "Blessed are the peacemakers, for they shall be called the sons of God."

In the Greek "called" means "owned." God "owns" the peacemaker as his very son. "This is my beloved Son, with whom I am well pleased" (Matthew 3:17).

"Sons of God" is a Jewish manner of speech. In Acts 4:36, Barnabas is called a "son of encouragement." It is a Hebraic way of saying Barnabas was an encouraging man. Likewise, Jesus is the "son of man," or fully human, incarnate. So in the text to be a "son of God" means to be doing a godlike work.

What does the seventh beatitude mean? "Blessed ... fulfilled ... doing what God created you to do ... blissful is the man who is a peacemaker, who brings people together ... Happy is the man who creates a nourishing atmosphere that leads to spiritual, psychological, and social peace. He shall be owned by God for he is doing a godlike work."

Suggested Prayer
Lord, help me to make peace, for Jesus' sake. Amen.

The Bliss Of A Martyr's Way

Blessed are those who are persecuted for righteousness' sake, for theirs is the kingdom of heaven. Blessed are you when men revile you and utter all kinds of evil against you falsely on my account. Rejoice and be glad, because your reward is great in heaven, for so men persecuted the prophets who were before you.
— Matthew 5:10-12

In the beatitudes, Jesus says a Christian's pilgrimage is much like climbing up one side of a mountain and then descending the other side. One begins with a sense of his own abject spiritual poverty before God. Then he learns to care and to grieve over sin. Next he is meek and filled with humility. Finally, the Christian reaches the peak of the mountain he has hungered and thirsted to attain, and he is satisfied.

However, God will not allow us to sit upon the heights savoring our relationship with him alone. He directs us down the other side of the mountain. Hence the next four beatitudes deal specifically with our relationship with people. The first step down is mercy. As I have myself received mercy, I am urged to offer mercy to others. Next my motives are called into question. Are they pure? I climb downward to be a peacemaker and to be a nurturer. Finally, I come all the way down among sinful humanity to where I am persecuted. The thanks I get for my trouble to be merciful, pure, and a peacemaker is to be misunderstood, slandered, rejected, imprisoned, and perhaps slain.

The eighth beatitude is an odd one in that it is not a description of some positive character trait found in a Christian. It is rather the Christian life: suffering at the hands of people.

Ah, but one must marvel at the sheer honesty of Jesus Christ. Today, many preachers tell us that if we believe in Jesus our sins will not only be forgiven, but we'll become a "king's kid" — prosperous, never sick, always loved and appreciated. This is not what Jesus told the twelve at their ordination. Quite the opposite! Our

Lord said we'd be "reviled," "persecuted," and "victimized" by people "uttering all kinds of evil against" us.

This is not exactly a popular message to preach, but Jesus is honest. He tells us up front what to expect: The Christian life is not only hard, it is unpopular and will likely get you in at least as much trouble as it will get you out of in this life! All through our life with Christ, we must remember that God is not so much interested in making us comfortable as he is in making us holy.

With this in mind, let's take the last step off the mountain down into the eighth beatitude and see what is there for us.

What Is Persecution?

In the Greek, "persecution" means "to pursue," "to press toward." Hence, persecution means pressure. Three words or phrases in the text aptly describe it: "revile," "persecute," and "utter all kinds of evil against you." What Jesus is saying is this: "If you live with the character of these beatitudes forming in your person you can reasonably expect society to put you under pressure."

Persecution takes various forms. It can be verbal: "all kinds of evil uttered against you!"

Early Christians were slandered by outsiders who believed they were cannibals and given to sexual orgies. Since they met in secret, ate the Lord's supper as Christ's body and blood, and were so affectionate with one another, it is easy to see how such talk got started.

Still today, Christians are victimized by the lies and slander of the human tongue. Just look how believers are portrayed in mass media as ignorant, intolerant, easily led, no fun, hypocritical, and having a low view of women.

Persecution can surpass mere talk. It can be economic. A certain early Christian stonemason was offered a contract to build a pagan temple. He needed the work. But there was a conflict between his faith and his business interests. He laid the problem before his pastor and concluded with the remark, "What can I do? I must live!" "Must you?" asked the pastor.

It is the same today with Christian doctors and nurses called upon to perform abortions, Christian grocers pressed to stay open on the Lord's Day, a convenience store clerk asked to sell pornography, or a waitress asked to dress in a suggestive manner and serve plenty of alcoholic beverages to lusty clients.

Sometimes a Christian must say no and suffer the economic consequences.

Persecution can also take the form of social pressure.

In the ancient world, most parties were held in pagan temples. An invitation might read, "I invite you to dine with me at the table of our lord Serapis." A lamb was killed with a small portion burned to their god. A part was given to the priests. Then the rest was eaten at a dinner party. The whole affair began with a prayer to idols and a cup of wine poured out to Serapis.

Christians could not participate in such affairs. All too often their social life dried up and they became lonely and ostracized.

Family pain is yet another form persecution takes. Often a man became a Christian but his wife did not, so a religious division developed in the household. Thus values, holidays, and worship became a source of contention.

How often I have watched young men and women at college convert to Christ, spend a year growing up, and then go home over the summer to mildly religious parents who scorn their newfound faith.

Persecution can also become political in nature. When the Christian church was young, the Roman empire was experiencing disunity. The emperors tried to use religion, specifically emperor worship, to unify the nation. It became law that each citizen must pledge his first allegiance to the state. The image of Caesar was set up in each town and once a year each person must stand before it, burn a pinch of incense, and bow down saying, "Caesar is lord!" Having done so he was given a certificate allowing him to buy and sell as a loyal Roman citizen.

For Christians such an act was a defilement. Only Jesus is Lord. So they went without the certificate and were thus considered outlaws. Many were hunted down and killed. Others were thrown to the lions as sport in the arena. Others were wrapped in oily rags and used as human torches in Nero's palace gardens.

It is very possible that we shall see such terror rear its ugly head again in our generation.

What, then, is persecution? It is pressure brought to bear on Christians that is meant to hinder or destroy. It can be verbal, social, economic, even political.

Where Does Persecution Originate?

Some persecution comes from outside the church.

In 286 AD, Emperor Maximan of Rome ordered the army to take part in a pagan sacrifice and then assist in purging Christianity from Gaul. A certain legion of over 600,000 soldiers, all Christians, refused. The emperor ordered a decimation. Every tenth man was killed — over 60,000 men! The rest of the army stood by Jesus. A second decimation was ordered. The rest of the army stood firm in the faith, so Emperor Maximan ordered the entire legion slaughtered.

Persecution almost invariably arises from people who have something to lose. In this case it was an egomaniacal emperor who refused to allow any God but himself.

Persecution does not just come from outside the church. Often as not, it originates inside the church. Jesus' worst tormentors were religious Pharisees. If you study church history, there is a corrupt and bloody side to it that is most depressing. As it usually happens, the church slides into corruption and ineffectiveness. A reformer steps forward. There is a response of jealousy, anger, and a panic attempt to maintain one's own position. Then the persecution starts.

During the English Reformation, Thomas Cranmer set out to cleanse the church in Great Britain by calling her back to the Bible. He was arrested and tortured and eventually recanted. For his signature on a document denouncing his reform efforts, he was given his freedom. He shortly came to his senses, reannounced his reforms, and was rearrested and burned at the stake. As he faced death he said, "Now I come to that which troubles my life more than anything that I ever did or said in my whole life, and that is that through fear of death I signed with my hand what I do not believe in my heart. When I come to the fire, this hand shall be the first to burn." Thomas Cranmer went to the stake smiling. When the fire leaped up, he held his right hand in the flame until it was burned away.

Let's face it: Whether persecution comes from inside the church or outside, it is Satan who inspires it. The devil has hated Jesus, his words, and his people from the start and he'd like nothing more than to destroy it.

Why Does Persecution Come?

This eighth beatitude is often grossly misunderstood. It doesn't say, "Blessed are the persecuted." It says, "Blessed are those who are persecuted for righteousness' sake." You see, this beatitude gives Christians no license to be dumb, to go "asking for it," to be immature, to be ill-tempered and rude, or even to do something wrong.

Too often, Christians call persecution down on their own heads. Because of self-righteous and objectionable behavior we deserve the pain we receive! I well recall a group of high school students who sat proudly in the center of the school cafeteria and both prayed and read scripture loudly. You can imagine the rest of the students' reaction ... persecution!

This beatitude says we're blessed when we become so like Jesus that people take offense at us. Jesus said, "If the world hates you, know that it hated me before it hated you. If you were of the world, the world would love its own; but because you are not of the world, therefore the world hates you. Remember the word that I said unto you, the servant is not greater than his lord. If they have persecuted me, they will also persecute you" (John 15:18-20).

Never forget that people tried to stone Christ, to throw him over a cliff. He was rejected in his hometown, a murderer was chosen over him, a friend betrayed him, and he was executed on a cross. All this and Jesus said we could expect more of the same. He said, "You will be hated by all nations for my name's sake" (Matthew 24:9). He even said there'd come a day when people kill Christians and think they've done God a favor!

Our persecution should never be because we are immature or guilty of wrongdoing, but because we are like Jesus, the result of a clash between two irreconcilable kingdoms, two different value systems, and we become a threat to the sinful way things are.

How Do We Respond?

So far we've asked of persecution: What is it? Where does it come from? Why does it come? Now, we must inquire: How do I respond to persecution?

None of us wants to be hurt, rejected, tormented, misunderstood, or jailed. When we are, what's our reaction?

Some opt for avoidance, wallowing in the fear of involvement. I like the cartoon that has a Roman Christian being led out to the lions in the arena. "Okay," he says to the guards, "I'll admit to being a Christian, but I never served on any boards or anything like that."

Shame is another response. "I must be a bad person if this is happening to me."

Then there is anger at God. "I deserve better than this. What sort of father are you if you can't take any better care of your children?"

I could go on chronicling pity, depression, and all manner of retaliation. But the text says our response should be to "rejoice and be glad." In the Greek it means "to leap up exceedingly high for joy!"

Why?

"For so men persecuted the prophets who were before you," Jesus said. In the early church, to suffer for Christ was considered a privilege, a badge of honor that men like David, Noah, Gideon, Elijah, Stephen, Paul, and Jesus wore.

Polycarp, the 86-year-old leader of the early Turkish church, was arrested for being a Christian. He was given the choice to worship Caesar and live, or profess Jesus and die. "Eighty and six years have I served Christ and he has done me no wrong. How can I blaspheme my king who saved me?" He was burned at the stake. His last prayer? "I thank thee that thou has graciously thought me worthy of this hour."

Jesus said we could also rejoice because "your reward is great in heaven." This world is not all there is. There is an afterlife, a heaven, a paradise with Christ. One may take my life, my car, my job, my loved ones, my reputation, my money, but no one can rob me of Jesus and my reward.

Another reason we can rejoice in our persecution is that by our struggles we can make things better for those who follow. There is a World War II soldiers' cemetery in England. The gate sign reads, "Remember all you who pass by, we gave our tomorrows for your todays." Certainly there are sacrifices, hurts, and forfeitures any Christian worth his salt must offer up to Christ these days. But why? Why? The answer is: We do it for our children and our grandchildren.

Yet another cause to leap for joy in our trials and tribulations is because of how such pressure forms our character. In 1 Peter 1:7, our persecutions are described as trial by fire. In Malachi 3:2, God says he is Lord of the refiner's fire. I have ventured to Israel and seen the street vendors who take silver coins, melt them in their small firepots, and refine them into jewelry. Every few minutes the silversmith will look into his pot and take a spoon and skim the impurities off the top. He knows his silver is pure when he can see his face in the molten silver.

Likewise God uses pain, the furnace of affliction, to refine us. How does he know when we are done? When he can see himself in us.

Stand Tall And Straight

The eighth beatitude is the longest of them all and the only one with a commentary attached. This one is simply so hard it has to be explained.

Notice that the eighth beatitude is uttered in the third person to people in general. But the commentary is uttered in the second person. It is specifically directed to the disciples, as it is now to you and to me so directed.

It seems strange to go from peacemaking to persecution, but Jesus is saying if we live like him the world will certainly recoil in hostility simply because our life is a public rebuke to sin.

Over the last 100 years there have been so many martyrs. In fact, more Christians have been killed in the last 100 years than in all the former 1,900 years put together. And it is predicted by church experts that the near future will see more persecution than ever before.

Steel yourselves. Settle it in your minds beforehand. You will suffer for the faith.

Peter wrote, "Don't be surprised at the fiery ordeal that is coming upon you as if something strange is happening to you ..." (1 Peter 4:12). Jesus has warned us beforehand.

Those who've survived years of torture in prisoner of war camps say the worst pain doesn't come from beatings, starvation, or brainwashing. The torture that breaks a man quickest is a prison cell so small that a man must crouch; he cannot rise to his full height.

Jesus is telling the church to stand up tall and straight! For such are the times that would pressure us to stoop.

Suggested Prayer

Jesus, you are God the Lord of me. Help me to stand up tall and straight for you this hour. Amen.

No Salt In The City?

You are the salt of the earth; but if salt has lost its taste, how shall its saltiness be restored? It is no longer good for anything except to be thrown out and trodden underfoot by men. — Matthew 5:13

The Sermon on the Mount begins with eight "Blessed are the ..." statements. Now it continues with two "you are" statements.

Last fall the phone rang in my study. It was a newspaper pollster doing a survey on church and society. His main question was, "What would your city be like without the church?"

I was tempted to be funny in my reply. Like the cartoon that shows a pack of wolves howling at the moon. A wolf on the back row is looking worried and asks another fanged friend, "Do you think we're doing any good?" Sometimes I feel like that when the church seems to be ignored or irrelevant.

Yet any time one feels he is small and can't have much of an impact, just remember what it's like going to bed with a mosquito in the room!

Actually, I told the phone researcher that a city without the church would be like life without salt. Why do I say this? In the Sermon on the Mount, Jesus said to his disciples, "You are the salt of the earth." That was quite a compliment in Jesus' day, for salt was very rare and highly prized.

Greeks called salt "the second soul of meat." A half pound of salt was worth more than a human being. Soldiers were often paid in salt. The word "salary" is derived from "salt." This is where we get our saying, "He's not worth his salt."

So, when Jesus said, "You are the salt of the earth," the compliment must have "wowed" the apostles. They were valuable to God and society. As we say today, "They were worth their weight in gold."

What does it all mean practically speaking? Jesus knew what salt can do as well as we do. So, let's look at what Christ had on his mind.

Flavor

Consider the flavor enhancing properties of salt. Why, what are french fries without salt's flavor? How bland! And as salt adds zest to a meal, so Christians are the spice of life at school, at the office, in the classroom, and down at the local club.

The good Lord never meant for Christians to be dull, lifeless killjoys. Why, Jesus was the life of the party! Not only was he invited to the wedding feast of Cana, he served up some pretty good wine! Jesus explained, "I came that you may have life, and have it abundantly" (John 10:10).

Yet, how many Christians walk about looking like they've been weaned on a dill pickle? All of this prompted Mark Twain to comment, "I'll take heaven for climate and hell for society."

When I was in college, I joined the Sigma Alpha Epsilon Fraternity. Few of my brothers were Christians. At mealtime, we gathered in the commons and told jokes around the table. During the spring of my sophomore year, I got into a joke duel with Hank. He'd tell a dirty joke. I'd counter with a clean joke, just as funny. We bantered back and forth for two months until he was spent. Then he said to me privately, "Stephen, I've never met anyone like you. You have a good time without being dirty-mouthed or drunk. What have you got that I don't have?" I told him of Jesus and how he adds spice to life. In Christ, fun becomes funnier, love lovelier, and truth even more voracious.

De-Icer

Not only can salt add flavor, it also owns the property of melting ice. A snowstorm barrels across our city and road crews busily spread salt on our bridges to melt the ice.

In our day, human hearts have grown frosty, long icicles of indifference suspended like daggers from our lives. We have our cliques, our racial walls, our cold-blooded murders. We say, "I don't care about God. I don't even care about you. All I care about is me!"

It takes salt — Christian salt — to thaw out a society.

A young lady in our church was looking forward to attending a concert. She and three of her friends had tickets and the day neared.

In casual conversation, she found out two other students really wanted to go but couldn't find a ride. They had room in their car. But these two were of a different race. They ran with a different crowd and lived on the other side of town.

When she suggested to her three chums they take the two with them, she was met with a stout, "No!" Undaunted, the girl pressed on about how the two were human just like themselves, how it was time to build some bridges of kindness in their high school, and how there should be enough of her to love three friends and two new ones to boot!

Now, that, my friends, is salt!

Thirst

What else can salt do besides add flavor and thaw ice? It can induce thirst.

If you take a date to the movies, just about the time the movie is getting good, you'll feel an elbow in your ribs. "Popcorn!" she will say. So you scramble out to buy some. But don't be cheap! While you're out, you might as well purchase a drink, for the popcorn is so salty that after four bites, you'll get the elbow again. "A drink," she'll command.

There's an old saying, "You can lead a horse to water, but you can't make him drink." True. But you can add plenty of salt to his oats, and he'll find the water trough soon enough.

When Kathryn and I first married, we lived in a tiny three-room apartment in Atlanta. The complex had about 300 people in it, mostly blue-collar workers — divorcees, homosexuals, alcoholics, the unemployed. Looking back, it was a rough place, though it didn't seem like it at the time. There was always a domestic spat, a drug bust going down, or a break-in. The swimming pool was unfit to swim in. Beer cans strewed the lawn, paint peeled everywhere, and there was no gospel in the neighborhood. Come Sunday morning, you could sleep in the middle of the road and not get run over by a single person going to church.

Kathryn and I lived there two years. That's where our first baby was born. We were without any insurance, so I got a job picking up trash, mowing grass, cleaning the pool, and painting to make ends meet.

Come Thanksgiving, just before Kathryn gave birth, we decorated for Christmas. Nobody ever did that there. But it's as if seeing our wreath and colored lights stirred something long asleep in those people. Before many days, the apartment complex twinkled with festive decor.

When spring came, Kathryn asked me to make her a window box for her flowers. I did so, and all summer, banks of lovely flowers spilled over our porch. One by one I began to see hanging baskets and flowerpots added to other apartments.

After graduation, we said our good-byes and moved to work in a church in Virginia. It was six years before we had a chance to visit our Atlanta neighborhood again. But as soon as we turned the corner and saw it, we burst out laughing! Flower boxes were everywhere, the lawn was newly mowed, and the swimming pool was in pristine condition. The resident manager, Ann, told us she'd become a Christian and showed us her 3-D picture of Jesus hanging over her television.

See how salt works quietly? We just live our lives before a watching world, and they get thirsty for our Savior.

Healing

What does salt do? It flavors, thaws, and promotes thirst. But it also heals. Recall your childhood sore throats and how Mom made you gargle with salt water? Though it stung, it ultimately brought soothing relief.

Christians are like that in society.

Jesus called Christians "the salt of the earth."

If you study history, you'll find Christians going where the hurt is, killing germs, and healing sickness.

As a Christian intellectual I'm alternately befuddled, bemused, saddened, and outraged at how the elitist world of the mainstream media depicts Christians as dung.

In movies, the serial killer wears a cross and uses the Bible to justify his homicidal lust.

On television, Christ is blanked out as an irrelevancy except in moments of heated passion when his name is used as an expletive.

Newsprint frequently refers to Christians as intolerant, one-or-two-issue political zealots, and uneducated Neanderthals.

Yet, a cursive view of history proves this is nothing but a smear job. Christians, in reality, have historically been earth's salt!

When one is sick, a hospital can be a fine thing, and who built some of our region's finest healing centers? Bowman Gray Medical Center in Winston-Salem is Baptist. Duke University Medical Center is Methodist. Then there is Presbyterian Hospital in Charlotte.

Next, take the orphanages. Helpless children have long been gathered at Thornwell Orphanage in South Carolina or Elon Home for Children in central North Carolina. Both were started by Christians. Name a single such ministry the atheists have built! Has the *New York Times* constructed such a humane habitat? No.

Another example is ignorance. Christians have long known that uneducated people are difficult to govern. Scripture teaches, "The wisdom from above is open to reason." So it was the dying Puritan preacher, John Harvard, gave his books to the Massachusetts Bay Colony in the 1600s and Harvard University was founded. In rural New Hampshire, as "the voice of one crying in the wilderness," Dartmouth College began as a school to evangelize Native Americans. In New Jersey, Log College, now known as Princeton University, was chartered to train Christian clergy. This educational phenomena carries down the entire East Coast — Duke, Davidson, Wake Forest, Furman, and Emory. So, don't go telling me Christians are dumb!

The ranks of people claiming a kinship with God and humanity by repentance from sin and faith in Jesus' atoning death include such stellars as Bach and Handel in music, T. S. Eliot in poetry, Rembrandt and van Gogh in art, and Jimmy Carter and Ronald Reagan in politics. This is not to say Christendom hasn't had its flaws. It is to say, rather, to an arrogant and hostile press, "Think again!" When you attack Christ and his churches as intolerant, ignorant, and unworthy of anything but marginalization, you are forgetting what salt Christians have provided in the land for hundreds of years.

Last spring, drinking got out of hand at a local college. After a party, a young man crashed his car and died. The campus was numb with grief. That's when some Christians began the Greek Christian Fellowship and made it their goal to educate the campus on alcohol abuse, not to let friends drive drunk, and to show their friends how to party drunk on God's Spirit and not on liquor.

Salt! Glorious salt! Flavoring, thawing, inducing thirst, healing!

Preservative

Salt is also a preservative. If you cure a ham with salt, it can last indefinitely, rather than spoil.

Stick your head out the door and you can catch a whiff of our society spoiling.

In New York City, more than 830,000 people are on welfare (a total bigger than the population of all but ten US cities), 366 cars are stolen each day, and over 200,000 people a day jump the turnstiles to ride the subway free. There are over two million warrants out for people who failed to show up in court. The public school system has more administrative staff than all of Europe. New York has 500,000 drug addicts. It is the AIDS capital of the world. The illegitimacy birth rate in Harlem is 80% and rising. Over 10,000 babies a year are born "toxic," which means their mothers were crack cocaine addicts, and it will take at least $220,000 per baby in remedial medical attention just to get them started in life. There is a robbery every six minutes. There are at least 93,387 armed robberies each year, with twenty-one cab drivers being murdered.

What's going on in New York City is but a foreshadowing of where our nation is headed in Los Angeles, in Dallas, in Charlotte, and one day right in your own town.

Now is the time for salt — to preserve marriages, to initiate and sustain friendships, to be an effective parent, to renew racial dialog, and to preserve values in public schools.

If we withdraw, if Christians cocoon themselves, if we keep our salt to ourselves, then our children's world won't be fit to live in!

In the 1930s, as Hitler rose to power as a Nazi dictator, Albert Einstein watched with growing alarm. He expected the newspapers to expose Hitler's corruption, but the media was quickly silenced. Einstein looked to the universities to stop Hitler. Instead, they went along. In the end, only the church stood squarely in Hitler's path. Einstein wrote, "What formerly I had no use for, I now praise unreservedly." It was the salty church of our Lord and Savior, Jesus Christ.

George Gallup, the famous pollster, writes that fewer than 10% of Americans are deeply committed Christians. "These people are a breed apart. They are more tolerant of people of diverse backgrounds. They are more involved in charitable activities. They are more involved in practical Christianity. They are absolutely committed to prayer." And they are "far, far happier than the rest of the population." Then he goes on to say that such devout Christians exert an influence on our society that far outweighs our numbers.

Just like salt. It only takes a pinch to do the whole job!

Quite a compliment, eh?

Jesus didn't say we were the sugar of the earth. He called us salt! And of its wonderful properties we share!

Along with the compliment comes the warning: "But if salt should lose its saltiness, how shall it be restored? It is good for nothing but to be thrown out and trodden under foot by man."

Heed well Christ's warning, my friends, and be what you are for the need is great!

Suggested Prayer

Lord, restore my zest, and make my life count for Christ. Amen.

Light! More Light!

You are the light of the world. A city set on a hill cannot be hid. Nor do men light a lamp and put it under a bushel, but on a stand, and it gives light to all in the house. Let your light so shine before men, that they may see your good works and give glory to your Father who is in heaven. — Matthew 5:14-16

If one rushes home after Sunday morning church services, he or she can see a television news show known as *Meet The Press*. Each week, some leader is given the hot seat and thoroughly questioned on issues. Let's do the same thing with Jesus and the text. Let's play *Meet The Congregation.*

Before we commence, some background. The world to which Jesus came was dark and difficult. Sixty percent of the population were slaves. Rome was in power. There was an emperor and no constitution. The army enforced Rome's will with force and violence. There was no set tax percentage. The tax gatherer made up the rules as he went along. There were no public schools. Only a fragment of the population could read. There were no hospitals, no rest homes, no orphanages, and there was no gospel. Man worshiped imaginative myths and slew animals and read their entrails to discern the future.

And we think we have it bad today!

To such a world as this, Jesus was born. His first thirty years were spent quietly in Egypt, then in Nazareth as a carpenter. By age thirty, Christ was baptized and launching his public ministry. This, the Sermon on the Mount, is Christ's first sermon.

"So, welcome Mr. Jesus to *Meet The Congregation.* Obviously our world is in a mess! Some questions...."

What Are You Doing About It?

The central word in the text is "light." In John 9:5, Jesus said, "I am the light of the world."

Several years ago, I went on a 185-mile rafting expedition through the Grand Canyon out west. I stopped by K-Mart and purchased a $1 flashlight beforehand. Big mistake! The first night out we camped riverside in a boulder field. About 2 a.m., I awoke and needed the portable toilet we had placed across the field, downwind, in some scrub trees. I grabbed my trusty one-buck light and ambled over. When I needed to return to my bed roll, the light wouldn't come on again. I fiddled with it and it flickered weakly, then went dark for good. So, here I was, 200 yards from my bed, it's inky dark, and no one can hear me yell over the river's voice. I know that rattlesnakes come out at night to soak up the warmth of the boulder field. Talk about feeling helpless! I'll never take light for granted again!

So it was in Jesus' day. There were no street lamps, no car headlights, no flashlights, and no wall switches. There were only flickering oil lamps. And as it is with light, so with knowledge.

In John 8:12, Jesus said, "He that follows me shall not walk in darkness, but shall have the light of life." But how does one gain this light, this truth? How can I shed light on death? How can I light the path toward a good marriage? How does one know life's meaning? What is right and wrong? Is there truth from God? Does he even exist?

There are two ways to discover truth. One is by human speculation. This can be very casual or highly academic as man tries to figure things out himself. The second means of finding truth, light to live by, is divine revelation. What Jesus is saying to a world in the dark is, "I have come to light your way so you can walk in reality."

This is what the prophet Isaiah said, "The people who walked in darkness have seen a great light."

Who?

Now, for a second question. "Jesus, who will aid you in shedding such light?" In the text, Jesus says, "You are the light...."

My friend, this is a huge compliment! For the same Jesus who said in John 9:5, "I am the light...." Now turns to his disciples and affirms, "You are the light...." In other words, "You are what I am!"

To whom was Christ speaking? To Peter and James — fishermen. To John — a merchant. To Paul — a sailmaker. To Nicodemus

— a court officer. To Luke — a physician. To Lydia — a textile importer. To Martha — a housewife and Timothy — a teenager. To such as these Jesus compliments, "You are my continuation! You are the light of the world."

Sadly, the church has lost something of this today. A mill worker complained to me, "One can't be a Christian and work where I work." I was introduced recently as a minister. "Oh," the man said, "You're one of those paid to be a Christian!" Our thinking, you see, has become, "I cannot be God's light of truth where I am, but the preacher can. He has studied. He gets paid. He's the professional."

Jesus will have none of it! To common folk like you and me he breathes, "You are the light."

If you look into the nighttime sky, scientists explain that some of the light has journeyed billions of miles and hundreds of years to reach your eye. You see, light ranges far from its source. In the text, Jesus is explaining that the light of God's truth in him finds its continuation in you and moves on further to others.

During the nineteenth century, a forgotten Sunday school teacher in Chicago led a shoe clerk to Jesus. The teacher's name was Kimball, and you have likely never heard of him. The shoe clerk was Dwight L. Moody.

Moody became an evangelist and over his ministry he had an influence on F. B. Meyer. Meyer began to preach on college campuses. One of the students he impacted was J. Wilbur Chapman, who worked with the YMCA.

Chapman, in turn, brought a former pro-baseball player named Billy Sunday to preach in Charlotte, North Carolina. The revival was so successful local churches arranged for a second meeting with the preacher, Mordecai Hamm.

A crew foreman on a dairy farm, Albert McMachon, persuaded some of his summer help, some local high school boys, to attend with him. And that's how Billy Graham became a Christian.

"You are the light...."

Where Do We Shine?

Now, for a third question: "Where? Where do we shine?" And Jesus answers, "You are the light of the world." We shine at church, for certain. We shine in classes, in small groups, at prayer, and in meetings. But our light carries out to the world of clubs, marinas, factories, schools, and housing developments.

Living shore-side, we're aware of local lighthouses. For ships at sea, a beacon of light across a dark, stormy ocean can be a lifesaver.

Exploring our region, I've found three lighthouses. One is the little-known Paige's Creek Lighthouse. During 1864, in the Civil War, federal gunboats shot the top out of it, and it has never been fixed. "Old Baldy" is the second lighthouse, the oldest one on the East Coast. It, too, no longer works. Only a very low-wattage bulb illuminates the top. Then there is the Oak Island Lighthouse, which is working at full strength with its light beam visible from miles away to guide ships to the harbor.

These area lighthouses symbolize us and our area churches. Some of us have quit shining because we've been hurt. Others of us have replaced the light of Jesus Christ with some low-wattage, unbiblical message. Yet, thankfully, there are some churches and Christians who light the way boldly, consistently as a working lighthouse.

In Matthew 5:13, Jesus called us the salt of the earth. The Greek word for "earth" means "geography." God has given us each a piece of geography to flavor with Christ. In Matthew 5:14, Jesus calls us the "light of the world." In Greek, the word "world" is *kosmos*. To the Greeks it meant order. Their idea of beauty was orderliness. Indeed, we get our word "cosmetic" from this. So, the essence of beauty is order.

God is saying, "What I want is beauty and order. I will bring it by shining it through you." Thus, in Christ, we become living demonstrations of godly order in our lifestyles, in our singleness, in marriage, at work, and at play.

Clearly, then, all of us are a witness to Christ's light in everything we say and do. As Jesus said, "A city set upon a hill cannot be hid."

I was at a conference waiting to speak. We were having a banquet. We were awaiting the opening prayer when I noticed a big slice of pecan pie at each place setting. I love pecan pie and I was starved, so I began to nibble on my dessert. A few minutes later I became aware of a real tussle going on between a mother and her child. The mother was saying, "No, you can't eat your dessert first! It'll spoil your dinner." With that the child pointed at me and said, "He did!"

Our witness cannot be hid.

How?

We've asked the what, who, and where of Christ in the text. Now, let's ask how. "Jesus, how do we shine?" And Christ replies, "Let your light so shine before men that they may see your good works."

It is vital to remember that we are not saved by works. We are, however, saved by faith in Jesus for a life of good works. James 2:17-18 warns us, "Faith without works is dead." A person who claims to be a Christian, yet has no accompanying works is highly suspect.

Consider the works of Jesus. He healed the blind, the deaf, the lame. Maybe you're to serve as a physician. He taught the masses preaching. Is this your calling? Okay! Perhaps you're not a preacher or a physician. Maybe you can wash dirty feet, serve drinks at a wedding, or teach twelve how to pray.

In John 14:12 the Lord confidently predicted, "Greater works than I do will you do." Think about it! Our Lord only had three short years to minister here. So far, I've had over 34! It is likely I've had the chance to preach to more people than Jesus! Ditto for doctors and healing — and servants who cleanse dirty feet.

When I was a young child my parents bundled me into the car once a month and took me to Hickory, North Carolina, for a weekend visit to my grandparents and my great-grandmother. Sunday morning came, the visit was brief, so we skipped church, choosing instead to cozy together around the breakfast table. That is, all except my great-grandmother Espey.

Mrs. Espey got dressed and sat in her chair in the living room waiting for her ride to church. I watched her struggle to fit her swollen feet into high, lace-up shoes. As she huffed and puffed, I quietly wondered, "Why does she go to such lengths to attend worship? Why would she leave us to go? What is so important about church?"

Mrs. Espey was the first to witness Jesus to me. She was the light of my life! Now, years later, I know Jesus and worship and why it is all well worth the struggle!

Why?

Now for a final question in our interview with Jesus, *Meet The Congregation*. "Why?" "Why do we shine?" And the Lord replies, "Let your light so shine before men that they may see your good works and *glorify your Father who is in heaven*." In other words God's light in us is for his glory and not our own.

An interesting contradiction presents itself here. In Matthew 5:16, Jesus urges us to "Let your light shine before men." But later in Matthew 6:1, Jesus cautions, "Beware of practicing your piety before men in order to be seen by them." Which is it, Jesus? To show or to hide? Is this, indeed, a contradiction or a caution for balance?

I think Jesus is saying enigmatically, "When tempted to show off, hide. And when tempted to hide, show forth."

Some examples: When offering a tithe, a large one, that could garner you great prestige in the church, hide! Give in secret!

On the other hand, in the classroom when abortion is being debated and the Christian pro-life position ridiculed, speak up!

Always make certain your motivation is to God's glory and not your own. Every preacher should forever remember that only God is great. Our goal is never to get people to say, "What a great preacher you are!" But "What a great God we serve!"

In science there is an observable phenomenon known as phototropism. You may observe this by noticing how a plant will grow toward the light. When we become the light of the world people grow toward Jesus.

Conclusion

Over 1,600 years ago, Ambrose tutored a lost boy given to wild excesses. When the youth began to grow up, he converted to Christ and wrote his life story: *The Confessions of St. Augustine*.

Of his tutor he wrote, "I began to love him, not at first as a teacher of truth, which I despaired of finding in the church, but as a fellow creature who was kind to me. He did not use any arguments. He built a bridge of love from his heart to mine, and Christ walked over it."

Ambrose was Jesus' light to Saint Augustine.

In 1832, when German author, Goethe, lay dying, his last words were, "Light! More light!" And such is the cry of our world today.

Let's be what Jesus says we are.

Suggested Prayer
Lord Jesus, shine through me! Amen.

From Legalism To Obedience

Think not that I have come to abolish the law and the prophets; I have come not to abolish them but to fulfill them. For truly, I say to you, till heaven and earth pass away, not an iota, not a dot, will pass from the law until all is accomplished. Whoever then relaxes one of the least of these commandments and teaches men so, shall be called least in the kingdom of heaven; but he who does them and teaches them shall be called great in the kingdom of heaven. For I tell you, unless your righteousness exceeds that of the scribes and Pharisees, you will never enter the kingdom of heaven.
— Matthew 5:17-20

And I will tell you a modern fable ...

The earth was in crisis. Rivers were polluted. The air was fouled, the food chain poisoned. An AIDS epidemic was killing millions. City streets were battle lines in a race war. Civil courts were clogged with the most uncivilized behavior — lying, cheating, stealing, and divorce. Churches were half attended. Family values were dead. And taxes were climbing over 40% as big government threw money at problems.

What to do? The president called a summit of the nations' best mayors, lawmakers, police chiefs, and professors. All of their gathered input was fed into a computer and the key was pressed requesting solutions. The powerful main frame began its electronic ruminations, then slowly began its printout.

"You shall have no other god but God."
"You shall not bow to a graven image."
"You shall not take God's name in vain."
"Remember the sabbath day."
"Honor your father and mother."
"You shall not steal."
"You shall not kill."
"You shall not commit adultery."

"You shall not covet."

So it is we come to the law of God as discussed by Jesus in the Sermon on the Mount. There are three key phrases we must master if we are to comprehend what Jesus said.

The Law

The first is "The Law." "Think not that I have come to abolish the law," Jesus said. What exactly is "the law" to which Jesus is referring?

In the Old Testament there are three groups of laws.

First, there are the health laws, found mostly in Leviticus. God promised his people, "If you obey my commandments ... I will put none of these diseases among you which I put upon the Egyptians" (Exodus 15:26). Then God proceeded to reveal health and nutritional habits that science has only affirmed in the last 150 years. Check it out: Sterilization (Leviticus 13:52), the quarantine (Leviticus 13:45-46), purification (Leviticus 13:54), meat spoilage (Leviticus 19:5-7), and further laws about revenge, sexual expression, and diet.

In the year 1348, a ship pulled into the harbor of Genoa, Italy. It had been trading for spices in distant Mediterranean ports. As she was tied up to the wharf, the bodies of several sailors, recently deceased, were carried ashore. The healthy crew members offloaded their cargo and went ashore themselves.

Soon, even the healthy crew became sick with wheezing and rosy patches on their skin. They, too, began to die.

The epidemic spread to households, merchants, schools, monasteries ... and other cities.

Some citizens went to bed well, got sick in their sleep, and died before daybreak.

The mysterious illness began with rosy patches on the skin ringed in red, then the victim began to sneeze, and death came within days at most.

Children began to play games in the street and chant, "Ring around the rosey (the symptoms), a pocketful of poseys (flower petals thought to cure), ashes, ashes (cremation of dead bodies)! We all fall down!" (The grim result of the plague.)

Between 1348 and 1350 at least one third of the population between India and Iceland perished in what became known as "The Black Death." Entire villages were wiped out. Some urban areas lost half their populations. There were so many corpses there weren't enough workers to bury the dead.

Why was this sickness ravaging the world? Doctors thought it came from poisoned wells. The Jews were blamed. Thousands of Jewish innocents were massacred. Others thought it came from someone giving you the evil eye. Soon, no one was making eye contact.

It was the monks of the monastic orders who eventually abated the plague. They did so by restoring the health laws of Leviticus to medieval society.

Fourteenth-century European towns were built tightly together. Raw sewage was emptied into city streets from chamber pots. The sick were not quarantined. People ate with unwashed hands. Rats foraged in unburned trash.

The monks taught villagers to dispose of human waste outside the city. They insisted clothes be washed regularly. Quarantines were imposed. General sanitation improved, and the plague lifted.

It would be another 500 years before science understood what the sickness was, how it killed, and how to prevent it. Now we know it was the Bubonic Plague, caused by flea bites from the fleas nesting on rats that were brought in on ships. When the monks taught villages to clean up, the rats left and so did the fleas and the plague.

The Ceremonial Law

Besides the health laws of diet and sanitation, there are the ceremonial laws of the Old Testament. Many of them are found in the book of Numbers, but you'll find them throughout the first five books of the Bible.

The ceremonial laws deal with things like the calendar year and certain seasonal repetitious celebrations of God's mighty deeds — Passover, Pentecost, Day of Atonement, and Hanukkah. The priesthood's calling and training is prescribed along with dress code, music, and specific acts of worship such as praise, fasting, confession, and reading God's word.

The point of all this is plain. God exists, and he desires a balanced relationship with his people. But he is holy and we are warned not to come into his presence casually, but reverently, and on his divinely revealed terms.

Ah, but here's the sticking point! We all want God ... but on our own terms. I was discussing worship with a gentleman recently, and he said, "I think people should find a church in which they are comfortable and dress like they please." The problem with such thinking is that it is backward. It is man-focused instead of God-focused. It asks, "What do I want?" not "What does God want?" It asks if I am comfortable, a rather Hedonistic question, but it overlooks the more important consideration, "Is God pleased?" The ceremonial laws answer that question.

The Moral Law

Besides the health laws and the ceremonial laws of scripture, there is yet a third body of law taught in the Old Testament and that is the moral law. Technically called the decalogue, we know it more popularly as the Ten Commandments, found in Exodus 20.

The first four moral laws deal with one's relationship with God — priority, worship with mind and body, religious speech, and time.

The last six of the laws deal with our relationship with people — respect for authority, respect for property, marriage, truth, life, and a warning against greed.

So, when Jesus mentioned "the law" in his sermon, he was likely referring to the health laws and the ceremonial law as well as the decalogue.

Now, to further complicate matters! In Jesus' day "the law" could mean one of four things ...

1. It could refer to the Ten Commandments.
2. It could refer to the first five books of the Bible, the Pentateuch, literally in Hebrew, "The Five Rolls" or scrolls of the Old Testament.

3. It could refer to the whole of scripture, including the prophets. This is, obviously, what Jesus was meaning, because in the text, he actually refers to "the law and the prophets."
4. However, there is a fourth law. It is the oral or scribal law of man's interpretation.

For instance, in the fourth commandment work is forbidden on the sabbath. But what constitutes work? The law has to be interpreted. So a sect of scribes developed in Judaism whose purpose was to interpret the law.

Scribes defined work on the sabbath as carrying money in your pocket. They decreed it was unlawful to carry more weight than a dried fig, drinking more than a swallow of milk, or writing more than two letters of the alphabet. They even taught that in treating the sick, it was sinful to heal on the sabbath. One could stabilize the patient but must not seek to cure him.

By 300 AD, the scribes had written over 800 pages of laws known as the "Mishnah." Later, to further explain the "Mishnah," twelve more volumes were produced known as the "Talmud."

A cult known as the Pharisees grew up around the law. Their name means "The Righteous Ones." These men were 100% committed to keeping God's laws and thus earning their salvation by correct behavior.

A cartoon best sums it up. It is titled "How a Pharisee witnesses." In it a Pharisee is piously asking a sinner, "Have you heard the 4,973 spiritual laws?"

All of this, yet in the Sermon on the Mount Christ speaks of the law with reverence.

Not Come To Abolish The Law

That is something of what God's law is. Jesus says he did not come to abolish the law.

In his sermon, Jesus assured his listeners, "Think not that I have come to abolish the law." Indeed, he mused, not even a "jot or tittle would pass away." These are tiny Hebrew alphabet marks, like our dotting an i or crossing a t. Clearly then, Jesus expressed God's law to be eternal, even to the tiniest of details.

In the complexity of all this, don't miss the simple truth. God is, and he is a personal God calling to himself a people, the Jews. God selects Israel to be the land wherein they dwell. He gives them a law, a social contract, the living of which singles them out from among the people of the world. They would be healthier, wiser, more prosperous, and more just than any people around the globe. As the prophet predicted, "Nations will come to the brightness of your rising" (Isaiah 60).

Today, our society antagonizes anyone trying to structure our lives by law. But we've got to live by someone's rules! For instance, what traffic laws will we obey?

What if I stop on red and go on green, but you decide to do the opposite? Others stop on yellow. Still others stop at nothing, while everyone makes up their own speed limits. At the first intersection there is a snarl of traffic, human carnage, and general immobility. Matters become worse as citizens take things into their own hands.

I tell you, the highways would be full of people trying to get out of the city, not into it!

To avoid such anarchy, God gave his law. It is a civilizing social pact limiting certain behaviors and encouraging others. Its result among the living is order, prosperity, and community.

However, there is something hidden in the law that is also very wonderful. For the law reveals what God is like in what he allows or disallows.

Example: If you visit my home, I'll likely request you leave your muddy shoes at the door. I like a fire in the hearth but guard carefully to keep the flames off the living room rug. You won't hear lewd rap music or see pornography lying about. You see, what I limit and permit reveals my character. As it is with me, so it is with God. His laws bespeak of his nature, the content of his character.

God's health laws reveal his practical compassion for our physical well-being. His ceremonial laws reveal his desire for well-rounded fellowship with us in worship that is both reverent and beautiful. His decalogue reveals his character of community, order, truth, and justice.

Who God is, as revealed in this law, is best described as "holy," and Jesus assures us God's law and character are eternal. Such cannot be abolished by kings or politicians in congress, nor will the ravages of time weaken it, nor will the fickleness of cultural trends cause it to go out of fashion. "Not a jot nor a tittle shall pass away," Jesus assured.

Fulfill It

So far, Jesus has mentioned the law and said he did not come to abolish it, but he makes a third point. "I came to fulfill it," Christ said.

When I look in a mirror, it tells me my face is dirty. But can I use the mirror to wash my face? Of course not! It has diagnostic powers but not cleansing qualities. I must find soap and water for washing.

Likewise, when I look into the law I realize I am a lawbreaker, a sinner before God. But can I wash in the law? No way! Hebrews 7:9 says, "The law never made anything perfect." The law, like a mirror, can diagnose my problem, but it can't fix it. I go from the law poor in spirit, mourning my sin, hungry for mercy. And where do I find cleansing forgiveness? In Jesus Christ!

As I read the New Testament and come to the cross, I understand on some level that Christ took the punishment for sin that I myself deserved. I trust him and find forgiveness, and he sets me free. But free to do what? To continue breaking his law? No! Out of the incredible relief of mercy, for sheer love and gratitude, I've a new desire to obey God's law.

Take a teenager, just turned sixteen, with a new sports car. He drives it with glee! Sadly, he doesn't take care of it. Turning corners on two wheels, no oil changes, tires underinflated, grinding the gears, and then one day the car quits. It's towed to the dealer, still under warranty. The mechanic asks to see the maintenance schedule. The teen responds with a blank look, "What maintenance?"

The warranty is voided. The engine has seized up — it's a total loss. The teen is on foot. He can't buy his way out of this fix.

That's when the father steps in. He forgives his boy, purchases a new car, and puts the child in it. He also gives him an owner's manual and says, "Read this. And this time keep the rules!"

Will that son waste his second chance? Probably not! Out of sheer gratitude the child will keep the law not because he "has to," but because he "gets to" please his father.

When we realize God the Father's love for us on the cross, we must answer it. "Christ is the end of the law," Paul wrote in Romans 10:4. Augustine had a fine way of putting it. "Love God and do as you please," he spoke. When we love Jesus, indeed, it becomes our desire to please him.

Conclusion

So far Jesus has spoken of the law, how it is eternal, and how he fulfills it. Next Christ gives six very meddlesome examples of the fulfillment of the law. They are the six "you have heard that it was said, but I say" statements dealing with murder, adultery, divorce, swearing, revenge, and love. We will turn to these in detail in later chapters.

My friend, Harvey, was laboring in his garden breaking stones. "That pile doesn't seem to shrink," I observed. "No, Stephen, these stones are like the Ten Commandments. You can go on breaking them, but you can't get rid of them."

Alas, for our society's attempt to get rid of God's law. Until 1978, schools in Kentucky posted the Ten Commandments on classroom walls, but the Supreme Court ruled 5-4 that such was unconstitutional. Since then the law has become increasingly obscure.

The results? Prior to 1978, the two worst problems in the classroom were talking out of turn and chewing gum. Today, however, our besetting classroom problems are disrespect for teachers, drugs, theft, profanity, guns, and cheating — and pregnancy.

For those of us in Christ, we have the urgent mandate as salt and light, to live forth the law not to save us, but because we are saved.

Paul wrote it well in Romans 6:12-14: "Let not sin therefore reign in your mortal bodies to make you obey their passions. Do not yield your members to sin as instruments of unrighteousness;

but present yourselves to God as those alive from the dead, and your members as instruments of righteousness to God. For sin will have no dominion over you, since you are not under the law, but under grace."

Suggested Prayer
Jesus, save me from self-righteousness to your righteousness. Amen.

Do The Old Rules Still Apply?

> *"I am the Lord your God, who brought you out of the land of Egypt, out of the house of bondage. You shall have no other gods before me. You shall not make for yourself a graven image.... You shall not take the name of the Lord your God in vain.... Remember the Sabbath day to keep it holy...."* — Exodus 20:24, 7-8 (RSV)

Grandma was well into her eighties when she saw her first basketball game. It was a high school contest in which two of her great-grandsons played. She watched the action with great interest. Afterward everyone piled into the van to get some ice cream and a grandson inquired, "Grandmama, what did you think of the game?" "I sure liked it fine," she chirped. And then a little hesitantly she added, "But I think the kids would have had more fun if somebody had made the fellow with the whistle leave the players alone!"

I wonder when it comes to God's law, do most of us feel the same way? We'd all enjoy our lives much more if we could do away with the rules!

Yet think two minutes about playing a basketball game with no rules: Anything is fair. It would be trip, gouge, cut, shoot, elbow, slug, and even kick! A little of that and soon the game would become chaos! Players would be walking off the court in disgust, refusing to play in a game that is no fun!

It is the same with playing by the rules of life. Israel was a slave in Egypt when God through Moses freed them to become a new nation. Then at Sinai the Lord gave them the Ten Commandments with this introduction, "I am the Lord your God who brought you out of the land of Egypt, out of the house of bondage." "I freed you," God said, "and now I give you these simple laws to keep you free!"

Very simply, the Ten Commandments are a fence God places around our behavior and inside of it the good things of life can run wild.

Looking at God's law, it is immediately noticeable they were written on two tablets of stone. The law is divided into two parts. The first four laws deal with one's relationship with God. The next six deal with one's relationships with people. In this chapter we will deal with the first four.

Priority

Law one reads, "I am the Lord your God. You shall have no other gods before me."

"I am," God affirms. "I exist!" And, "I am the Lord *your* God." Straightaway we learn God exists and he is a personal God calling us to a relationship with himself.

Malcolm Muggerridge, the fine British intellectual, journalist, and author, became a Christian late in his life. When asked why, he explained, "I didn't want a God. I was not looking for God, but I had to come to terms with the fact that God wants me and came looking for me."

That's exactly what Adam and Eve discovered. When they sinned, they turned from the Lord to themselves and hid from God. Yet the Lord walked in the cool of the evening and called out, "Where are you?" He sought the twosome until he found them. "I am," he intoned. "And whether you like it or not, I am your God!"

You see, God is not like broccoli that you may decide if you want him on your plate or not. He is God, the most important fact of the universe, and he calls us to relationship with himself.

"I am the Lord your God. You shall have no other gods before me." Actually, the Hebrew word for "before" can also be translated "beside." "You shall have no other gods before me or beside me." God simply asks that he be our number one relationship, our first priority.

Many years ago, I was sitting in a movie theater with my girlfriend. We were watching James Michener's *Hawaii* when the main character wept to his wife, "I have sinned, because I love you more than God!" Immediately I was smitten by the Holy Spirit in my heart. By that time in my life I was a Christian. I loved the Lord. It's just that I also loved my girlfriend, football, clothes, money, myself, cars, and a dozen other things. Frankly, God was fifth or sixth down on my list of priorities. The result was that I was unhappy. So was God — and he was calling out to me like an anguished lover.

Try this experiment. Go home and turn your radio on. Tune it to a beautiful symphony with long stretches of pristine harmony. Enjoy! Now, turn the tuner dial just a tad to the right so that you're still receiving the signal, but you're also mixing it with another channel along with some static. The raucous sounds will cause you to do one of two things: either tune in or turn it off! That's what Jesus meant when he said, "No one can serve two masters." "You can't serve God and mammon." God wants our first love with no rivals, no static, in full tune. All other loves of our life aren't even close! (Matthew 6:24).

Is that how you love God now?

No Fixed Image

Law two requires us never to make a graven image of the Lord God and bow to worship it. It's with a great sense of relief that we come to this law because most of us think we're not about to break it. But look twice!

Precocious Nancy, in the first grade, sat in her Sunday school class hunched over her drawing paper working eagerly with crayons. "What are you drawing?" The teacher inquired.

"I'm drawing a picture of God!" the child confided.

"That's silly," the teacher said. "No one knows what God looks like."

To which the child replied, "They soon will!"

We laugh, but we all still think we've got God's picture. Ancient man experienced God in his conscience and through nature. He was awed. The Lord had a voice of thunder, the strength of a bull, the bosom of a mother, and the wisdom of the aged. Ancient man tried to symbolize God by creating a statue of him. Trouble was, when humans reduced God to an image, they soon elevated their image to the status of God. It became a snare.

Though not many of us make statues of God and bow, often we have fixed inner conceptions of who God is. Many today see God as a grandfatherly figure, tolerant, busy, who likes Baroque music, the sort of mahogany found in church pews, and big theological words like "ecclesiastical." In other words, God is an Episcopalian gentleman ... or Baptist ... or Pentecostal ... or, you fill in the blank!

Fact is, no human can ever fully conceptualize God. That's like trying to capture the Pacific Ocean in a thimble! Even the apostle Paul was humble here. In 1 Corinthians 13 he wrote of knowing God, saying, "Now we see through a glass darkly." Paul is saying we view God through a very dirty window. Sure, Jesus said, "If you've seen me you've seen the Father" (John 14). Still, of all God is, we know but the dimmest outline. Of his love, his grace, his wisdom, his holiness, his majesty we cannot completely comprehend. So, law number two requires us to remain humble, to worship God open-endedly with ever expanding wonder and awe!

Many years ago in the Louvre Museum in Paris, I watched a schoolteacher take her class of six blind students up to the famous Venus de Milo statue. The students felt the smooth white marble contours of the statue's feet and marveled at all of what it must be. In a real sense we worship the Lord just like that. We know him. We have a grip on him in Jesus, but he is so magnificent and we are so small. There is so much to see and our vision is through a dirty window.

Is God for you a neatly packaged theological concept you've entirely figured out and stacked on a closet shelf marked, "irrelevant for daily life," or is he a growing, consuming, emerging, relevant deity you can't learn enough about?

Reverence

The third commandment reads, "Thou shalt not take the name of the Lord thy God in vain." In the Hebrew, to take God's name "in vain" means to say it idly, emptily, with no sense of reality.

You have a name and when you hear it called, you turn to that person, giving them your attention. Aren't you disappointed when the person who used your name did so out of mockery?

Jewish people know God as Yahweh, a name so Holy that it is unspeakable. God's name must never be used without a deep reverential sense that he is listening!

Today in Jewish courts, when a witness is sworn in, the judge says, "Remember, the earth trembled when God spoke the third commandment."

There are two major ways we violate the third commandment today. One is profanity. I watched a movie in which Jesus Christ's name was used quite regularly. But they weren't talking to my Lord. How many of us salt our conversation by telling God what to damn and such? Profanity is basically trying to establish my own authority at God's expense. It reduces God's name to a swear word. It destroys reverence.

The second manner in which we violate law three is in lip service. We call Jesus Lord then live as we please. We sign our name into covenant "in the name of God" then keep it as only it is convenient. We stand before the Lord and vow to wed in the name of the Father, Son, and Holy Spirit, in sickness and in health, for richer or poorer, for better or worse, until death us do part. Then we divorce when something better comes along, or we get tired of trying.

Soon neither our words nor our vows or prayers mean anything. Reverence is completely destroyed by our easy familiarity.

Law three brings back the spine-tingling awe of the reverent use of language to and about God ... "our Father, Jesus, Holy Spirit, almighty God, or the one who hears me speak." When you say these words do you mean them reverently?

Sabbath

The fourth law reads, "Remember the sabbath day to keep it holy." The Hebrew word, *sabbath*, means "to desist." "Remember the day to desist and keep it holy."

Pharaoh's cruel taskmasters had put Israel to forced labor seven days a week, literally worked them right into the ground. When Moses liberated them, God sat them down at Mount Sinai and said, "You are not slaves, you're my children. Work, to be sure! But take a day off, a sabbath to desist, to rest, and keep it holy! Keep it separated unto the Lord."

When I went off to college, I had to learn to wash my own clothes. That means you let everything you have get dirty and pile up in the bottom of your closet. Then you wear it for six more weeks. Finally you decide to wash, because it's hard to catch the foxes when you smell like the hounds. You bundle everything up, walk to the laundromat, open the lid, and drop it all in together — jeans, tennis shoes, white shirts, red plaids. It all kind of swishes together in soapy suds and comes out ... *gray*.

That's what happens to life when we treat the sabbath as just another day. We no longer keep it holy, separated unto God, so it is secular — just another day to work, run to and fro, play a game, or shop. And what happens? The bright, crisp, holy white of the Lord's presence in our lives greys until there's no knowledge of God in our lives or in our culture.

In the mid-1800s, an English safari made its way into the African interior. For six arduous days the explorers and their bearers slashed their way into the jungle's heart. Come day seven, the leaders were up early to be at it again. But their porters wouldn't pack up. No amount of coaxing or threats would make them move. Finally the black tribal leader explained, "Day seven we stop here and rest. Let our soul catch up with body."

There you have it. Refusing to let the material outpace the spiritual, allowing the spiritual time to grow amidst the secular.

Look at it this way. If I want to obey law one and put God first, and if I want to be careful how I conceptualize God and expend my physical energy bowing and pursuing him, and if by law three I am careful with my tongue not to destroy reverence as I talk about God, then there is only one thing more I lack — time. There must be time to put God first. There must be time to bow down. There must be time to think, to study, and to talk of him in worship. Hence, remember the day to desist, to keep it holy, separated out from the rest of human affairs like work and shopping, traveling, and so on; a day set aside for rest and worship that I might know God.

Conclusion

If you break the laws of agriculture the crop fails. Break the laws of architecture and the building collapses. Break the laws of health and your body suffers. It is the same with God's moral laws: the Ten Commandments. Just look around you today and you will see in our society the results of our breaking these first four commandments.

But here is the good news! While the law tells us what man must do, the gospel tells us what God has done.

Man has sinned but God has come to redeem. Man has turned from the law to go his own way only to end up in ruin. But Christ has come calling us to turn back to God. In the end he paid the penalty for our sins on the cross.

A student said to me, "Why did Jesus die on the cross? Why didn't God just forgive us? I mean, after all, he is God. He can do anything he wants!" I told the student that God does love us — but his nature is also just. He loves us with the love of a judge.

I was riding in my car through the little town of Ware Shoals, South Carolina. I was doing about 45 miles per hour in a 35 miles per hour zone and a policeman coming toward me pulled me over. He said, "You're speeding. You're under arrest. You'll have to come with me." He took me to the local justice of the peace who was also a barber who was shaving a man at the moment.

He told me to sit down, the court would be in session in a few minutes. Sure enough, when he finished shaving the man, the barber stepped over to a desk in the corner, rapped a gavel, and said, "The court's in session. What's the charge?"

"Speeding," the officer accused.

"Guilty or not guilty?" the judge asked me.

"Guilty, your honor," I said.

"That'll be $65," he said, without looking up.

I reached in my wallet to get my money to pay the man, when suddenly the judge looked up, stared at me, and a look of recognition crossed his face.

"Don't I know you?" he inquired.

I said, "I hope not, your honor."

"Aren't you Stephen Crotts, the minister who spoke to our South Carolina State Fellowship of Christian Athletes Convention?"

I said, "Your honor, sir, I regret to admit, that's me."

He stood up and said, "Put her there, pal!" He shook my hand vigorously. He went on to say how much my sermon had meant to his son and how welcome I was in his town.

I slipped my wallet back into my pocket and felt relieved. He offered me a soda and a pig's knuckle, and we chatted amiably for thirty minutes. Then I reminded him I was in a hurry. After all, that's why I was here in the first place. "Another town in which to preach the gospel," I assured him.

As I turned to leave, he said, "That'll still be $65!"

He liked me. He was my friend, but he was still a judge. What sort of judge would he have been if he'd have winked at the law? The crime had been committed. The penalty had to be extracted. So, I paid dearly.

And what of this universe, God's law, and our lawlessness? God has taken three $20 bills and a $5 bill and put them in the drawer himself. "You've broken the law. But I'm going to pay the penalty for you." That's what it means when Jesus died for our sins. He suffered the death penalty for sin we deserved.

All of us have sinned and fallen short of the glory of God. We deserve to die, to be separated from God, forever. However, Christ stepped in and took our places. All we can do now is turn from sin to God by faith and ask Christ to save us. Then God does a wonderful thing. He not only forgives us, he fills us with his Spirit and causes us to want to obey him, to live out his law — not to save us, but because we are saved.

Perhaps there is one of you here today who'd like to get in on this gospel. Right now, right here, you'd turn to Jesus and accept his grace and devote yourself in gratitude to putting him first, worshiping him spiritually, and using your days to reverently know and speak of him.

The old laws still apply!

Suggested Prayer

Jesus, Lord, forgive my sins. Fill me with your Spirit as you write your laws upon my heart that I might walk in them. For Christ's sake. Amen.

Anger: The Misunderstood Emotion

> *You have heard that it was said to the men of old, "You shall not kill; and whoever kills shall be liable to judgment." But I say to you that everyone who is angry with his brother [without cause] shall be liable to judgment; whoever insults his brother shall be liable to the council, and whoever says, "You fool!" shall be liable to the hell of fire. So if you are offering your gift at the altar, and there remember that your brother has something against you, leave your gift there before the altar and go; first be reconciled to your brother, and then come and offer your gift. Make friends quickly with your accuser, while you are going with him to court, lest your accuser hand you over to the judge, and the judge to the guard, and you be put in prison; truly, I say to you, you will never get out till you have paid the last penny.*
> — Matthew 5:21-26

My sermon topic is Emmanuel Kant's deontological categorical imperative with poly-syllabic profundities from the floating pericopes of the ancient Eucharistic text. Aren't you just aquiver with anticipation?

According to recent polls, the big reason people do not attend church is that it all seems so irrelevant. But starting with Matthew 5:21, Jesus gets relevant, and personally so! Like the small town news editor who had some extra space and printed the Ten Commandments as a filler. Within a week he had 103 complaint letters. "Cancel my subscription. You've become meddlesome."

In the last chapter, we studied God's law, how Christ did not come to abolish it but to fulfill it. Now the Lord shows us just how thoroughly he plans to do just that — to fulfill the law in us so that our "righteousness exceeds that of the scribes and Pharisees" (Matthew 5:20).

The next 27 verses describe an unsurpassable obedience that the Pharisees, for all their outward show, could not even imagine.

In this portion of his sermon Christ uses the formula, "You have heard it said, but I say...." He does this six times, using intensely personal examples of anger, lust, divorce, swearing, revenge, and love. In this chapter we'll grapple with the first — anger.

What Is Anger?

In Matthew 5:21, Christ quotes from the Decalogue, Exodus 20:13, "You shall not kill." "You have heard that it was said to the men of old, 'You shall not kill,' but ..." and this is the shocker ... Christ keeps going! "But I say ... everyone who is angry with his brother shall be liable to judgment." Clearly Jesus was equating the outward act of homicide with the inner attitude of anger. Both are destructive and liable to the same punishment by God, he says.

In the Greek, there are two words used for anger. One is *thumos*, defined as "a fire in dry straw — quick kindling, burning hot, but just as suddenly gone."

A woman once confessed to Billy Sunday, "I've a bad temper. I blow up over the least little thing. But it's over in a minute."

Sunday said, "So is a shotgun blast. It's over in a second, but look at the terrible damage it can do."

The other word for "anger" is *orgizesthai*, defined as "a cold, calculated anger" — nursed, long-lived with a slow burn. This is the word Jesus uses in the text.

In United States law, both forms of murderous anger are recognized. First degree murder is premeditated, the cold, calculated stalking of one's victim. Second degree murder is the sudden, irrational variety of homicide. A man looks at your girl in the bar. You say something to him, he takes a swing at you, and you stab him to death.

What Jesus is doing in these verses is linking our deeds with our thoughts. He is saying the one is just as vital to righteousness as the other. The Pharisees, you see, never killed, but, like us, they liked to think about it, to fantasize about striking someone in the face, getting even, dispatching someone to an early grave.

In a local novelty shop, for $3.95, one may purchase "The Traffic Avenger." Battery operated, dashboard mounted, and quite harmless, the owner can press a button and hear the sound effects of ridding oneself of the car in front of you. The choices are "Flame Thrower," "Sidewinder Missile," and "Vaporizer." It's the latest in road-rage chic.

Jewish scribes in Jesus' day believed as long as you didn't do the deed all was okay. But Jesus raised the bar — if you think it, if you cultivate it inside, then you're just as guilty!

Plato described people as charioteers being pulled by two horses, one Reason and the other Passion. It is up to us to decide which one leads.

Modern psychiatrists teach that if we sow a thought, we reap an act. If we sow an act, we reap a habit. If we sow a habit, we reap a character, and if we sow a character, we reap a destiny. Thus, as Jesus said, all homicide starts with thoughts.

So, what is anger? Jesus defines it as a murderous emotion, a loss of control in our inner life that leads to destructive behavior.

Righteous Anger

Not all anger is bad. In Matthew 5:22, Christ carefully delineates, "But I tell you anyone who is angry with his brother [without cause]...." Some translations add "without cause." Others delete it. Nevertheless, Ephesians 4:26 instructs us to "Be angry, but do not sin."

Jesus waxed angry at the money changers in the temple. He took a whip and drove them out, overturning their tables.

Certainly the sin of our day is angerlessness. We lack passion. We are slumped in indifference.

Scour the Bible and you will find at least eight instances of anger properly used.

1. Moses' anger at Israel's idolatry in the valley of resting (Exodus 32:19).
2. Jonathan's anger at Saul's plans to kill David (1 Samuel 20:34).
3. Anger at innocent children being harmed (Nehemiah 5:6).
4. Elihu's anger at Job's condemnation by three friends (Job 32:2-3).

5. The prophet's indignation at Israel for not heeding God's word (Jeremiah 6:11).
6. Christ's wrath at hypocrisy (Mark 3:5).
7. Paul's ire at an evil doer hindering the gospel (John 2:16).
8. Jesus' anger over false doctrine (Revelation 2:15).

I think the spirit of our age, our lack of righteous indignation, is best captured in Ralph Coingold's novel, *Two Friends of Man*. A friend chides his companion, "Hull, do try to moderate your indignation and keep cool. Why, you are all on fire!"

Hull responds, "Mr. May, I have need to be all on fire, for I have mountains of ice about me to melt."

Unrighteous Anger

We've looked at what anger is — a fire in dry straw or a simmering pot. We've also considered angerlessness as a sin, and the need for righteous indignation. Now let's look at unrighteous anger.

In verse 22, Jesus warns, "Anyone who insults his brother is answerable to the Sanhedrin. But anyone who says 'You fool' will be liable to the hell of fire."

Go grab a book of matches. How does one ignite a match? Strike it! Rub it slowly over an abrasive surface, and you'll get a spark that will cause the match to burst into fame and be consumed. This is how our tempers work. We rub by someone. There is friction. Heat! A right is violated. Our tempers spark. And there is a flare-up.

The first evidence of anger is often our tongue. It has the dubious distinction of being the only part of our anatomy that has two of the Ten Commandments governing it.

Jesus said anger with someone comes in the form of insults. Literally, to call someone "*Raca!*" This is neither a Hebrew or Greek word, but Aramaic. It is essentially untranslatable. It has to do with tone of voice, contempt for someone, insult. It is like calling someone "a brainless idiot."

The rabbi tells the story of a young student returning to his home from school. An old man's cart has broken down and is blocking the road. Angry at delay, the youth snarls at the elderly driver,

"You imbecile! *Raca*! How dare you delay me. You're such a peawit. Are all of your race so *raca*?"

To which the cart driver replies evenly, "Why don't you go and tell the maker how ugly is the creature he made!"

You see, God created. He made man in his own image (Genesis 1:26). He judged us to be "very good" (Genesis 1:31). To kill another human being is an act of rebellion. It is to fling creation back in God's face. "I won't have it!"

Jesus is saying that to insult a human is to start down the road to murder. We must not even put our foot on that path.

Further expanding on our inner life, Jesus describes how we call one another names like, "You fool!" In the Greek it is *moros* from which we get our word, "moron." Psalm 14:1 says, "The fool says in his heart, 'There is no God.' " It is the same word. We even get our word "morals" from this. *Moros* gave us our words "morals" and "moron," which means "to deride someone by calling them a fool is to pass moral judgment upon them."

To call someone "*Raca*!" is to insult their nature and personhood. To cry "Fool!" in someone's face is to judge them morally. The one is like calling someone "Bastard!" The other is like saying, "You go to hell!"

Jesus is saying murder starts with ill will in thoughts. It pops out of our mouths as insults, gossip, and slander. It is to speak ill of whom God has made. If left unchecked, it will eventually lead our hands to murder.

Christ declares in the text a "righteousness that exceeds that of the Pharisees." One is not righteous if he does not kill. He must not nurse thoughts of ill will and speak words of insult. "Nip it in the bud!" Jesus is saying.

Let it sober you in verse 22 when Christ Jesus three times reminds us God will hold us accountable for our thoughts, words, and deeds. "Liable to judgment." "Answerable to the council." "In danger of the fire of hell." See how seriously God takes our behavior toward one another? Even our inmost thoughts are under the Lord's scrutiny!

For the Pharisee, religion was an exterior show. "Just don't kill!" But for Jesus religion went deeper. The purest of religion invades the mind, the emotion, and will with God's word and Spirit. When the inner life is right, so the outer life is proper as well.

Now for verse 23. In the NIV, it begins with the word, "Therefore." Each time you come to this word in the scripture, you should ask, "What is the 'therefore' there for?" Clearly there has been an argument. Now Jesus is drawing conclusions: "Therefore, if you are offering your gift at the altar, and there remember that your brother has something against you, leave your gift there before the altar and go; first be reconciled to your brother, and then come and offer your gift."

Have you done something you know of to anger someone? Have you swindled, betrayed, insulted, slandered, or abused? Then go make it right, Jesus says.

You see, the Bible is a book of relationships. And we of the church should be about relationships as well.

The great commandment in Mark 12:28-31 bids us love God and love our neighbor as ourselves. There is a balance here. One cannot fully love the creator unless he fully loves the creation. Worship, Jesus says, is reflected in our human relationships. A tithe offering is a fine thing. But fixing a relationship of anger is finer still.

I have a pastor friend who was sexually immoral before he entered the ministry. He told me one of his biggest fears was to be in the pulpit preaching on marriage and sexual purity and look out in the congregation and see one of his former girlfriends. She'd be waving a handkerchief and saying, "Yoohoo! Remember me? Preach it, brother!" Before this dimension of his ministry could flourish, he had to go do some homework. He had to go back and ask forgiveness.

The best way, then, that we can worship God is by serving God's people, by valuing them, and by drawing them into healthy relationships.

Now Christ gives us some free legal advice. "Make friends quickly with your accuser, while you are going with him to court." If not, Christ sagely points out, you won't get out of the legal system until your pockets are emptied. When tempers get involved, truth matters little, and in the end you'll both lose.

Conclusion

Seneca called anger, "a brief insanity." Anger is like jumping into a wonderfully equipped sports car, gunning the motor, taking off at a high speed, then discovering the brakes don't work.

Anger manages everything badly. But truth and love manages everything well.

Proverbs 16:32 explains, "He who is slow to anger is better than the mighty; and he who rules his spirit than he who takes a city."

In Mexico City, tour guides will show you a volcano and say, "This would have been our tallest mountain if it hadn't blown its stack."

Suggested Prayer

Come inside, Jesus. I need you! Amen!

Adultery: Saying No And Knowing Why!

You have heard that it was said, "You shall not commit adultery." — Matthew 5:27

Cheating has become America's national pastime. Statistically, 65% of men have affairs by age forty. For women, it's 35%.

In his Sermon on the Mount, Jesus quotes Exodus 20:14, "You shall not commit adultery." Why? What's so wrong with sexual adventuring: Why must we live within single or wedded boundaries? Clearly, Jesus wants us to say, "No" to adultery and know why.

Talking with a pastor who had demitted the ministry due to sexual misconduct, he confided, "I never thought it could happen to me. But it did. For fifteen minutes of rolling in the sheets I sacrificed everything precious in my life — wife, children, reputation, ministry, even my health."

Another friend confided in me after adultery, "Stephen, it just happened! It just happened!" I said, "No, it didn't just happen. You let it happen!" In every affair there is a choice, steps taken, roadblocks crashed, and red lights run. For a very poignant look at the process that leads to an affair, read 2 Samuel 6-12. There the anatomy of David and Bathsheba's affair is laid bare before one's eyes.

In walking through this epic story of wrong, I want to make my points with all "E's" The point is, an affair is *easy*.

Estrangement

The first step is *estrangement*. David and his wife, Michal, are on the outs. He is excited about bringing the Ark up to Jerusalem. He danced for joy, but Michal belittled him. "My, how the king has lowered himself before the people today, dancing half naked like an ape!" From that day on, Michal and David barely spoke.

Most marriages that fail do so not from a blow out but from a slow leak. We get into marriage with such high expectations. We're in love, choosing to act in one another's best interests. "Forsaking all others I will keep myself only unto you so long as we both shall live." Early marriage is exciting, and we pursue it with verve!

Then there is a fight, some disappointment, and resentment settles in. A slow leak.

As a poet has written, "'Twas not love's going hurt my days, but that it went in little ways." The snap is gone. Sex becomes routine. She can't remember a tender time. He can't recall her support. So they quit trying together.

Two single men were talking. One remarked, "If I ever get married, I want a wife who is an economist in the kitchen, a lady in the living room, and a bobcat in the bedroom." He did marry several years later, and his friend asked him if he got what he had wanted in a woman. "Yes, but garbled," he replied. "My wife is a lady in the kitchen, a bobcat in the living room, and an economist in the bedroom."

Syracuse University has spent considerable time researching marriage. Of the ten most important things couples say they want in a marriage, sex is ninth. Caring, a sense of humor, and communication are tops.

Among men, the top five things they want in a wife are:

1. Respect — "She makes me feel capable." "She is proud of me!" "She is willing to follow my lead."
2. Domestic support — a home that is a refuge from the stress of the world; a home that's fun, pleasant, and tasteful.
3. Companionship — as in walks and talks, entering one another's world.
4. Sexual fulfillment — "She responds to me. She studies what is mutually pleasing, gets good at it, makes time for me, and takes sex seriously."
5. Attractiveness — clean, does her hair, cares how she looks, stays in the best shape she can.

Naturally, all of these values are constantly coming in and out of focus; but a good wife is always monitoring, adjusting, caring, and trying. She keeps her marriage fresh.

If these are what a man wants of a wife in marriage, what does a woman want of a husband?

1. Affection. According to Genesis 1-2, the first thing God didn't make out of dirt was a woman. Ephesians 5 explains that wives are made to be "cherished." This means romance, a steady stream of hugs, pats, compliments, kisses, and courtesies. At an airport, I saw a woman wearing a button that read, "This is my husband's idea of jewelry." Contrast that with William Jennings Bryan's hair over his ears. When asked why he wore it so since it was unfashionable, he said, "When I was courting my wife, she thought my ears stuck out funny and asked me to grow my hair long to cover them, so I did." To which his pal replied, "But that was years ago!" "Sure," Bryan said, "but the romance is still going on!"
2. Conversation on a "feeling" and emotional level.
3. Honesty and openness, not sullenness — "A person who won't close the door on me."
4. Financial support.
5. Family commitment — not a Dagwood Bumstead who passively sleeps and eats, but an active man who puts time and energy into the marriage, the children, the family.

On my wedding day, Joseph Paul Aiken, my grandfather, said to me, "Stephen, if you treat your wife like a queen, you'll get to be the king." He was paraphrasing the golden rule: "Do unto others as you would have them do unto you." Such does not come naturally. We have to work at it, strive to keep the marriage pumped up.

This is why happily married couples read, study, talk, and ask, "How am I doing?" They listen, acquire role models, and keep marriage among their top priorities. Without such action, the marriage develops a slow leak, until, like David and Michal, an ice age sets in, and they make the perfect couple — he's a pill and she's a headache!

Encounter

David and Michal were estranged. Next in the anatomy of an affair comes the *encounter*.

King David is middle-aged. He's lost a step on the battlefield, so he stays home while the whole army marches to war. Having slept late, he broodily walks his patio, and from there spies his neighbor's wife, Bathsheba, immodestly bathing in her rooftop garden.

Don Wharton, a friend of mine who is a songwriter and performer, told me other musicians constantly tell stories about how women throw themselves at them. Don said it never happens to him. He first thought he must be ugly or unsexy or something like that. Then he realized how in every one of his concerts he mentions his wife, how much in love they are, and sings some love song about her, Don realized how he is sending out signals to other women. "I'm spoken for." "No chance with me!" "I've got what I want!" His love for his wife simply jams other women's radar.

Some experts believe man has a hormonal lack only his wife can provide with respect. And similarly, woman has a hormonal lack only her husband can provide with cherishing. If the spouse does not provide it, a hunger sets in. And according to 1 Corinthians 7:5, Satan will try to provide it with an affair. This is what you have in the text. David is estranged from Michal, while Bathsheba's husband is absent, away at war. Both have pent up anger, sending out signals of their lonely dissatisfaction, and they encounter one another.

Empathy

Next on the list comes *empathy*. Look at the action verbs in 2 Samuel 11:1-5. David *saw*. David *sent*. David *inquired*.

It used to be that women were quite sheltered. They never went out in public without a chaperone and only then with their hair up and veiled. Now, with women joining the work force, dressing to show off their figures, and their hair down, encounters are much easier.

Two *starved* people meet, sparks fly in their looks, in a whiff of perfume, in a chance touch. In and of itself, these things are not bad. But if the sparks land in dry lives, then a flame is quickly kindled.

What we are talking about is a bonding or a meeting of needs between two people never meant to relate on such a level. It may be a hand on the shoulder or words like, "Sometimes I don't want to go home" or "You have a nice figure." He volleys in her court. She responds. The two begin to flirt and to look for opportunities to be around each other at the desk, on the phone, or at the water cooler. Feelings sent. Feelings received. The hook is set. He makes her feel cherished. She makes him feel respected.

Enjoyment

David "saw from the roof a woman bathing; and the woman was very beautiful." The Bible says he enjoyed it and wanted more. So, "he sent messengers."

This is the adventurism, the flirtation, the infatuation of an illicit romance. The deceptive sweetness of forbidden fruit. Like a moth drawn to a flame, we fly closer. "I'll just carry her bags up to the hotel room. That's all." "I'll just stay ten minutes and leave. I can handle it."

We now begin to live in a fantasy world. We wonder how it might be. We undress them in our minds. Our thoughts are ripe with the pleasure of them.

Expedition

Romans 13:14 warns, "Make no provision for the flesh to gratify its desires." This is a roadblock we crash quite brazenly. It began with estrangement, encounter, empathy, enjoyment, and now, *expedition*. David actually sent for Bathsheba and she came to his palace. It was like granting Satan an easement across his property.

We decide to go to a weekend business conference. She is there, too. We arrange to stay in the same hotel. Go out to dinner together and share a couple of drinks.

Or we decide to ask her to work late at the office.

"I'll just drive her home."

Bolder and bolder we become. "You have nice shoulders."

"Why, thank you. I sure could use a back rub."

Expression

The next step is *expression*. The text says, "So David ... took her ... and he lay with her." They stepped over the line. Thoughts became action. Fantasy turned into sex.

Now the two adulterers become obsessed, totally addicted, so that they often lose all sense of judgment. Nothing else matters but to be together — not spouse, not children, not church, not reputation. She swills in the cherished feelings. He is inebriated with her respect.

In a nearby town, a certain banker was having an affair with his secretary. At lunch he would go out to her car backed against the shrubs and stealthily climb into the trunk and close the lid. She would come out ten minutes later and drive the Cadillac out to a secluded woods where he would pop the trunk, climb out, and join her for an amorous time. Well, as fate would have it, she was low on gas one day, stopped at a filling station, and he, thinking they were at their rendezvous, popped the trunk lid and climbed out, to an audience of laughing customers and attendants. What fools adultery makes of us!

It's easy. Estrangement, encounter, empathy, enjoyment, expedition, and then expression, then suddenly, you're a fool!

Adultery is not purely a sexual sin. It is at the root the inability to deal with normal feelings of romance toward someone who was never meant to meet those needs. The problem is not *between* two people, but *in* two people. They will not nurture a relationship so that it lasts.

Effects

An affair is not over with the sexual experience. There is one step further: the effects. Second Samuel 12:7-14 explains how Bathsheba became pregnant, how David murdered her husband, Uriah, and lived a cover-up for a good year. "I can get away with it," David thought. "Nobody will have to know." Ah, but God knew! And he judged.

David and Bathsheba's child died, and Nathan, the prophet, said to David, "Because you have utterly spurned the Lord, the sword shall not depart from out of your house."

David's daughter, Tamar, was raped. His son, Amnon, was murdered. His boy, Absalom, rebelled and was slain. His next-in-line-for-the-throne, Adonijah, was killed. Solomon wed over 1,000 wives and they turned his heart away from the Lord. My, my! What an awful legacy of immorality David thrust upon his children.

A man utterly broken from the effects of adultery once moaned to me, "If I knew how far down it would take me, how long it would hold me, and how deeply it would hurt me, I would never have done it." Adultery is like a rat nibbling the cheese in a trap. The food is great but the service is terrible. Just how terrible adultery can be is eloquently described in the following quote, written by the husband of an unfaithful wife.

> *One reason it feels so good to be married is the sense of being chosen. Out of all the people in the world, she chose me. Me to touch. Me to express intimacy. Me to share life's deepest sighs and groans. When I'm with her, I keep thinking what a gift she is. I keep telling myself, "No one else gets to see this, to feel this. This relationship is exclusively ours." I feel confidence because I can please her, satisfy her. And when I wake up in the morning, she's still in my arms. She brushes her hair back and smiles at me and soothes, "I love you." And I know all is right with the world.*
>
> *After she had the affair, I felt de-chosen. My entire confidence was shaken. Could I not please her? How could she take what was exclusively ours and give it to another? The thought of her in another's embrace, another man seeing her, holding her, inside her, left me so hurt, so confused, so suspicious, so angry, so emotionally eviscerated I wanted to die. But I wasn't even sure death could remove the pain. I still torture myself, asking, "Where did I go wrong? How did I fail her? Why was I not enough?"*
>
> *Shakespeare's* Othello *called being victimized by adultery "cuckolded." I call it the great betrayal. It's like taking two who've become one and making them a diluted three. Like walking with a rock in your shoe,*

adultery leaves a sharp object in your marriage bed, in your memory, in your loins.

Now when I hold my wife, I'm tormented by the thought she's comparing me with another lover. What used to be a mutual embrace of exclusive intimacy is now so much less.

Conclusion

A poll of 250 ministers who admitted having affairs discovered they only had one thing in common. They all thought, "It can't happen to me."

I once met Billy Graham. It happened to be during the televangelist sex scandals. He was asked, "Mr. Graham, thank you for all your years of purity in ministry. How is it you have managed to stay scandal free?" To which Mr. Graham replied, "It's because I constantly run scared."

That's not bad advice for you and for me. Never say, "Never!" An affair is all too easy, and it begins when we allow our own marriages to grow stale.

Drink water from your own cistern, running water from your own well. Should you spill your springs of water in the streets? Let them be yours alone, never to be shared with strangers. May your fountain be blessed, and may you rejoice in the wife of your youth, a loving doe, a graceful deer — may her breasts satisfy you always, may you ever be captivated by her love. Why be captivated, my son, by an adulteress? Why embrace the bosom of another man's wife? For a man's ways are in full view of the Lord, and he examines all his paths. The evil deeds of the wicked man ensnare him; the cords of his sin hold him fast. He will die for lack of discipline, led astray by his own great folly.

— Proverbs 5:15-23 (NIV)

Suggested Prayer

Lord, keep me true! For Christ's sake. Amen.

Lust: The Fire Inside

But I say to you that every one who looks at a woman lustfully has already committed adultery with her in his heart. If your right eye causes you to sin, pluck it out and throw it away; it is better that you lose one of your members than your whole body be thrown into hell. And if your right hand causes you to sin, cut it off and throw it away; it is better that you lose one of your members than your whole body go into hell.
— Matthew 5:27-30

How can a young man keep his way pure? By guarding it according to thy word. With my whole heart I seek thee; let me not wander from thy commandments! I have laid up thy word in my heart, that I might not sin against thee. — Psalm 119:9-11

There is a woodstove in my home. Beneath the door is a stern warning in bold print: **"Warning!"** it reads. **"Always keep door closed during operation. Failure to do so may cause excessive heat and create a fire hazard."**

In our lives there is a firebox that God built into us to contain our sexual passion. Likewise, if we leave the door open to every desire, lust will ignite in our passion, meltdown will occur, and our lives will be consumed.

There are too many of us walking around out there with our door open. From many directions, the world is shoving logs into our passion: the internet, cable television, pornographic magazines, the cinema, risque gentlemen's clubs, provocative clothing, dirty jokes, 1-800 dial-a-porn. In Jesus' day, the Pharisees gloated that *they* didn't commit adultery. But Christ said, "That's not good enough! For if you nurse lusty thoughts in your mind, you're just as guilty!" As with anger and murder, Christ connects thinking with deeds. And here he connects lust with adultery. When he says, "looks at a woman lustfully ... in his heart" (v. 28), Jesus is saying the righteousness God expects starts with pure thinking. Thus does Jesus deepen God's standard beyond what the Pharisees expected.

So, what's a person to do? The answer is found in scripture: Psalm 119:9-11.

A Standard

First, the Bible tells us there is a moral standard. "How can a young man keep his way pure?" Hear that? The fact that the Bible uses the word "pure" is evidence God has a code of right and wrong. In Hebrew, the word for "pure" means "cleansed, innocent, or translucent (as opposed to muddy)."

On campus, a professor of philosophy ran into a colleague, a doctor of music, each morning at 7:45 a.m. in the faculty lounge. "What's the good news?" he asked every morning. The music teacher ignored the nervous remark for months, until, one day, he just couldn't stand it anymore. So when the philosopher chirped, "Good morning, professor! What's the good news?" He grabbed him by the arm, pulled him to his study, picked up a tuning fork, struck it with a mallet, and smiled with pleasure. "The good news is that's a C-note. It was a C 10,000 years ago. It is a C now. And it will be a C in 50,000 years!"

As with musical notes, so with morals. God's standards are eternal.

Singleness has always been a moral lifestyle. So has romance, marriage, and sexual fulfillment in wedlock. But homosexuality, fornication, lust, adultery, pedophilia, and casual divorce was, is now, and ever shall be, immoral.

Our society has lost its ethical moorings. We think we are our own moral authority and we can do as we please. Contrary to popular belief, there is still a God, he has his Ten Commandments, and he will judge our behavior.

Pope John Paul II preached, "We must not make the faith up as we go along." The text mentions purity, a standard God provides.

We Must Guard Our Lives By God's Standard

If you shop the Arab bazaars of the Middle East, you'll eventually come to the silk merchant. Customers walk into the dimly lighted store, select a dress, and walk abruptly out into the street with it. You think they are stealing at first! Yet, the merchant is unbothered. The customer out in the street holds the silk dress up to the sunlight and closely examines the fabric. He is looking for flaws, gauging the dress's quality. Only after he is satisfied with the quality of the goods will a purchase be arranged.

Likewise, we, too, must learn not to think every thought that pops into our minds. Rather, we closely examine each thought, holding it up to the light of God's word, and refuse to buy or wear any thinking that is seriously flawed.

Example: I see my neighbor's wife sunbathing while I'm out emptying the trash at the curb. She is altogether lovely, and I appreciate her physique and poise. Why not? The Bible says, "God looked on all that he made and said, 'Behold! It's very good.' " There is nothing wrong with such behavior.

But when I look twice, when I begin undressing her in my mind, when I leeringly imagine taking something that is not mine, then I begin to sin.

The word "lust" in Hebrew is *khaw-mad* and means "to covet or delight in or desire someone you can't rightfully have." In Greek "lust" is *epeethoomeho* and it means "to set the heart upon."

"How can a young man keep his way pure, translucent, and unsullied? By guarding it according to thy word" (Psalm 119:9 cf). The Hebrew for "guarding" means to "take heed." This means as you guard the amount of wood you put in your fire stove, you guard the thoughts you allow into your mind.

Would you put a stick of dynamite in your woodstove? No! You'd wreck your home! Likewise, allowing pornographic thoughts into your mind can explode in passion.

Serial killer, Ted Bundy, likely murdered over fifty women. He was executed in Florida in 1988. Interviewed just prior to his death, Bundy confessed, "I've lived in prison for a long time now and I've met a lot of men who were motivated to violence just like me. Without exception, every one of them was deeply involved in pornography."

God's way is pure, translucent, innocent married love — not sordid, filthy lust. Love's way is God-blessed; lust's way is God-damned. God's way is Spirit-filled. Lust's way is echoingly hollow.

Norman Cousins wrote, "The trouble with this wide-open pornography is not that it corrupts, but that it desensitizes; not that it unleashes the passions, but that it cripples the emotions; not that it encourages a mature attitude, but that it is a reversion to infantile obsessions; not that it removes the blinders, but that it distorts the view. Prowess is proclaimed, but love is denied. What we have is not liberation, but dehumanization."

There is a standard of proper and improper conduct. And we must guard our lives by it.

Scripture Helps Keep Us Pure

The psalmist with us complains to God, "How can a young man keep his way pure? By guarding it according to thy word ... I have laid up thy word in my heart that I might not sin against thee."

I have in my mind a conveyor belt, not unlike those you see at the baggage claims at airports, and it is constantly moving. On it I've placed hundreds of scripture verses I have memorized. As I live my life, I find I am tempted to step out of line with God's law. That's when the conveyor speeds up to suddenly stop while a red light flashes over a scripture verse.

For example, if I see a pretty lady on the street, my mind flashes a fantasy, and suddenly Proverbs 5:15-19 pops into my mind. Now, no man can think two thoughts at the same time, so I have a choice to make. Either I will lust or affirm God's word. I choose to think through the memory verse, "Drink water from your own cistern ... and rejoice in the wife of your youth ... Let her affection fill you at all times with delight, be infatuated always with her love!" Thus do I snap back to reality.

Another example is if I am teaching at a university on sexuality. Afterward a lovely woman, deeply troubled, asks to talk. "My car is in the lot. We can sit privately," she declares. Immediately, the conveyor belt springs forward and halts, the red warning light flashes Romans 13:14. "Make no provision for the flesh to gratify its desires." So I suggest we talk in the commons with a third party — the chaplain.

Here is another biblical passage that will keep you strong! When King David committed adultery with Bathsheba, the prophet,

Nathan, held him accountable. For his sinful behavior God judged, "The sword shall never depart from your house."

Just look what happened! Amnon, David's son, raped Tamar, Amnon's half sister. Absalom, another of David's sons, then killed Amnon. Absalom went on to ferment revolution, seeking to depose his father. "After all, if Dad does not have to play by the rules, why do I?"

Absalom failed and his throat was slit in battle. Adonijah was next in line for the throne. Yet, it was given to Solomon, who slew his brother, Adonijah. Over the years, Solomon wed every woman he could fit into his harem and foreign wives turned his heart away from the Lord.

See! David left the door open to lust and not only his life went up in flames, his heritage was consumed as well. Is that the heritage you want for your children?

Conclusion

Christ is so adamant about avoiding the destructive activity of lust, he actually warns, "If your right eye causes you to sin, pluck it out and throw it away; it is better that you lose one of your members than that your whole body to be thrown into hell." The Greek word meaning "causes you to sin" is *skandalon* from which we get our word, "scandal." It means to "bait a trap" for one to fall into.

Over the centuries, Christians have struggled with Jesus' meaning here. Origen, an early church father, took it literally and castrated himself to gain sexual control. So many brothers were mutilating themselves that by 325 AD, the church council of Nicea forbid any such further acts, decreeing that Jesus meant it figuratively, not literally. Indeed so! Removing your sex organs doesn't free you from the most erotic of your members — the human mind!

What Jesus said is simply to take sin seriously. If you're having trouble with cable television, rip it out. If pornography on the internet is your snare, then, guess what? You can't have an unsupervised computer. Be decisive! Deal with sin before it deals with you!

Proverbs 4:23 warns, "Keep your heart with all vigilance, for from it flow the springs of life." In most American homes there is a life-saving device called a smoke alarm. Ever vigilant, it whiffs the air for any hint of smoke and lets out an ear-piercing alarm if it detects any.

Most American homes have smoke detectors, but, sadly, 60% of them have dead batteries and do not function. Psalm 119:9-11 is a challenge to install a lust alarm in your life and see to it you keep fresh batteries there.

Suggested Prayer

O Lord, cleanse me of lust and guard my life in your word! Amen.

Divorce: The Deadlock Of Wedlock

It was also said, "Whoever divorces his wife, let him give her a certificate of divorce." But I say to you that every one who divorces his wife, except on the ground of unchastity, makes her an adulteress; and whoever marries a divorced woman commits adultery.
— Matthew 5:31-32

Last year there were over a million fresh divorces in the nation. Nearly half of all marriages will end with the drop of a divorce court judge's gavel.

The tragedy is, fewer of us are taking divorce seriously. I saw a bumper sticker that read, "How do you spell relief? D-I-V-O-R-C-E!" In a cafe, I heard a young woman say to her companion, "It's a friendly divorce. He gets to keep whatever falls out of the back of the truck as I drive away."

Did you know some churches have even begun to offer sacred services of divorce recognition? It has even become fashionable to mail out engraved divorce announcements. One reads ...

> *It's official,*
> *Colleen and Mitchell F. Amor have parted*
> *Amicably and without rancor.*
> *Colleen is once again happily Ms. Colleen Ibsen*
> *Residing at the Bradley Creek Towers.*
> *Mitchell's permanent residence is now on his boat, I Pagliacci*
> *Where he will continue to drift aimlessly ... forever.*

I asked a young man about the divorce of his wife of eleven years. He replied, "It works for me!" And I shot back, "But does it work for God or for your wife? Does it work for your children, for society, or for your grandchildren?" In all of our own noisy opinions, what does the Bible say?

As always, I am reluctant to discuss divorce. It is so widespread. There is so much hurt, and I do not wish to trample upon anyone. But as Jesus dealt with divorce in his sermon, so must I. I promise to try to be truthful and sensitive.

At the outset, let me assure you that God knows all about you. He knows what you have done. He knows what has been done to you. He still loves you, and he is more eager to forgive you than he is to judge you. In fact, Jesus Christ is able to meet you where you are and still bring a blessing out of your life!

Some of you have not chosen divorce. It was thrust upon you by an unfaithful spouse. You are, as Shakespeare put it, "More sinned against than sinning." You've been torn, halved, sundered, and in all this I write to remind you that you are beautiful to God. Jesus is coming for you soon as a groom. He promises, "I will not leave you desolate. I will come to you" (John 14:18).

With these mercies ringing in our ears, let's look at Christ's words.

Divorce

"It was also said, 'Whoever divorces his wife, let him write her a certificate of divorce.' " Jesus is quoting Moses' words from Deuteronomy 24:1: "When a man takes a wife and marries her, if then she finds no favor in his eyes ... let him write her a bill of divorce." All it took was one hastily written paragraph given to her in the presence of two witnesses and the marriage was over.

In Christ's day only a man could do this. The right of divorce was not given to a woman to initiate except in rare instances.

The area of argument among the Pharisees was what Moses meant when he said a man could divorce his wife, "If she finds no favor in his eyes." There were two schools of thought on the matter — the one liberal, the other more conservative. Rabbi Hillel led the liberals, explaining that a marriage could be dissolved over the slightest infraction: if she spoiled your dinner, if she put too much salt on your food, if she was quarrelsome, or if the man found someone better. Meanwhile, Rabbi Shammi taught strictly that a marriage could only end over adultery.

Which school of thought became the most popular? The lax view. In Jesus' day there was widespread sexual immorality with plenty of divorce and broken homes, and it was not just the Jews coupling and uncoupling in matrimony; the Greeks were the worst. Men, you see, married, had children, and their wives ran the household.

Women weren't allowed to be public figures. Education was denied them. They were kept at home to feather the nest and live a life of seclusion.

Meanwhile, men enjoyed harlots and kept mistresses. It was a double standard. Wives must remain pure and at home. Men were expected to cad about.

Some of the writings of this day are quite revealing. Socrates wrote, "Is there anyone to whom you entrust the more serious matters less than to your wife, and is there anyone to whom you talk less?" Another male denizen spoke, "The happiest day of my life was the day I wed. The next happiest was the day I buried my wife."

The Roman empire was built on the civilizing influence of the family. One early Roman official said, "Marriage is a lifelong fellowship of all divine and human rights." For the first 500 years of Roman history there is no record of divorce. The earliest mention of a failed marriage came in 234 BC. A fellow named Ruga dismissed his wife because she bore him no children. By the second century BC, divorce was as common as marriage and it was nothing for a man to marry five or six times over his life.

By Jesus' day, Greek immorality had infected Jews and Romans. The sanctity of marriage had so eroded that women were held in low regard as objects of lust, afternoon carnal refreshments to be used and discarded like food wrappers. There were no moral absolutes sexually. The family was torn apart by divorce, incest, illegitimacy, and lack of parenting.

On all of this, Jesus comments, "You have heard it said if your wife displeases you, write her a certificate of divorce. But I say he who divorces his wife and marries another commits adultery."

I think I learned something of what adultery is when I was four years old. I had watched my grandpapa put fuel in his car. When we got home, I enlisted my younger brother's help in adding some sand and water and gravel. We didn't know one had to be selective. We just thought anything worked. The next day on the way to church, the car came to a grinding halt. The fuel had been adulterated. We do the same thing when we divorce and remarry — we contaminate things.

God, you see, conducts a grand redeeming strategy of human redemption, and marriage is central to his plan. The scriptures teach that history began with a wedding in the Garden of Eden (Genesis 2:18-24). Christ launched his public ministry at the wedding of Cana where he turned water to wine, his first miracle (John 2:1-11). Afterward, Jesus began to call himself the groom and to speak of the church as his bride (Ephesians 5:21-33). Revelation 19 teaches that history will end soon at the wedding supper of the lamb.

Hence, marriage is a lesser relationship that points to a greater relationship. It is the little picture God uses to point to the *big* picture. Thus is God greatly upset when anyone contaminates his grand redeeming strategy with adultery.

Consider how divorce ruins what God plans.

First, there is the adultery of sexual union. The two cannot become one because of flashbacks, mental comparisons of how it was with someone else. Frankly, when two divorced people remarry, four people get into bed together. So there is no pure, unblended bond, but, rather, a mishmash of comparisons.

Then there is the adulteration of finances. For, as with most working class mortals, when finances are cut in half, neither makes out very agreeably.

Then there is the adulterated self-worth. One of the reasons it feels so good to get married is the sense of "chosenness." "Out of all the people, she chose me!" But one of the reasons it feels so awful to get divorced is the feeling of being de-chosen. Divorce is such a terrific body blow that some never recover their self-esteem.

Don't overlook the contamination of children and the authority structure of the home. For when divorce and remarriage blends his, hers, and our children, how does one exercise parental control? "You're not my real daddy!"

Yes, there is the mixed adultery of commitment. Children see parents quit when it gets tough, so they live like that, too.

Finally, there is the adulteration of culture, the contamination of the foundation on which society is safely built. Martin Luther wisely observed 500 years ago, "What is a city but a collection of houses? Where fathers and mothers rule badly and let children have their own way, there neither city, town, village, district, kingdom, nor empire can be well and peacefully governed."

Two minutes of thought will tell you that a brick building's strength is in the integrity of its bricks. If enough of the building blocks are broken, then the structure is unsafe. Marriages are the building blocks of society. When enough of them are unsound, no society can stand.

Danny DeVito said it well in *War of the Roses*, a movie about divorce. "Civilized divorce is a contradiction of terms."

Christ Jesus stunned those of his day when he said, "No" to lust, "No" to adultery, and "No" to divorce. His world was not used to any rules of sexual conduct. They did as they pleased and in the end no one was pleased — not God nor man nor woman nor children nor society!

Southern novelist, Pat Conroy, divorced his wife, Barbara. As a means of coping, he wrote a book about the ordeal: *Death of a Marriage*.

> *Each divorce is the death of a small civilization. Two people declare war on each other, and their screams and tears infect their entire world with the bacilli of their pain. The greatest fury comes from the wound where love once issued forth.*
>
> *I find it hard to believe how many people get divorced, how many submit to such extraordinary pain. For there are no clean divorces. Divorces should be conducted in surgical wards. In my own case, I think it would have been easier if Barbara had died. I would have been gallant at her funeral and shed real tears —*

> *far easier than staring across a table, telling each other it was over.*
>
> *It was a killing thing to look at the mother of my children and know that we would not be together for the rest of our lives. It was terrifying to say good-bye, to reject a part of my own history.*
>
> *When I went through my divorce, I saw it as a country, and it was treeless, airless; there were no furloughs and no holidays. I entered without a passport, without directions and absolutely alone. Insanity and hopelessness grew in that land like vast orchards of malignant fruit....*

Now you see why God declares in Malachi 2:16, "I hate divorce." He does not say he hates divorcees. He says he hates divorce. He hates what it does to men, women, children, church, society, and his own breaking heart.

Exceptions?

In verse 32, Jesus seems to leave the door ajar to divorce on the grounds of sexual immorality. "Except on the ground of unchastity," he says. In the Greek, the word for "unchastity" is *porneia*. We get our word "pornography" from the same word. It means "uncleanliness," and it is usually translated as adultery.

Aye, but here is where Christians who take the Bible seriously, quarrel. There are three camps of interpretation.

Camp one stoutly holds out for singleness as one man for one woman for life. No divorce is allowed for any cause. These scholars point out that the gospels of John, Mark, and Luke do not issue any qualifier as Matthew does. In Hosea, the prophet is asked by God to take back his wife spoiled in harlotry. For Christ, our groom, will never dismiss us, his soon-to-be bride. Our steadfastness in matrimony should simply match God's.

Camp two likewise holds up singleness as a laudable way of life. One man for one woman for life is the ideal. Yet when there has been adultery, the marriage bond is severed as Jesus says here in verse 32. Sometimes Paul is quoted in 1 Corinthians 7 as adding desertion as a grounds for divorce.

Camp three fully agrees with the other camps as to singleness and the sanctity of marriage. But it points out that the list of things that lead to divorce according to the scriptures is likely not inclusive, but indicative. *Porneia*, they say, is uncleanliness, and that's not just adultery. It can be pedophilia, homosexuality, even serious drug abuse or trafficking in the occult.

Whichever camp you come to, no serious student of the Bible can justify divorce as a first recourse and on flimsy grounds. Divorce must be an extreme last resort, and only then on the grounds of serious *porneia*.

Personally, I try to do three things here.

1. Hold high the standard! Singleness, as one man for one woman for life.
2. Enable people to reach God's ideal for the single or married life.
3. Minister to those who fail. As Jesus, in John 4, cared for the Samaritan woman worn out with bad relationships, so must we, too, care for those suffering in divorce.

Conclusion

One hundred years ago divorce was almost unheard of in the United States. People married for better or for worse until death did them part. Fifty years ago couples wed and remained so until they simply couldn't stand it anymore. Then they reluctantly divorced. Now we get married and stay so until something better comes along, and we're fast becoming little more than a nation of yard dogs led about by our passions. Jesus stood up in a culture like ours. He preached against lust, adultery, and easy divorce. He said we must not casually flick off our relationships with a manmade certificate. There is something of great value in marriage — something God wants — and we should embrace it.

I have a houseplant that once bloomed beautifully, but it wilted and died. Rather than throw it away, I pruned it, fertilized it, and nurtured it in a sunny window. Over time, it has bloomed again. Jesus is saying that we should find a way to nurture our own marriages again and again to good bloom. My suspicion is that many people simply conclude they are *unable* to do so when, in fact, they are *unwilling*. They say the pain is too great, but it isn't. First Corinthians 13 teaches, "Love suffers long." It doesn't say how long, but it is longer than we think.

In the end, divorce is not a solution but an exchange of problems. You give up one set of woes only to take up another. And, believe me, the frustrations that come with divorce are almost always worse than any in marriage.

Suggested Prayer

Lord, help me to take my relationship seriously. Show me the way through, not out, and give me compassion for those who fail. For Christ's sake. Amen.

A Woman's Place

... everyone who looks at a woman....
— Matthew 5:27

In 1959, Betty Friedan published *The Feminine Mystique*. She pointed out that up until then the popular notion was that if you gave a woman a husband, several children, a home, and a kitchen she would be fulfilled. Friedan, however, argued that such ideas have stunted women's growth.

Many single and childless women, even divorced women, already knew they could find fulfillment in school, in Jesus, in friendships, and in careers. Betty Friedan issued a call for women to broaden their horizons from traditional family values. Get out of the house! Get away from children, diapers, toilet brushes, and hot meals! And get into the world of business, art, law, politics, and medicine. Exert yourselves!

Indeed! Over the last half century women have done so! The feminist movement has brought us child care, the push for equal rights, abortion on demand, unisex clothing, female vice-presidential candidates, a female UN Ambassador, and Secretary of State.

Ms. Friedan has since published a second book in which she pointed out that women can do everything, but do they have to? They're tired, Friedan observes. Women labor outside the home. They jog, lead a club, cook, parent children, are an incredible bed partner to their husband, and are so very exhausted. Hence, some women are beginning to ask if feminism isn't some sort of a mistake.

The women's issue needs to be addressed by the church. In a day of confusion we must ask, "What does it mean to be a woman in Jesus Christ in today's world?"

Three huge concepts must be grasped from scripture.

Woman's Identity As Revealed In Creation

Females are first mentioned in Genesis 1:26-27. God said, "Let us make man in our image ... and let him have dominion ... So God created man in his own image ... Male and female he created them."

Hence, both man and woman are bearers of the divine image. God's nature is not contained in the male image alone. The full reflection of God is seen in both male and female. It takes both genders to reveal all the attributes of God.

Note this balance in the New Testament. In the Lord's Prayer, Jesus identifies with God as "Father" (Luke 11:2). That's the masculine. But in Luke 13:34, Jesus says, "How often I would have gathered your children together as a hen gathers her brood under her wings." Hear the feminine? Not a rooster, but a hen.

So, God created woman as a cobearer of his divine image. He blessed her and commissioned her to rule alongside man. All this is best described with the word, "egalitarianism." It means "man and woman are both equal before God."

Genesis 1 gives a general view of creation. It is often called the Eloheim view because that is the word in Hebrew it uses for God. In Genesis 2, there is a more close-up, focused view of creation. This is often called the Yahweh view since Yahweh is the word used for God.

Some biblical critics point out these two creation stories — one general, the other specific — and call them contradictory. I see it as a literary device. The first tells the story broadly, while the second is a reiteration of the same. It's not unlike watching a football game on television and seeing the play from the Goodyear blimp, then watching the same play from an endzone camera.

In Genesis 2, man is created single. And God, in the first negative statement from the Bible says, "It is not good that man should be alone" (Genesis 2:18). See? Man without woman is no good. "I will make him a helper fit for him" (Genesis 2:18). The Hebrew word for "helper" is untranslatable. It means something like "an ideally suited compliment." "Helper" should not convey "assistant" or "sub-ordinate." It may help you to know that in other places God is called the "Helper of Israel" (Psalm 10:14; 30:10; 54:4; Hebrews 13:6).

Now read through Genesis 2:19-23. Adam was made from the soil. His name means "red clay." Then woman, Eve, "the mother of all living," was made from Adam. She is the first thing God did not make from dirt. Eve was made *for* Adam *from* Adam.

Be careful with two popular false notions here.
1. Woman was made from man, therefore she is subordinate. So? Man was made from dirt. Is dirt better than man? No.
2. Woman was made second, therefore she is subordinate. So? Grass and animals were made before man. Is he, therefore, inferior?

There may be a slight hint of subservience of woman to man. In Genesis 2:22, God brought the woman to the man. The man named her just as he did the animals. Does this imply hierarchy? Possibly. Yet it is vague at best.

So then, what is real femininity? It is to recognize woman as created by God, a cobearer with man of God's divine image, blessed, commissioned to rule, made from man for man, and now man is made from woman. She is equal to man, but a vague subordination is at least hinted.

Now we come to the second large concept that must be comprehended from scripture.

Woman's Identity Obscured By The Fall

Read through Genesis 3, the temptation story. Why did Satan pick on the woman first? She was the youngest, the least experienced. Adam was older, more experienced. He named the animals. He'd heard God's word firsthand, and we do not know how thorough a job he did in instructing his new wife as to God's restrictions.

Satan singles out the woman getting her to question God's word (v. 1). Meanwhile, Eve quotes God's word back to Satan (vv. 2-3). But notice it takes her forty words to say what God said in 36 (2:16-17). Satan sees that Eve is fuzzy in her knowledge of God's word. She's actually added to it, making God's demands more legalistic than he wills. Satan makes three quick promises (vv. 4-5).

"You will not die." "Your eyes will be opened." "You shall be as God." Break it down and you notice the devil, in disobedience, promised her pleasure, power, and prestige.

There is great drama here. Whom will Eve believe? God her creator who promised her life within certain boundaries? Or a beautiful, talking serpent who speaks with authority and promises a better life without restrictions.

Eve weighed all this in her intellect. She eyed the tree, the food, the delight of more with less restrictions, and she believed Satan and so indulged herself.

But wait! The man is now tempted by his wife. Eve's tempting required Satan himself. He got at her through her intellect. All it took to tempt man was a woman. And he just wanted to please his wife. His temptation was more on an emotional level.

Let me hear one of you say, "Woman is the weaker sex. Man is stronger, more cognitive, while woman is driven by her emotions." Not necessarily. For it is definitely Eve who comes out looking better in this whole episode!

It is interesting what happens next (Genesis 3:8-13). Though the woman sinned first, God calls Adam first to account for his misdeeds. Remember the implied hierarchy of man in Genesis 2? Since Adam was in charge, he is held responsible first.

However, Adam blames God and his wife for the malaise (v. 12). God calls the woman to account. Verse 13 shows her straightforward honesty in confession, and God begins to pronounce judgment as well as to announce his plan of the ages, a divine redeeming strategy that included Eve and it includes all women. Genesis 3:15 is God's first promise after the fall. God told the serpent Satan that he and the woman would constantly quarrel. A descendant of Eve would crush him while being wounded in the fight himself. This is the first prediction of a Messiah in scripture. Someone born of Eve's lineage would crush Satan, but he'd be wounded in the fracas. Do you see the cross of Jesus in this? If you study the genealogy of Jesus in Luke 3:23-38, you'll notice it traces Christ back to Eve and Adam through the Virgin Mary.

Though Eve is chosen to help bear the Savior, she is judged by God for sin and in verse 3:16 experiences the difficult stress of childbearing. She desires her husband, yet is told, "He shall rule over you." This last point, rulership, is important to ponder. Here's why: Is this statement of God, "He shall rule over you" prescriptive or descriptive? Is God prescribing man's rulership by saying, "I'm going to fix it so woman is ruled by man"? Or is it descriptive? Is God only lamenting, "Oh no! because of sin and the ensuing anarchy, man is going to ride roughshod over females?"

I personally think it is only descriptive. Whichever way you interpret it, your theology will move in a particular direction.

Following quickly in scripture, woman is denigrated. In Genesis 4:23, she is victimized by polygamy. In Genesis 12:10 following, Abraham tries to give his wife to the pharaoh to save his own skin. Then in Genesis 19:8, when a group of sexual predators plan to attack Lot's house and rape two male visitors, the man offers to satisfy them with his daughters. In Genesis 17, circumcision is mandated as a mark of the covenant, but it is only for males. By the receiving of the Ten Commandments in Exodus 20, a woman is reduced to a list of man's possessions. "You shall not covet your neighbor's house; you shall not covet your neighbor's wife, or his manservant, or his maidservant, or his ox or his ass."

By Jesus' day, Jewish males rose to pray in the morning, "I thank thee, Lord of heaven, that thou didst not make me a slave or a Gentile or a donkey or a woman." The rabbis had a saying: "It is better to burn the Torah than teach it to a woman." Aristotle thought that females were born from deficient male sperm. Even the reformation hero, Martin Luther wrote, "If a woman suffers and dies in childbirth, it matters not because that is why she exists."

A. W. Verrall, renowned classical historian, wrote, "One of the chief diseases from which ancient civilization died was a low view of women." The Greeks, the Romans, and the Hebrews allowed themselves to slip into an immoral view of the feminine. Hence, as Jesus preached in Matthew 5:27-32, habits, mentality of lust, adultery, and divorce are not honoring to God or woman. We must say, "No" to reducing a woman to a piece of meat. We must say, "Yes" to women in God's plan.

All this is surely uppermost in Christ's mind when he preaches the simple phrase, "... looks at a woman...."

So far we have looked at woman in God's image before the fall and at woman in God's image obscured by the fall.

Woman's Identity Restored
In The Redemption Of Jesus Christ

The gospel of our Lord rolls back the consequences of sin. Genesis 3:19 mentions work "by the sweat of your face." Now we have air-conditioning. It mentions weeds and thorns as a result of sin (Genesis 3:18). But we have weed killers. It mentions disease and death (Genesis 3:19). But we have strong medicines to postpone dying. The point is, if we can "have dominion" (Genesis 1:28) over the consequences of the fall — heat, weeds, and disease — can we not also roll back the consequences of the fall for women? In Genesis 3:16, God promised the woman pain in childbearing. Do we do wrong to administer them anesthesia?

Both the Old Testament and the New Testament promise a new order, that Eden, the kingdom of God, will come again.

Joel 2:28-29 predicts a time when God will pour out his Holy Spirit on all flesh regardless of gender, age, or economic status.

Acts 1 is a fulfillment of God's prediction. The Holy Spirit came to the disciples gathered for prayer in the upper room. Acts 1:14 tells us women were there.

Then there is that great magna carta of scripture Paul wrote in Galatians 3:28. "There is neither Jew nor Greek, slave nor free, male nor female, for you all are one in Christ Jesus." F. F. Bruce, the conservative Evangelical Bible scholar, says, "Anything written about woman must be seen in the light of Galatians 3:28. This is a banner verse."

It is true that Paul told women in the immature Corinthian church to "keep silence" (1 Corinthians 14:34). But in Galatians 3:28, he said "in Christ" gender is of as little consequence as social status and race. So, to put it bluntly, I'd rather be in Christ than in Corinth.

Christ's treatment of women is interesting to study through the gospels for he is constantly challenging his culture's norms.

For example, a woman in public with her hair unbraided was considered immoral. Yet Jesus allowed a lady to wet his feet with her tears and wipe them with her unpinned hair. And he affirmed her! (John 11:2; Luke 7:38 ff).

In Luke 10:38 following, Jesus allowed Mary to sit at his feet and learn the gospel right alongside the rest of the men. Martha was nonplused. She wanted her sister to get back in the kitchen where a woman belonged. But Jesus commended Mary, said she had "chosen the good portion."

In John 4:9, Christ shared the gospel with a woman and then sent her into the town to tell everyone the gospel.

In Luke 24:10, Christ entrusted the message of his resurrection first to women.

A few years ago I received a poll in the mail from a Christian magazine. It was enquiring as to the role of women in the church. "May a woman keep nursery?" Check. "May a woman teach six year olds?" Check. "May a woman teach a married couple's class?" You get the point! "Where is the cutoff point?"

If, as the prophet Joel said, "The Spirit is poured out on all flesh" (Joel 2:28), then the fullness of God's presence and ministry gifts are on women. So just about anything a man can do a woman can do as well, better, or worse: pray, teach, sing, encourage, administrate, heal, evangelize, preach.

I challenge you to read through the book of Acts and mark in orange the mention of women. You'll be amazed what women do. In Acts 1:14, women pray with men in the upper room. In Acts 5:14, women factor heavily in church growth. In Acts 12:12, a church meets in a woman's house. In Acts 21:9, Phillip's four daughters preach.

Clearly, women in ministry is not an issue in the New Testament. However, authority is. Consider: Jesus selected twelve males to be his apostles. First Timothy 3 gives elder qualifications as male. For some reason our Lord chose males to exercise authority in his churches. If I were doing it, perhaps I'd have done it differently. But God selected males to rule, to exercise over all authority. This is true both in the home and in the church (Ephesians 5:23, 27).

Conclusion

On a certain Pacific island before World War II, it was required of women to walk humbly ten paces behind their men. After the war, women walked ten paces in front of their men. It seems that the Japanese had mined the island and men used their wives to safely clear a path.

Where today in the home and church should we place women? They are created by God, a bearer of the divine image, commissioned to rule creation alongside man, very good, a compliment to man as he is to her, a fellow sinner struggling with the consequences of the fall, equally loved, redeemed, and filled with the Holy Spirit by Jesus. Women are given the talents of the Spirit to serve, to be encouraged to become all God desires, yet meant to function in an orderly way under proper male authority in the home and church.

The technical term for this scriptural view is egalitarian authoritarianism. But be very careful with it. Women comprise more than 50% of the church's membership. I lay awake nights fearful that somehow I may be burying someone's talents, especially those of women!

Suggested Prayer

Lord, let me play my role in life. Grant that I be an encourager of women to fulfill their role, as well. For Jesus' sake. Amen.

Don't Waste Your Breath!

> *Again you have heard that it was said to the men of old, "You shall not swear falsely, but shall perform to the Lord what you have sworn." But I say to you, Do not swear at all, either by heaven, for it is the throne of God, or by the earth, for it is his footstool, or by Jerusalem, for it is the city of the great King. And do not swear by your head, for you cannot make one hair white or black. Let what you say be simply "Yes" or "No"; anything more than this comes from evil.*
> — Matthew 5:33-37

After Jesus finishes with the subjects of lust, adultery, and divorce, he takes up the subject of the human tongue.

How much of our well-being as humans depends upon truth-telling by the tongue? When shopping for a pound of hamburger and the butcher hands you a package, how would it be to get home and find a quarter pound of pork? What's it like to make an appointment at 8 a.m. and your associate doesn't show up until 8:45? What about business contracts? "Send 10,000 dozen socks at 31¢ each by May 1. I will pay in full by July 1." You do, but he doesn't. Or we stand here and say to a missionary, "You take your end of the rope and go down into the darkness and bring the light. We'll stay here and hold our end of the rope." But we seldom give or pray and within a year we drift to another church and promptly forget the missionary.

What about our oath here at the chancel before God in marriage? "I take thee in sickness and in health, for richer or poorer, for better or for worse, till death us do part." Inside two years we're ready to quit the marriage. Think how vital it is to take the witness stand and promise to tell "the truth, the whole truth, and nothing but the truth."

In the text, Christ addresses the issue of the human tongue in his day. He points how sinfully out of control one dimension of the tongue had gotten — swearing.

There were two sorts of swearing in the Lord's day — binding and unbinding.

Binding

A binding oath occurred when one used God's name in a promise.

"As God is my witness, I swear...."

"As Jehovah sees me, I promise...."

"I thee wed in the name of the Father, and of the Son, and of the Holy Spirit."

"I promise to tell the truth, the whole truth, so help me God."

The idea was that the use of God's name lends strength to our words. By invoking God's name, God became a partner in the deal.

Unbinding

Ah! But the Jews were clever! They'd developed evasive swearing. If one made an oath without using God's name, the promise was unbinding.

"By heaven, it's true!"

"I swear to you by Jerusalem!"

"I stand on my mother's grave and pledge to you...."

Jewish businessmen had swearing down to a fine art. If you weren't up on the subtleties of it, there were those who'd take advantage of you. We call it getting the short shrift, being shafted, being "had." As such, in Christ's day, Jewish businessmen had a bad reputation. You counted your fingers after you shook their hands. As Paul wrote of the Jews in Romans 2:24, "For, as it is written, 'The name of God is blasphemed among the Gentiles because of you.' " It's hard to believe in the God of one who has swindled you.

In the midst of his sinful society Jesus stood up for a greater righteousness. "You can't cut God out!" He said. The Lord is everywhere! He won't be marginalized in any of your deals!

Woe to you, blind guides, who say, "If anyone swears by the temple, it is nothing; but if anyone swears by the gold of the temple, he is bound by his oath." You blind fools! For which is greater, the gold or the temple that has made the gold sacred? ... So he who swears by the altar, swears by it and by everything on it ... and he who swears by heaven, swears by the throne of God and by him who sits upon it. — Matthew 23:16-22

A Simple Yes Or No

Jesus says confusing or obscuring business contracts with clever language and swearing is a waste of breath. It is evil.

The Roman historian, Josephus, wrote, "They that cannot be believed without swearing are already condemned." Make your words count. Let your pledge be clear. A simple "Yes" or "No" will do. And by your integrity you'll never need to buttress your language.

Wow! Do we ever need to mature here ourselves! In Exodus 20:7, God asks us not to take his name in vain. "In vain" means "emptily, insincerely, with a lack of reality." So, how does our language miss the mark here?

Profanity

One way we do it is by taking the sacred and lessening its value with calloused use. We do it by reducing God's name to a swear word, a casual flippant exclamation. Our halls at school echo with it. Movies scream divine words turned to obscenity. Our private conversations are littered with it.

The result is we've destroyed reverence. We've trivialized God by frivolous use of language.

Profanity by definition is simply this: trying to establish my authority at the expense of God's glory.

During the American Civil War, President Lincoln rounded a corner in the White House and bumped into a soldier. Both were knocked to the floor. The soldier got up cursing foully. Mr. Lincoln listened and then chided softly, "My young man, there is something wrong with you on the inside."

One thing wrong is a poor vocabulary. To the profane it is hot as hell, cold as hell, slow as hell, hard as hell, fast as hell, and raining like hell. Come, now! Really? Where are your powers of description?

Furthermore, profanity reveals not just a poor vocabulary, it identifies a lack of self-control. When our rights are violated and we respond with an ugly stream of obscenities, where is our poise? Where is our purity?

If you squeeze a tomato, what comes out? Tomato juice. When Christians come under pressure, what comes out is what's in us. Obscenities are always disappointing. But Jesus is always a sign of inner maturity.

Lip Service

A second way we void our word is in lip service.

The bane of religion is that talk is easy, behavior is not. Jesus said of Israel, "This people honors me with their lips but their heart is far from me" (Matthew 15:8).

We call him "Father," but do we act like his children? We call him Lord, but do we act like his servants? We join a church promising the sacrifice of our lives, but really mean, "As it is convenient." We vow in marriage "to love, honor, and cherish" but mean to do as we please.

In the end, our words come to mean so very little. What Jesus is saying, tongue-in-cheek, in the text, is that Christians who speak by the yard and perform by the inch, should be dealt with by the foot.

Lying

Another way that we destroy truth is with lying words.

"You shall not bear false witness against your neighbor" (Exodus 20:16).

Satan was the first liar (Genesis 3). Then Cain picked up the habit (Genesis 4). Now lying is widespread and an art form.

One sees it in the supermarket. "Jumbo Shrimp." "Giant Sized." "Extra Fancy."

One sees it in little white lies, like the sign in a Chapel Hill bar: "Charges for telephone answering service: Just left — 25¢; on his way — 50¢, not here — $1; and who? — $5."

Then there is bribery. A news cartoon shows a Navy ship with the caption, "The best ship that consultant costs, lobbying fees, entertainment write-offs, kickbacks, and political pay offs can buy."

Don't forget half-truths. One purchases a huge box of cereal, only to get home and find it two-thirds full. The fine print on the box explains, "Sold by weight, not volume, contents may have settled in shipping."

Of course, there's the out-and-out lie, recreating the truth to fit your advantage. I overheard a teenaged shop clerk say to her loitering friend, "I was an hour late coming in last night. So I locked my keys in the car and called my dad to come get me so I wouldn't get in trouble."

We could go on and on with gossip, slander, even conspiracy of silence. But the point is clear — we've a culture awash in untruth, lies, and scandal. The result is a growing cynicism, a building chaos of confusion, a snarled legal system, an insecurity, a societal breakdown.

Conclusion

In 1723, Maryland passed a law against lying. For the first infraction, the offender was bored through the tongue with an awl and fined twenty pounds. The second offense was public flogging and six months in jail. The third offense earned death without benefit of clergy.

Obviously our forefathers, along with Jesus, respected the importance of truth in society. They took seriously the power of the tongue to corrupt. It is time we do so, too! Let your "Yes" be "Yes," and your "No" be "No," Jesus said.

If you read the Ten Commandments in Exodus 20, you'll discover one body part that is so unruly God gives two laws to govern it — the tongue. Yet Acts 2 teaches that on Pentecost it was the Holy Spirit who seized Peter's denying tongue, yes, even his profane tongue, and used it to proclaim the gospel.

There is hope.

We can't cure our tongues in our own strength, but God can. Peter is living proof. Let's be that proof, too, in our generation, as our words come to mean something.

Suggested Prayer
Jesus, help! Take my tongue and fix it! Amen.

You Guys Are Really Gonna Be Different!

> *You have heard that it was said, "An eye for an eye and a tooth for a tooth." But I say to you, Do not resist one who is evil. But if any one strikes you on the right cheek, turn to him the other also; and if any one would sue you and take your coat, let him have your cloak as well; and if any one forces you to go one mile, go with him two miles. Give to him who begs from you, and do not refuse him who would borrow from you.*
> — Matthew 5:38-42

In this text, we reach the high point of the Sermon on the Mount. These are the words for which Jesus is either the most admired or the most resented. For here is where Jesus teaches total love for "one who is evil," and for one's "enemies" (vv. 39, 44).

"Divine logic!" shout such heroes as Tolstoy, Gandhi, and Martin Luther King Jr. "Utterly ridiculous!" "Naive!" shout a chorus of others.

Let's get into Jesus' words. And let's allow them to get into us.

The Oldest Law

You will notice the text begins with, "You have heard it said, 'An eye for an eye and a tooth for a tooth.' " This is humankind's oldest law, the *Lex Talionis*. In 2250 BC, it was published in the *Code of Hammurabi*.

I call it the "tit for tat rule." If I get in a fight with you and knock out your tooth, the law says one of my teeth must be knocked out. If I get drunk and drive my car into yours and your wife loses an eye, then I shall forfeit one of my eyes. You will find this law laid down in Exodus 21:23-25 and again in Leviticus and Deuteronomy.

Before you call this law cruel, bloody, and revolting, let me hasten to point out it was made to limit violence and to stop blood feuds between tribes.

Recall Shakespeare's *Romeo and Juliet*. Two prominent families with a rivalry that spills blood in a sword duel, and suddenly there is the prospect of escalating war! The *Lex Talionis* limits retaliation to a proportional response. It takes retribution from the streets to the law courts. If you lose an arm, you do not kill in retaliation. The penalty is to do what was done to you.

Over the course of time, the *Lex Talionis* moved to a financial settlement. "Blood money," we call it. If you lost an eye due to my negligence, rather than gouge my eye out, we'd strive to arrive at a financial settlement. There are five points used to determine the suit: injury, pain, healing, loss of time, and indignity.

It all sounds strangely modern! When we're involved in an automobile wreck and it's our fault, we have insurance agents, courts, attorneys, and arbitrators who go to work sorting things out and bringing about an equitable solution. Our nation is awash in such litigation!

A New Way

In the text, Jesus seems to abolish all this. "You have heard it said, 'An eye for an eye, a tooth for a tooth.' But I say unto you, do not resist one who is evil" (vv. 38-39a). We are to give up our right to revenge, to absorb the blow, to refuse to retaliate, and to suffer the injury.

To drive home his point, Jesus gives four examples.

The first has to do with insults. "If any one strikes you on the right cheek, turn to him the other also" (v. 39b). Think about it. To be hit on the right cheek is not to be punched. It is to be backhanded. This is a blow of insult. Christ is pointing out that by the law of Talionis, to be insulted releases one to insult in return. But Jesus is now telling us, "You guys in the God kingdom are really gonna be different! For instead of lowering yourself to the level of insult, you simply absorb it, and literally turn the other cheek."

During the American Civil War, President Lincoln had a churlish but talented cabinet member who constantly undercut him and derided him as a "baboon." A friend asked Abraham Lincoln what he thought of the fellow. Mr. Lincoln said he was a capable worker. Surprised, the man asked if the president knew of the man's ugly words. Lincoln said he did. "Then why do you say nice things about him?" the gentleman inquired. Old Abe replied, "I thought you were asking me what I thought about him."

The second cameo has to do with lawsuits. Jesus said, "If any one would sue you and take your coat, give him your cloak as well" (v. 40). The coat was an inner garment, a sort of "long shirt," and even the poorest had two. But a cloak was an outer garment, a sort of blanket or tunic. The average person owned just one. It served as his raincoat, winter wrap, and blanket at night. Exodus 22:26-27 warns businessmen that if you take a fellow's tunic in pledge, be sure to return it by nightfall lest they be cold. What Christ is saying is this: If someone is suing you for the shirt off your back, give them your coat, also. The law of love demands you shiver through a sleepless night rather than keep a legal fight going.

The third cameo Jesus shared has to do with impositions. "If any one forces you to go one mile, go with him two miles" (v. 41). In Christ's day, Israel was a conquered nation. The Roman army occupied the land. To keep the Jews from forgetting their subservient status, the Romans decreed a forced impressment. Any Roman soldier could stop you on the street, interrupt your schedule, and force you to carry his pack for a mile. By treating you as a pack mule, it insured two things. You knew Rome was the boss, and the soldier arrived at his post rested.

One can imagine how unpopular such forced impressment was. Here you are clean, shaved, dressed up, and walking four blocks to a dinner party at your girl's house, when a burly Roman soldier shouts, "You! Carry my load." There's hatred in his eyes, his hand is on his sword, so you take up his dirty pack and walk sweating the full mile, then stagger back to your dinner party late, dirty, and tired. Such was humiliating and provoking.

But Jesus says rather shockingly, "Go the second mile." Do not do the least expected. Don't ask, "How little can I get away with?" Do more than expected. Do it without resentment. Do it cheerfully.

Simon of Cyrene was forcibly impressed by a Roman soldier. He found himself carrying the cross of Jesus to Golgotha (Matthew 27:32).

Now for the fourth cameo. Jesus said, "Give to him who begs from you and do not refuse one who would borrow from you" (v. 42). Deuteronomy 15:7-11 gives careful instructions about not hardening your heart, but opening your hand to the poor in your midst. The idea is that all people are made in God's image and therefore have value. Poverty is defacing. It is a responsibility of the wealthy to minister with their wealth, not to simply consume it all upon themselves. Generosity and kindness must be the mark of the Christian.

Suffering Servanthood

"You guys are really gonna be different!" Jesus is saying.

The old way is tit for tat, an eye for an eye. But now there is a new and living way! And Jesus sums it up, "Do not resist one who is evil" (v. 39). The word "resist not" in Greek is *anthistemi*. It means "to not oppose, not to withstand, not to set oneself against."

Scripture teaches us to "resist not God" (Romans 9:19; 2 Timothy 3:8; Acts 6:10). It does teach us to "resist the devil" (Ephesians 6:13; 1 Peter 5:9; James 4:7). The idea is quite clear in scripture. We are to give God his way, to refuse to give Satan his way. When it comes to people, "Resist not one who is evil who insults, sues, forcibly impresses you, or begs" (vv. 38-42 cf). In other words, don't fight with people. As a Christian, I have only one enemy — Satan.

During the naval battle of Trafalgar, Admiral Nelson had two officers who constantly bickered among themselves. Exasperated with their conduct, he took them both by the sleeve to the bow of the warship, pointed to the Spanish Armada gathering on the horizon, and said, "Gentlemen, the enemy is out there!"

Fight with the devil, sure! But not with people.

Dietrick Bonhoeffer called such a lifestyle, "Visible participation in the cross." Charles Spurgeon, speaking of this verse, remarked, "We are to be anvils when bad men are hammers."

Let's say a business deal goes bad. You have been used and abused! When you inquire politely and request that the contract be honored, you are insulted and sued, and your name is slandered about the business community. What are you to do?

There are four possible responses.

1. He hurt me. I'll hurt him more. I'll go after his jugular. Revenge is my aim — nuke him!
2. He hurt me. I'll pay him back in kind — tit for tat. I'll give him a taste of his own medicine — exact retribution.
3. He hurt me. I'll ignore him. I'll treat him as a non-person and write him off — freeze him out.
4. He hurt me. I'll love him anyway and find a way to serve him.

This fourth way is what Jesus is lauding. It is the story of the Bible. God created man good and allowed us to frolic in the Garden. When we sinned and hurt God, he didn't ignore us or hit back. He loves us and always acts in our best interests.

This is precisely what Jesus did in his passion.

The soldiers struck Jesus on the cheek. He offered them the other.

He was mocked, crowned with cruel thorns, and stripped naked of his shirt and cloak. He did not resist. He let it all go.

He was impressed forcibly by Roman soldiers to carry a cross. He lifted it all the way to Golgotha.

When sinful beggars came to him destitute, with hands out for any mercy from God, he gave. He gives, freely!

When we hurt Jesus, he responds in love. "For God so loved the world that he gave his only son, that whoever believes in him should not perish but have eternal life" (John 3:16).

From the cross, God saw us at our worst, our most hating, rebel-hearted, demonic selves. Ah! On the cross, we see Christ at his best, his most loving, gracious, and forgiving self.

In the text, Jesus is asking us to behave like him.

We are forever standing on our rights, clutching privilege to ourselves, militant, punishing, ready to sue to preserve our status. But Jesus says if we follow him we must give it all up and become a servant to others.

I like how Peter put it: "Jesus set us an example that we should follow in his steps" (1 Peter 2:21-23 cf).

Conclusion

In the book, *Seven Habits of Effective People*, Don Covey touts not *reacting* to situations, but being *pro-active*. When a sinner hurts you, the reactive lower themselves to that level. You allow them to set your agenda. In retaliation, you provide just one more worldly example of human sin.

The *pro-active*, however, let God set their agenda. They act in positive love by turning cheeks, non-resisting, refusing to sue, giving generously, and going that extra mile. In doing so, they witness Jesus. The world has seldom seen the likes of such!

You say, "That's so weak! It's an invitation to be a doormat!" Quite the contrary! The Bible says of Jesus, "Have this mind among yourselves which is yours in Christ Jesus, who, though he was in the form of God, did not count equality with God a thing to be grasped, but emptied himself, taking the form of a servant, being born in the likeness of men. And being found in human form he humbled himself and became obedient unto death, even death on a cross. Therefore God has highly exalted him and bestowed on him the name which is above every name, that at the name of Jesus every knee should bow ..." (Philippians 2:5-10).

Clearly, if we try to exalt ourselves all we can do is fight. But when we become servants one to another, God himself, is careful to exalt us.

Is your cheek burning from some slap of insult? Has someone torn the shirt off your back in court? Is some burly warrior using you as a pack mule? Has the world come begging at your door?

Will you act or react? Will you live like Jesus or live like the world?

Arthur Ashe, the African-American tennis star, was victimized by racial prejudice. He contracted AIDS from a blood transfusion during surgery, and he died without malice, a Christian. Before he perished, he said in a speech, "True heroism is remarkably sober, very undramatic. It is not the urge to surpass all others at whatever cost, but the urge to serve others at whatever cost."

So let it be with all who name the name of Jesus!

Suggested Prayer
Include me in on all this, Lord! Amen.

How To Treat Your Enemies

You have heard that it was said, "You shall love your neighbor and hate your enemy." But I say to you, Love your enemies and pray for those who persecute you, so that you may be sons of your Father who is in heaven; for he makes his sun rise on the evil and on the good, and sends rain on the just and on the unjust. For if you love those who love you, what reward have you? Do not even the tax collectors do the same? And if you salute only your brethren, what more are you doing than others? Do not even the Gentiles do the same?
— Matthew 5:43-47

And Nabal answered David's servants, "Who is David? Who is the son of Jesse? There are many servants nowadays who are breaking away from their masters. Shall I take my bread and my water and my meat that I have killed for my shearers, and give it to men who come from I do not know where?" — 1 Samuel 25:10-11

Did you hear about the man who went into the preaching ministry, worked for seven years, then resigned to go back to medical school and become a doctor? "People," he explained, "don't want spiritual health. They just want to feel good." But after working as a physician for seven years, he again resigned, this time to go back to school. "I'm going to become a lawyer," he explained, "because, in the end, people don't want spiritual health, they don't even want physical health. They just want to get even!"

The world is like that! There is a growing surliness in our lives today. People are bristling with sarcasm, lawsuits, handguns, and nuclear warheads. We are a people at war in our relationships. From our marriages to our child-parent relationships, to our next door neighbors, to our work relationships and on beyond, we are a people doing combat.

Much of our energy is consumed in licking our wounds and plotting our revenge. We want to hurt back, settle the score, or get even.

Allow me to meddle in your lives by asking, "Who are you at war with? How have you been treating your foes?"

But you say, "Stephen! I'm a Christian. I don't have any enemies!" Come, come, now! Without enemies a person's Christian faith is highly suspect! Why, if you can live the truth in this untruthful world and not upset some pocket of evil, then you're probably not very salty or light-filled. Jesus, after all, didn't say, "You are the sugar of the earth!" He called us "salt"! And salt has a way of stinging. He called us "light" and light exposes! You can be sure that Christ had his enemies. So did Paul, Stephen, Peter, and others. In fact, Jesus said, "Woe be unto you when all men speak well of you" (Luke 6:26).

So, if you live for Christ, "The question is how shall you treat your enemies?"

For those answers we turn to the text in Matthew 5:43-47 and 1 Samuel 25, brilliant examples of Christ's ethic in the Sermon on the Mount.

David has grown up watching his father's flocks near Bethlehem. He has killed the Philistine giant Goliath, been anointed the next king of Israel by the prophet Samuel, soothed King Saul with his music, become a military hero, and made his reputation as a poet with Psalm 23.

David's success threatened King Saul. The man was jealous, he actually tried to kill young David, but David slipped into the desert and hid. Twice he had the opportunity to slay Saul and twice he refused.

David was driven to the edge of Israel. He was reduced to living in a cave. He was hot, thirsty, hungry, and chief of a band of renegades in search of survival. His enemy, Saul, was on one side and his arch enemies, the Philistines, were on the other side. What David needed was a friend, but as we pick up the story in our text here, what David got was another enemy.

Help

In the text, David asks a Jew named Nabal for aide. David has served as a peacekeeping force in the area where Nabal lived. His military presence served as a wall against invasion or local mischief. And David saw to it personally that his men didn't bully Nabal's workers, steal from his flocks, or rape his women.

But David needs a friend. He's at the end of his resources. As the future king who has dealt honestly in the land, he sends his servants to the rich man Nabal asking for some supplies. He's not asking for what Nabal cannot give. He's only asking for what he desperately needs.

Be careful to note here that David has been completely honest with Nabal. He's even helped the man out by guarding his territory. David is only asking Nabal to respond in kind, to do right by him. It's rather like an American tourist in Paris, France. The tourist, a former American soldier, helped liberate France in a past war. He has a right to ask for some respect, some small return for his labors from the French.

Drop Dead!

David asks for help. And what does Nabal do? The text tells us Nabal was right in the middle of shearing his flocks. He was making money hand over fist! So, when David's servants visit and ask for aide, Nabal's mood turns nasty. He mocks them saying, "And who are you that I should help the likes of you? These days everyone is breaking away from Saul and pronouncing themselves king! No! I won't give you a single fig or a swallow of wine! Starve, you worthless scum!" (1 Samuel 25:10-11 cf).

Has that ever happened to you? Do you know what it is to live righteously, to ask for your due, and be so utterly spurned that you despair of life itself?

I was sitting in the steam room at a health spa when a stranger in his mid-fifties entered. He sat down and began to tell me his troubles. For nearly 21 years he'd worked for a large textile industry, but his company had fired him last August, just a few years before he could retire with full benefits. It seems the company didn't want to pay full retirement benefits, so they singled out those who'd be getting it soon, pressured them with relocations and impossible responsibilities, hoped they'd quit, but fired them for incompetency when they didn't.

No, the world has not changed all that much since Nabal sheared his sheep.

Revenge!

Back to the text! What's David going to do? He's done right but he's been treated like an enemy. David goes into what we might call a "slow burn." When he gets hot enough, he tells several hundred of his men, "Strap on your swords!" They move to attack Nabal, to kill every man of his tribe before a day is out. They'll take what they need! My, my! Can't we identify with David here? We've a hair-trigger when it comes to doing battle over our "rights." We find revenge so sweet!

There is an author named James Clark. While visiting a coastal book store he found six copies of a boring 900-page historical novel on a bargain book table. The book was written by some other author who also happened to be named James Clark. He bought all six copies and mailed them to six of his enemies with the note enclosed, "I hope you enjoy this and won't mind the slight reference to you. James Clark." Ah! Sweet revenge!

Then there's the one I read about in "Dear Abby." A divorcee wrote to say that her newly married ex-husband threw a big party at his home. She was formally invited by mail and told to dress as for a masquerade party. She showed up dressed like a scarecrow and the maid ushered her into the ballroom where everyone else was formally attired. Yes! Sweet, sweet revenge!

We humans are well-equipped for revenge. Why, we've developed a huge stockpile of barbs, looks, ploys, lawsuits, cuts, and sword thrusts with which to get even.

Years ago, when former Soviet Premier Khrushchev was visiting a French cathedral, he remarked to a reporter, "There is much in Christ that is in common with us communists, but I cannot agree with him when he says if you are hit on the right cheek, turn the left cheek. I believe in another principle. If I am hit on the left cheek I hit back on the right cheek so hard that the head might fall off." And so do we.

Godly Advice

Here comes David with 400 men. He's going to teach his enemy a thing or two. He's going to waste him!

It is interesting that Nabal's name in Hebrew means "fool." But fool that he was, the text tells us he had a beautiful wife of wisdom and discretion. Her name was Abigail, and she will forever be known as one of the great women in ministry!

Abigail, you see, learns of Nabal's foolish slight to David. She secretly gathers together the requested supplies and rides out to meet David. One person counseling forgiveness against 400 hot after revenge — those are the odds!

Well, Abigail meets David and, giving him the food, reminds him of several things. "Why stoop to your enemy's level by fighting with him? Your conscience is clear, your sleep peaceful. Let God take revenge. Keep your own hand from blood guilt. What is more, you are the future king. God will provide for your needs even if Nabal doesn't."

We all need to be reminded of those truths from time to time, don't we? Indeed, like David, we are quick to set off to avenge ourselves, and in so doing we rob ourselves of sleep, of a clear conscience. We lower ourselves to the level of our enemies.

Comedian Buddy Hackett said, "I've had a few arguments with people, but I never carry a grudge. You know why? While you're carrying a grudge, they're out dancing!" The truth is: Revenge is a burden. Unforgiveness ends up hurting you worse than it does the other person. Hatred is like an acid. It ends up wounding the handler more than it wounds the one he tries to throw it on.

All this is what Abigail came to remind David. This is what God would remind us today. In Deuteronomy 32:35, God warns, "Vengeance is mine. I will repay."

Leave It To God!

So, what does David do? He's been slighted. His temper has flared. He's mustered the troops and gone out to get even only to bump into this woman who's brought him supplies and preached him a sermon.

What would you have done? There you are in front of 400 men. A woman with a message has stopped you. What would your troops think if you backed down?

Exhibiting a character that will forever make David a man after God's own heart, David hears God's word from the lips of a woman, repents of his revenge, and sticks his sword back into his scabbard. "Like you say, lady. I'll turn it all over to God. I'll let him judge between Nabal and myself."

There are many in our world today who point out that Christ's commands to go the second mile, turn the cheek, and forgive seventy times seventy are unworkable, impractical, in this dog-eat-dog world.

What happens when David walks in this way? David starved, Nabal got fat, and King Saul lived happily ever after, right? Wrong! The text says Abigail shared plenty of food with David. Nabal heard of his wife's generosity and died of a heart attack, then David married Abigail. It's just like the Bible says in Proverbs 16:7, "When a man's ways please the Lord, he makes even his enemies to be at peace with him."

After World War I, President Woodrow Wilson, as a Christian, urged a greater measure of gentleness in dealing with the defeated nations. French Premier Clemenceau, who felt much more vindictive, objected, saying, "You talk too much like Jesus Christ." So it was that a harsh revenge was meted out by allies on a fallen Germany, and the seeds were sown that led directly to World War II, a war that some historians say was really WWI fought twice.

Will we ever learn Abigail's lesson? If we can trust our souls to Christ, can we not trust our enemies to him as well?

Revenge fosters revenge. War breeds war. Getting even, one-upmanship, is a never ending spasm of pain. If you sow quarreling, you'll reap quarreling.

Take a lesson from the wise, old mountain goats of Switzerland. Two "billies" meet on a high and narrow mountain path. The one is headed up and the other is headed down and there is no room to pass. What do they do? Lower their heads and butt it out? That would most certainly send them both falling to their deaths below! No, here's what they do. One goat lies down on the trail and allows the other to walk over him. Then he gets up and passes safely on his way.

That is what the gospel teaches for you and for me.

Conclusion

In Matthew 5:30-48, the Sermon on the Mount, Jesus says, "You have heard that it was said, 'An eye for an eye and a tooth for a tooth!' But I say to you, do not resist one who is evil. But if anyone strikes you on the right cheek, turn to him the other also; and if anyone would sue you and take your coat, let him have your cloak as well; and if anyone forces you to go one mile, go with him two miles ... You have heard that it was said, 'You shall love your neighbor and hate your enemy.' But I say to you, love your enemies and pray for those who persecute you, so that you may be sons of your Father who is in heaven."

Then, in Romans 12:14 following, the apostle Paul adds this, "Bless those who persecute you; bless and do not curse them ... Live in harmony with one another; do not be haughty, but associate with the lowly; never be conceited. Repay no one evil for evil, but take thought for what is noble in the sight of all. If possible, so far as it depends upon you, live peaceable with all. Beloved, never avenge yourselves, but leave it to the wrath of God ... No, 'If your enemy is hungry, feed him; if he is thirsty, give him drink; for by so doing you will heap burning coals upon his head.' "

Many of us think that by doing good to our enemies we drive them crazy trying to figure us out. We think this is the meaning of heaping "burning coals upon" their heads. Actually, there's a different truth here for us.

In ancient Palestine, people heated their homes and cooked their meals with wood fires. Since there were no matches or "Bic" lighters or electric ranges, fire was a precious commodity. If a fire ever went out, it was difficult to get it going again unless you borrowed from your neighbor.

For this reason, when you went on a trip, you'd take some hot coals from your fire, place them in a firepot, sit it snugly in your turban, and go out on your journey. The warm embers kept your head warm, and when time came to camp for the night, you had enough hot coals to light your fire.

Furthermore, if you were visiting in my home and rose to go, I, as a hospitable person, would go to my fire, rake out a few glowing embers, and heap them on your head (in the firepot, of course). This was a token of my hospitality, a winsome sign of my concern for your well-being.

The Bible is saying this is the respect we would show our enemies. For, who knows the grace of God, but that our enemies can be turned into our friends.

Suggested Prayer

God almighty, give me the grace to love my enemies. For Christ's sake. Amen.

Is Pacifism Biblical?

Do not resist one who is evil. — Matthew 5:39

Love your enemies. — Matthew 5:44

Did you hear about the Irish Christian boxer who went into a bar for a drink? Recognized and challenged by a local brawler anxious to make a name for himself, he took a hard punch to his left jaw! Reeling for a moment, he steadied himself, looked full into the young aggressor's face and turned his other cheek, whereupon he received a second blow. Recovering, he said, "That's both cheeks. Now I have no further instructions from Jesus." And he lit into his opponent with relish!

Obviously, he missed the point. Yet the question remains: "How many times must I turn the other cheek?" Does the Sermon on the Mount, indeed, teach pacifism? Nowhere is the challenge to believe and obey greater in Christ's sermon than in verses 39 and 44: "Do not resist one who is evil." "Love your enemies."

Does "Do not resist one who is evil" mean we dismiss the police force? That we disband the army? That we forego self-defense?

Clearly, these two verses amount to two of Christ's hard sayings. There are those who have taken them literally in every situation. Like the monk who let the mice nibble him. Rather than kill them, he felt it was Jesus' mandate not to resist evil.

Pacifism

In 1884, Russian novelist, Leo Tolstoy, wrote, *What I Believe*. He said, "Left alone with my heart and the mysterious Book," the Bible, particularly the Sermon on the Mount, he became a Christian. What's more, Tolstoy decided Jesus meant exactly what he said. Tolstoy decided to follow him into his ethic of not using violence as an individual or as a member of society. He urged the disbanding of the police and army. The money could be better spent. His critics pointed out that if evil came, then many would be slaughtered. Tolstoy's retort: "No man will be found so senseless as to deprive of food or to kill those who serve him."

Count Tolstoy and Christ were a huge influence on Gandhi, the liberator of India. "It is the Sermon on the Mount that has endeared Jesus to me," wrote Gandhi. He put into practice Christ's nonviolent ethic with colonial India's English overlords. He called his followers the "Truth Force." They stood up for what was right and, when opposed by force, endured suffering willingly. If you want to see this portrayed splendidly, watch the film, *Gandhi*.

During World War II, the gentle Gandhi urged England not to resist Adolf Hitler's armies. The church disagreed, pointing out that Mr. Gandhi's quarrel in India was with Great Britain, a somewhat Christian-influenced foe. But the Nazis were a different sort of enemy without a Christian conscience. At his fingertips was an arsenal of tanks, rockets, and perhaps nuclear warheads. If Hitler wasn't arrested in his evil reach, then surely we'd all disappear.

Tolstoy and Gandhi greatly influenced America's Martin Luther King Jr. in the 1960s Civil Rights Movement. What could have easily turned into a bloody race war found blacks meeting hate with love. And, as with Christ, the lifestyle of truth and peaceful nonviolent, noncooperation, ended with King's martyrdom. At the Reverend Doctor King's funeral, Benjamin Mays spoke.

> *If any man knew the meaning of suffering, King knew. House bombed, living day by day for thirteen years under constant threat of death; maliciously accused of being a communist; falsely accused of being insincere and seeking limelight for his own glory; stabbed by a member of his own race; slugged in a hotel lobby; jailed over thirty times; occasionally deeply hurt because friends betrayed him — and yet this man had no bitterness in his heart, no rancor in his soul, no revenge in his mind; and he went up and down the length and breadth of this world preaching nonviolence and the redemptive power of love.*[1]

King's marches and protests were appeals for equal justice under the law. And they were the embodiment of Jesus' words to love one's enemies and resist not one who is evil. When hurt, his followers absorbed it. When provoked, they refused to retaliate. In the end, passive resistance won out over bigotry.

At the very least, what Christ is saying is that when wronged, our first recourse is not to insist on our own rights nor to fight. Our first duty is patience, mercy, and love. Some say we resort to violence only as a last resort, only after going the second mile and turning the other cheek.

Yet, be quite clear — true pacifists say there is never a time for war. So say Tolstoy, Gandhi, King, Ron Sider, and William Barclay. They point out Jesus never killed. He blessed only the peacemakers. At his arrest, he refused to defend himself. He caused his followers to put away their swords, decrying, "If you live by the sword you will surely die by the sword" (Matthew 26:47). And like a lamb led to slaughter, Jesus went to the cross. To be Christian, to really believe in Jesus' word, we must, therefore, act like Christ in every instance.

Critics of this position point out that human nature being what it is — sinful, aggressive, and evil — pacifism causes the very war it seeks to avoid.

I once rented a boat in London to take a girl rowing on an autumn evening. We got out on an island to stroll, and when we returned, the boat was gone. I reported it stolen. The police came, and I got a ticket! It seems I had forgotten to lock my boat. In my failure, I was fined for "tempting a thief."

The same idea comes into play by maintaining a credible army. If am strong, my foreign neighbors will behave. My strength and willingness to fight will serve as deterrence to war.

It is interesting how cleverly some pacifists get around things here. Like the Amish farmer who wakes up in the middle of the night to find an intruder in his home. "I have a gun," he yelled. "I am going to shoot downstairs. You better remove yourself or you could be hurt!"

Then there is the Quaker milking his cow. The cow put his foot in the milk bucket. Unperturbed, the farmer washed it out and started over. This time the cow kicked the bucket over. The Quaker, clearly bothered, simply stared over. The next time the cow kicked the Quaker hard, sending him sprawling. The farmer got up, brushed himself off, went to the cow's face, pointed his finger at her, and said, "Thou knowest that I be a Quaker and can do thee no harm. But if thou bother me hence, I will sell thee to a Presbyterian!"

Context

When one comes to a hard saying in the Bible, the best commentary is more scripture.

It is popular to think of Jesus' Sermon on the Mount as the perfect sermon, entire of itself. Yet no mere sermon, even a series of sermons, can capture the full expanse of deity.

I have heard people call the Lord's Prayer "the perfect prayer," yet, it includes no thanksgiving. Most certainly, gratitude is a vital portion of our interface with God.

Likewise, Jesus never even once mentions the Holy Spirit in the Sermon on the Mount. And how can one ever hope to be like Jesus without God's invasive power? Likewise, in this sermon Jesus does not mention the cross or the resurrection or even the second coming.

Clearly, then, the Sermon on the Mount must be placed in context with not only all that Christ said and did — the New Testament — but all that Christ quoted and obeyed — the Old Testament.

The Rest Of Scripture

King Solomon, the wisest of kings, wrote in Ecclesiastes 3:1 and 8, "For everything there is a season ... [There is] a time for war."

The psalmist even praised, "Blessed be the Lord who trains my hands for war ..." (Psalm 144:1).

Deuteronomy 21:10 explains, "When you go forth to war...." Not "if," but "when." Because of human sin, violence is inevitable. Wilbur McClean learned it the hard way during the American Civil War. In 1862, this peace-loving Virginia farmer's land was overrun in the first Battle of Bull Run. He surveyed the terrible carnage and decided to get as far away from battle as he could. He picked up and moved his family to the absolute middle of nowhere — a tiny crossroads hamlet named Appomattox Court House.

There, in 1865, one of the last battles of the war was fought on his property. Lee surrendered to Grant in Wilbur McClean's living room.

In Revelation 19:21, Jesus makes his second coming. He came first as a lamb, a suffering servant, a dying Savior. His second advent, he arrives as a lion, a conquering Lord. He is described as being astride a white war horse. He slays the wicked with the breath of his mouth. Christians ride in the army behind him.

It seems to me, then, that the question is not, "Will I kill?" Indeed, I shall. The question is more rightly put, "Under what conditions will I take another life?"

The Case For A Just War

Proverbs 20:18 counsels, "By wise guidance wage war." And there is no better counsel than that of Saint Augustine of Hippo, North Africa, writing over 1,600 years ago. He gave us the seven criteria for a just war.

1. Personal revenge is forbidden. "Vengeance is mine. I will repay, says the Lord" (Romans 12:19). The sixth commandment in Exodus 20:13, when it says, "You shall not kill," uses the word for "murder." We are forbidden to kill when sanctioned to do so by the state. We are simply to refrain from personal unauthorized human slaughter.
2. The taking of human life belongs to God and to his established governments. Take a hard look at Job 1:21 and Romans 13:1-7.
3. God will judge a nation that is oppressive, unjust, and that makes war for evil purposes. Check out Amos, chapter 1.
4. Before a nation resorts to war, peace must be sought, every effort at reconciliation must be proved. We must go the second mile, turn the other cheek, and give up our cloak. We must never be trigger happy. War must forever be our last recourse, not our first impulse.
5. A nation must make God her trust, not the army. In Deuteronomy 17:16-17, God forbade Israel to multiply three things — silver, horses, and wives. He did not want

his people turning in trust to family, war machines, and bank accounts. As the psalmist put it in Psalm 20:7, "Some boast of chariots, and some of horses; but we boast of the name of the Lord our God."

6. If one must fight, there should be grounds. Augustine lists several.
    a. Self-defense (Matthew 24:43).
    b. Protecting national interests. Such as when Joshua fought that Israel might have a homeland.
    c. To rectify wrongs. In Genesis 4:9, Cain asks, "Am I my brother's keeper?" The answer is, "Yes." And when a neighbor is being savaged, we are to go to their aid.
    d. The preemptive war. If you are a clear menace to me, and I know I will have to fight you eventually, I may strike you first before you have a chance to fully arm yourself. By this means there will be less bloodshed.
7. War must be proportional. This means we make war on the army, not the civilians. We use only enough war to reestablish peace.

Conclusion

No better conclusion can one come to than the words of Saint Augustine. "Peace ought to be your desire, war only your necessity. Hence, even in warfare, be a peacemaker. Let it be necessity, not your desire, which slays the foe in fight."

Suggested Prayer

Jesus, help me to put away my warlike ways and study peace where I live. Amen.

---

1. Benjamin Mays, eulogy at the funeral of Martin Luther King Jr., April 9, 1968. Taken from "April 1968: Benjamin Mays delivers King eulogy," from http://www.bates.edu/x49909.xml.

Confessions Of A Healed Perfectionist

You, therefore, must be perfect, as your heavenly Father is perfect. — Matthew 5:48

Let me describe a sick man to you. We'll call him Jeff. I first noticed he had problems when I saw him walk into church one Sunday. Coming up the sidewalk he'd turn aside to actually pull the weeds out of an azalea. At first I thought he was only showing great care for the Lord's property. But later, at his place of business, I saw his merchandise meticulously stacked in neat rows with him scurrying up and down every aisle tidying up after each customer. Next it was his wife who came by my study weeping. It seems she was worried about her man. She described him with words like "dissatisfied, driven, joyless, critical, and grouchy." Then one of his children developed a nervous disorder that the doctor traced to the father-son relationship, and Jeff and I found an opportunity to talk about things.

"I like things done right," he began. He went on to vent his deep feelings about hard work, all about how if a job was worth doing it was worth doing right and so forth. Then he told me how when he was a small boy his dad made him mow the lawn. He told me his father stood there and watched him the whole time, "And if I so much as missed one blade of grass, he made me mow the whole lawn all over again!"

What we're talking about is the problem of perfectionism. It's in the fellow who has to win all of the time. It's in the woman with a neurotic passion for a clean and orderly house all of the time. It's in the person who cannot accept the best one can do when it's not perfect. It's in the eye that walks into a room, passes over dozens of things that are right, and dwells miserably on the one thing that is out of place. Perfectionism is a growing problem in our midst today, and its end result for us is just what it was for Jeff ... joyless, critical, grouchy, driven, dissatisfaction, even the alienation of our close relationships.

Jeff and I had numerous long talks. We searched the scriptures together, and the Lord began to give us insight that helped us both. I'd like to share that with you now in the hope that it'll make the difference in your life that it has in mine.

A Perfectionist Is Homesick!

The first principle comes from Genesis 2. There the Bible tells of the creation of man and woman and how God placed them in the Garden of Eden. Talk about perfection! Eden was a flawless human habitat. Read through Genesis 2, and you learn of the harmony once had in human relationships. The man spoke poetry to his wife, "This at last is bone of my bone and flesh of my flesh ..." (v. 23). There is no mention of anger, cross words, misunderstanding, or jealousy.

Then, too, note the strong self-esteem. So self-accepting are Adam and Eve that they stand naked and unashamed. No mention whatsoever is made of inferiority complexes, drug abuse, or suicide.

Next, take a look at the perfect environment. Eden flows with pure water, fresh blossom scented breezes fill one's nostrils, and tasty fruits are ripe for picking. The man surveys and names all animals and there is no fear between man and beast. Nor is there mention of pollution, epidemic, nor death.

Finally, take a look at Adam and Eve's right relationship with God. The Lord's will is clear to them. There is obedience, lack of fear, the absence of guilt.

Clearly the Bible is saying that the human race began in a perfect atmosphere, a garden paradise called Eden. And somehow, even today we've a memory, a taste for all of this. Deep within each of us there is a sense of order, beauty, and harmony.

You can see this in how we buy copies of magazines like *Better Homes and Gardens*, go to movies with tidy endings, prefer new cars without dents, rattles, or dirt, and admire youthful models with hourglass figures, straight teeth, and pure complexions.

In short, our perfectionist tendencies are a kind of homesickness for Eden.

Eden Destroyed!

If this is true, then why be homesick? Let's just get up and go home to Eden! But the fact is, we cannot. Eden is no more. It was destroyed by sin.

You can read what happened to paradise in Genesis 3. There's the story we know so well: the serpent Satan's temptation, Adam and Eve's disobedience, and the awful consequences of sin.

The word "sin" in the Greek means "to fall short, to miss the mark, to be off target." Perhaps you'll recall a few years ago when a man walked into the Vatican with a hammer and began to whack away at Michaelangelo's "Pieta," knocking off an arm and badly marring other parts of the masterpiece before he was stopped. That is sin. It is to deface the plan of God for one's life, it is to miss the ideal, to fall short of his perfection. The Bible says it's not just Adam and Eve who have sinned. Romans 3:23 teaches, "All have sinned and fall short of the glory of God."

If you want to see what our sin does to the world, read through Genesis 3 and 4. Harmonious human relationships with poetry in them turn to bickering, blame, and murder. Self-acceptance turns to shame. Trust in God turns to guilt, fear, and avoidance. The environment turns cold, dusty, a breeding ground for thorns, and death is mentioned for the first time.

All of this and the Bible teaches in Genesis 3 that God literally expelled us from the Garden of Eden. He "drove us out" the scripture says.

The facts are plain. We don't live where God originally intended. Sin has shattered our home. Sin has given birth to the ugly. Sin has brought imperfection. We are left with homesickness, a deep longing for what we had but lost!

Refusal To Accept God's Judgment?

Now follow closely! A perfectionist is a person who misses what he left behind in Eden. He wants things right again. He'll work tirelessly to see that everything is put back in its place. But because of sin, because of God's judgment, that can never be.

Note, if you will, how in Genesis 3 God removed us from the Garden of Perfection. To keep us from returning on our own terms he placed an angel with a mighty sword. Believe-me-you, those of us that keep trying to get back to where things are perfect know so well the painful thrusts of that sword!

So, a perfectionist is one who is homesick. He is one who wants his home back, wants things right like they were in Eden. But he is also one who will not accept God's judgment. "I won't live in that!" "I deserve better!" "I won't be a part of this!" "I want the best!" "It's got to be done just right!" And our attitude strives against God's judgment that because of sin we live outside paradise.

An interesting story that has to do with all this is found in Genesis 2. It's the story of the Tower of Babel. There man says, "Come, let's make a name for ourselves. Let's build a tower to heaven!" So, with brick and mortar they organize and build their way back, and God stops their work by confusing their language. The project ends in frustration and human alienation. The half-built tower stands as mute testimony that man's quest for perfection forever falls short!

Contrast this with what you find in Revelation 21:1 following. There a new Eden, a new paradise, heaven, is described. But it is not built from the ground up by humans. It is pictured as "coming down out of heaven" (v. 2). The message is clear enough: God built Eden and human sin ruined it. And it's not man's effort that will build it back. The work is entirely God's. It "comes down" from above instead of rising from beneath.

So, you begin to see something of our human predicament. We live between two worlds. It is God's judgment that we now live between an Eden that was and an Eden that will be. In the interim, we'll all do our share of writhing with imperfection.

During an episode of *Hill Street Blues*, Washington, a police officer, had done his best to bring a criminal to justice, only to watch helplessly as politics in the system allowed the man to go free. Washington was upset. He wanted to quit but Captain Ferillo called the officer into his quarters and said, "Do you have to win all of the time? Do things always have to be right for you? Grow up, Washington! We lost one. Get on with it!"

You can see this same attitude in the life of Jesus Christ. He took God's judgment seriously. He came to this world "as is" and got involved.

Think of it! Jesus, the perfect human being, came to live in this fallen paradise we call earth. No, he didn't come with a critical spirit. Instead, he selected imperfect people to be his followers — Peter, that swaggering big mouth; the temper-prone twosome, James and John; Thomas the doubter; and, of course, Mary of Magdala, the former harlot. Note how Jesus did not ask for perfect faith. "A grain of mustard seed" will do, he said. Note, too, our Lord's patience in dealing with his follower's pride, their misunderstandings, fears, and failures.

Isaiah the prophet said of Jesus, "A bruised reed he will not break, and a dimly burning wick he will not quench" (Isaiah 42:3). Most of us will throw away a broken pencil and put out a smoky candle. But Isaiah said Jesus would have patience with such imperfections and even try to fix them.

What we've got in the life of Christ is a perfect man living in an imperfect world. What we've got is an example to follow. If Jesus is not too good to be born in a stable, live in an anthill of a town like Nazareth, and do the menial chores of a carpenter, how much more so we? If Christ could live among imperfect people, show patience, kindness, and helpfulness, then why can't we?

We'll Get There, By God's Grace!

Well, all of that by way of understanding our human predicament. But now a word of hope!

In Matthew 5:48 Jesus said to his followers, "You, therefore, must be perfect." That's not exactly the sort of saying one would want to comfort a perfectionist with, eh? But I tell you there's good news in it for the Christian!

You see, the Greek word for "perfect" is *teleios*. It means "functionally useful" or "fit for a purpose." See here how Jesus is telling us to be functional and useful in this fallen world?

A lamb without blemish, one fit for sacrifice in the temple, is *teleios* or perfect. Jesus is telling us to live as worthy sacrifices in this world.

A full-grown man, as opposed to a half-grown boy, is *teleios*. He is perfect in the sense that he is fully mature. Jesus is telling us to grow up!

The most exciting meaning of "perfect" or *teleios* is its agricultural application. You see, a tiny spring bud on an apple tree is *teleios* or "perfect" in the sense that everything necessary for the production of an apple is already found in that bud. Just give it time and a blossom will appear, later a tiny green apple, and finally a red, ripened apple. Jesus is asking us to be perfect like that bud, to have within us everything necessary for the final maturity we all so desperately desire!

The good news is that in the life of Christ, in his death and ascension, and in the indwelling fullness of the Holy Spirit each of us is made *teleios*. Just like that bud on the apple tree we are already in possession of everything necessary for the emergence of a fully ripened apple! Just give us time. Just give us the "son" and rain and summer and complete maturity will appear.

The apostle Paul recognized this promise. In Philippians 1:6 he encouraged, "And I am sure that he who began a good work in you will bring it to completion at the day of Jesus Christ." Hear that? "God has begun a good work" in us. Can he finish the job? Will he complete us? The text says, "He will bring it to completion at the day," that's the second coming of Christ the Lord!

So, you want to be perfect? Then come to Jesus by faith. He'll put within you his *teleios*, the seeds of perfection that will mature, blossom, and bear fruit.

Until then, what are we to do? Do we sit back, stifle our longings for perfection, and settle for a "gentleman's C" in the course? Do we become a part of this age's rank mediocrity? No. Jesus in the Sermon on the Mount gave us the beatitudes in which he told us to mourn, to hunger and thirst, to be meek as we strive for renewed peace and perfection (Matthew 5:3-11). The entire sermon encourages us to get and stay involved, to quest, to reach out, but to depend on God all the while we're doing it, because, in the end, he is the source of all renewal. Paul follows this same line of thought in Philippians 3:12 following, "Not that I have already obtained this or am already perfect; but I press on...."

I think the bottom line for a perfectionist is this: We've got to accept our part of the judgment for sin. We've got to realize that it is only Jesus that can put things right again. We've got to come to Jesus and let him make us *teleios*, people blooming toward perfection. But at the same time we've got to get and stay involved in this fallen world just like Jesus did.

Take a lesson. Moses was called as an imperfect, stammering, temper-prone man to go get an imperfect people out of Egypt. Paul, that nearly blind, whipped, eyesore of a man was called to work with the imperfections of the Corinthian church, a fellowship in which people sued one another, committed incest, and got drunk on communion wine. We are called to work in this imperfect world, too. It's not ripe yet, but it has *teleios* in it. Just give it care and time!

I think God realized long ago what we perfectionists are slow in seeing: Something doesn't have to be perfect to do its job. Take my lawnmower, for example. It smokes, the wheels wobble, and the cut-off control is broken, but it cuts my grass. The same is true of leaders, homes, mates, friends, businesses, churches, and cars. Not a one of them is perfect. We are condemned to live with them. If we proclaim Christ, where he is received, *teleios*, the seeds of perfection are sown, and in time a new Eden will ripen.

Conclusion

Martin Luther spoke eloquently and true of our lives when in the mid-1500s he said, "This life, therefore, is not righteousness but growth in righteousness; not health, but healing, not being, but becoming, not rest, but exercise. The process is not yet finished, but it is going on; this is not the end, but it is the road. All does not yet gleam in glory but all is being purified."

What about you? Are you struggling with perfectionism? Is your life like Jeff's? Joyless, critical, driven, grouchy, and exhausting? Does one blade of grass out of place tear your insides out? Does a child's hand print on the wall set you off? Does your having to always have things right drive your friends away? Then come to Jesus for healing. Let him put his life within you. Let him make things right. Then humble, relaxed, hopeful, involved, longing, and looking to God, you can await the new Eden, the new heaven and earth coming down out of heaven for you and for me! You can be like Jeff who writes,"Hey, I used to need terrific all the time. But, no more! I've let go and let God. It's up to him. I'm only his servant working to make things some better until he returns to make it the best!"

Suggested Prayer

Jesus, I come! Amen.

The Fine Art Of Giving

Beware of practicing your piety before men in order to be seen by them; for then you will have no reward from your Father who is in heaven. Thus, when you give alms, sound no trumpet before you, as the hypocrites do in the synagogues and in the streets, that they may be praised by men. Truly, I say to you, they have their reward. But when you give alms, do not let your left hand know what your right hand is doing, so that your alms may be in secret; and your Father who sees in secret will reward you. — Matthew 6:1-4

After Jesus teaches his disciples about anger, lust, adultery, divorce, lying, and hatred, he moves on to another meddlesome topic — money.

Did you hear about the $100 bill and the $1 talking in the man's wallet? The $1 asked the $100, "What have you been up to lately?"

The $100 exuded, "Oh, I jetted to Europe, spent two weeks on the French Mediterranean coast. In Paris, I bought a fine meal with wine, took in a show in London, then back to Chicago where I bought two tickets to see the Bulls. So, dollar, where have you been lately?"

"Oh, the same old, same old," the $1 bill sighed. "I've been to church, and I've been to church."

Money talks. And it sure talks when it goes to church. In the text Jesus explains.

Alms

In verse 1, Christ talks about "practicing your piety." This has to do with religious observances, Christian disciplines. Jesus says, "Beware!" Be careful. It's easy to become a "hypocrite" (v. 2). In the Greek, a "hypocrite" is an actor. They look genuine but are really not. It is a show, all fake, pretend. And such empty piety, devoid of real worship, is the peril of all Christian people. "Beware," Jesus said.

"When you give alms ..." Jesus said. Not "if you give," but "when you give...." It is expected that Christians will give. The word "alms" means financial acts of charity, of love.

When my son was in the first grade, his class was making valentines. They made one for each student, for the teacher, even for the headmaster. Then someone suggested they make one for God. So they did. "But how will we deliver it?" someone mused. To which my son said, "That's easy! We'll just put it in the offering plate!" Our money can talk to God. It can be an act of worship when offered. It can whisper, "I love you. I believe in your kingdom. I want to be a part of your labors locally, in missions."

Almsgiving not only speaks to God in worship, it also has something to say to people! Standing in line to get a prescription filled at a pharmacy, I noticed a poor-looking farm lady and her son in front of me. The boy had a rash, a particularly itchy case of poison ivy. While he literally writhed in scratching, his mother presented the doctor's papers to the clerk. The order was filled and the bill presented. The mother looked at the price, examined the contents of her slim purse, shook her head wearily, and turned away with her unsoothed child. That's when another person in line stepped forward. "I'll purchase that lotion," she said. "Here, ma'am. This is a gift for your fine son. Be well." And she quickly walked away without even giving her name.

Giving alms to people speaks volumes. It says, "I love what God made in you. I care for your well-being."

The scriptures warn us not to seek "refuge in ... wealth" (Psalm 52:7). It chides us saying, "You have given no water to the weary to drink, and you have withheld bread from the hungry" (Job 22:7). Thus God judges us, saying, "In the fullness of his sufficiency he will be in straits" (Job 20:22).

During the California gold rush of 1849, a steamboat loaded with miners struck a log in the river and quickly began to sink. Some men found safety in lifeboats. Others stripped themselves of their heavy clothing, dived into the river, and swam for the shore. However, one of the miners lingered aboard the doomed vessel looting the other miner's trunks. Having filled his pockets with gold, he leaped into the water, and began frantically trying to swim for the shore. The weight in his pockets pulled him silently to a watery grave. Greed blinded him. He forgot money is only a tool. If you cling to it, money will pull you down.

Write this down and stick it in your hatband. We make a living by what we earn. But we make a life by what we give.

Motives

In verses 1 and 2, Jesus spoke of giving "in order to be seen" and "that they may be praised by men." It is true we can give for reasons of pride and human adulation.

Sometimes we give because we are forced to do so. For instance, at work, the United Way campaign begins. Someone sets a goal for 100% employee participation, and you are simply shamed into a pledge.

Other times we give to be seen. Recall that scene in the movie, *Gone With The Wind*, where, at a Confederate ball, an officer stands up to make an appeal for monies for the Rebel cause. Everyone gives what they can. One of the belles, her husband far away on a battlefield, takes off her wedding rings and offers them. Watching all this is Scarlett. Unhappily married herself, and all eyes upon her, she puts on quite a show by removing her rings and offering them for the Southern cause. Such ostentatious giving is the bane of the church, too. It is giving more devoted to self than God.

Yet another reason we give is for pity's sake. Television heralds the fly-encrusted faces and bloated bellies of famine victims in Africa. Morose music plays, and a somber-voiced announcer gives out a telephone number to call in your pledge.

The real motive for giving is love. This motive and this motive alone will save us from the "what-a-good-boy-am-I" Little Jack Horner religion. The text mentions twice God the "Father." He is the one we seek. He is our love. He is our devotion. He is our worship. What alms we give are for him and him alone.

T. S. Eliot, in his play, *Murder in the Cathedral*, wrote, "The last temptation is the greatest treason: To do the right deed for the wrong reason." Thus, each time we give alms, Jesus is asking us to stop and consider our motives. Is it to be seen by men? To indulge our self-preening ego? Or is it to worship God?

In Secret

One safeguard Jesus offers in all this is found in verses 3 and 4. Give "in secret," and "Do not let your left hand know what your right hand is doing."

When in Jesus' day the Pharisees gave alms they did so publicly. A man might purchase a cartload of water, haul it to a village center, have a trumpeter blow a loud fanfare, and say aloud to the thirsty crowd, "Bless me who gives you this water. I am a true son of Israel, a keeper of the law!" To the applause of the people, he strode away as they slaked their thirst.

We've all seen such public displays of piety. The newspapers are filled with smiling captains of industry presenting an oversized check to charity. Jesus is saying, "Beware!" We in Christ are to do it differently.

Put up no plaques; let there be no pictures on the walls; do not name it after yourself. With no fanfare give, and give in quiet secrecy.

Reward

In the tiny, rural Virginia village where I began my ordained ministry, the church treasurer came to me one day concerned. It seems one of the poor widows living in a cabin on the edge of poverty had given a check to the church. "She doesn't have it to give, pastor." So he asked me to visit, explain how the church was on her budget, and she didn't have to give.

Well, I was young then and didn't know any better. So I returned the widow's check and explained how she didn't need to give.

I'll never forget how that old, old woman began to weep softly and to me she confided, "I didn't give it to you. I gave it to God, and now you're taking away one of my last dignities."

Indeed! Giving is a privilege. And three times in the text Christ the Lord mentions the word "reward." It seems there is a reward for giving. Jesus very plainly says God rewards those who give him the sort of service or piety or alms he desires.

In Acts 20:35, the apostle Paul quotes Jesus, "It is more blessed to give than to receive." How so? How are givers blessed? In

Malachi 3:10, God challenges us to give and "... put me to the test, says the Lord of hosts, if I will not open the windows of heaven for you and pour down for you an overflowing blessing." This is the only place in the compass of scripture where God invites his people to put him to the test!

Giving Christians speak of God's reward in terms of joy, a sense of dignity in being a part of God's work, continued provision, things not wearing out, peace. Read the scriptures through. You'll see such rewards again and again.

"Your Father who sees in secret will reward you" (v. 4).

Suggested Prayer
O my Father God, I commit it all to you in Jesus' name. Amen.

Prayer: Moving The Hands That Move The World

> *And when you pray, you must not be like the hypocrites; for they love to stand and pray in the synagogues and at the street corners, that they may be seen by men. Truly, I say to you, they have received their reward. But when you pray, go into your room and shut the door and pray to your Father who is in secret; and your Father who sees in secret will reward you. And in praying do not heap up empty phrases as the Gentiles do; for they think that they will be heard for their many words. Do not be like them, for your Father knows what you need before you ask him. Pray like this: Our Father, who art in heaven, hallowed be thy name. Thy kingdom come, thy will be done, on earth as it is in heaven. Give us this day our daily bread; and forgive us our debts, as we also have forgiven our debtors; and lead us not into temptation, but deliver us from evil.*
> — Matthew 6:5-13

Jesus begins his discussion of prayer by first pointing out how not to do it. Do not be a hypocrite, that is, an "actor," and stand up in public pretending to talk to God when all you're really doing is preening your religious feathers in public and talking to others and yourself in a self-congratulatory way (vv. 5-6).

Prayer is also not a whipping yourself into an emotional frenzy until you achieve the right feeling. In verses 7-8 Jesus said there is no need to be verbose, to "heap up empty phrases." God is not hard of hearing. He understands plain words. We can speak to him simply.

Prayer, rather, is a simple conversation between you and God. It's best done in a room with the door shut (v. 6).

As an example of authentic prayer, Jesus gives the Lord's Prayer in verses 9-13.

A couple of football players began talking about religion in the locker room. One of them seemed a bit more ignorant about the subject than the other. "You're so stupid," commented the first. "Why, I'll bet you $5 you don't even know the Lord's Prayer."

"I'll take your bet," said the other. "Now let me see, the Lord's Prayer?" He cleared his throat and began....

> *Now I lay me down to sleep*
> *I pray the Lord my soul to keep,*
> *If I should die before I wake*
> *I pray the Lord my soul to take.*

The other jock just shook his head in disbelief. "I didn't know you knew it! Here's your five bucks!"

We laugh and shake our heads at such foolishness. But do we ourselves really know the Lord's Prayer? Most of us repeat it once or twice a week. Yet the words roll over us and through us too easily. There are 66 words. It can be repeated in about 22 seconds. Yet the meaning can take a lifetime to understand.

Who God Is

First of all, study how the Lord's Prayer reveals the nature of God.

Jesus said when one prays we should approach God as, "our Father." In Luke's version of this prayer the Greek word used for "father" is *abunna*, which translates as "papa" or "daddy." It is the familiar or intimate form of parental greeting.

When Jesus taught this prayer to his disciples, they were surely shocked! Jews were used to calling God Adonai or Jehovah or Yahweh, the unspeakable one. To call God "Papa" was radical!

Yet this reveals Christ bought us with his blood. No longer must we stand far from the mountain and avert our eyes. Nor must we wait reverently outside the holy of holies. Jesus Christ has torn the curtain in two! Now we can come boldly into his presence!

Think of it! In John 3:16 we are told that Jesus Christ is God's only begotten Son. Yet here in the Lord's Prayer we are taught to pray as sons and daughters saying to God, "Our Papa." This means in Jesus Christ we can pray to the Father just like we are Jesus

Christ himself! We've been born anew. No longer are we strangers and aliens to God, but children!

In the New Testament the word "Father" is used for God 267 times. There is only one tiny book, 3 John, that does not speak of God as Father.

"Our Father [Our Papa] which art in heaven." And then: "Hallowed be thy name." The Greek for "hallowed" means "to make holy" or "to show great respect." C. S. Lewis wrote, "The prayer preceding all prayer is, 'May it be the real I who speaks. May it be the real thou that I speak to.' " This is not easy.

It is so natural to fake it, to put on a religious air, and to pray only as wishful thinking to a God we've created as a figment of our imagination. It is one of the Ten Commandments that reminds us not to take the Lord's name in vain. In every society it has been all too easy and popular to become so familiar with the word God that we toss it about as an explanation, a byword, even a profanity. It is the Lord's Prayer that reminds us in the first sentence that even though we can approach God with the easy familiarity of a child his papa, we should also pause and remember to set God's name apart in highest reverence — "hallowed be thy name."

At a nearby synagogue school, a student prankishly wrote the name "Yahweh" on the chalkboard. When the rabbi came to class and saw it, he was overwhelmed, for that name above all names was so reverent as to be unspeakable. Yet, what to do? It couldn't be erased. Nor should it be covered. It was unthinkable to look further upon it. A meeting of the elders was called and it was finally agreed to cut that portion of the chalkboard out and bury it. It sounds radical. But you understand the reverence attached to the name of God.

You see the intimacy, the familiarity with which we may approach God on the one hand — "our Father." On the other hand, you see the awe, the reverence, the deep sense of respect with which we approach him — "hallowed be thy name." It is in this unrelieved tension that our relationship with God transpires.

In C. S. Lewis' *Chronicles of Narnia*, Christ Jesus is portrayed as the great lion, Aslan. A child watching the huge, fierce, loving, and just lion asks his mother, "Is he safe?" "No," the mother replies. "He's not safe. But he is good!" And so is God — he is a hallowed papa. He is strong and gentle, good and tough, with righteous mercy. He is a terrible beauty, fearful majesty, and a holy redeemer.

There are other attributes of God revealed in the Lord's Prayer. Words like "kingdom," "power," "glory," and "forever" are used of him. It can be discerned that he is forgiving and a provider, as well. Yet, the key quality I want you to see of God, as revealed in Jesus' prayer, is servanthood.

Jesus taught us to pray, "Give us this day our daily bread." Can you imagine going up to an awe-inspiring lion of a hallowed papa and asking for anything? Much less something as mundane as daily bread? Yet Jesus invites us to do just that!

What Christ is revealing here is that God has the heart of a servant. If you want to see this in black and white, or better still, in the flesh, look at Jesus in Philippians 2:5-7. "Have this mind among yourselves, which is yours in Christ Jesus, who, though he was in the form of God, did not count equality with God a thing to be grasped, but emptied himself, taking the form of a servant."

So, what does the Lord's Prayer teach that God is like? He is a papa but also must be hallowed. He is a servant eager to care for your daily needs, even something as mundane as your bread.

Who People Are

Immediately one is confronted with the fact that we are offsprings of God. For only a child can call God Father. This means we are not self-existent. We weren't here first. We're in no sense self-made creatures, in charge and unaccountable.

Furthermore, it becomes quickly evident that part of what it means to be human is to have needs only our Father can fulfill. One of our needs is physical. In asking God for daily bread our need for material benefits like air, water, sleep, warmth, and food is made known. Yet the prayer shows that materialism alone is not the answer. For in praying, "Forgive us our debts" a moral dimension to our existence is revealed. And the very fact that we ask for forgiveness shows that we have a problem — sin.

Then there is a spiritual facet to our being. "Lead us not into temptation, but deliver us from evil," recognizes this.

Political needs are confessed, "thy kingdom come." Also, social needs are confessed, "forgive us our debts as we forgive our debtors."

So, what are we saying about ourselves when we pray the Lord's Prayer? That we are the offspring of God, sinful, and having all kinds of needs: physical, spiritual, social, moral, even political. We are looking to God to oversee us as any father would his child.

The phone rang at home during supper recently. A poor woman asked me for financial help buying some groceries. I said, "Of course we'll help!" I asked if she had a church home. "No." I asked if she'd come to our next meeting and fellowship with us, network with our people, make some friends, and let us help her get a good job. "No," she said. She just wanted to come by and get the check for groceries.

In Christ, we aren't just interested in meeting the needs of the stomach but also social needs. We are interested in meeting emotional needs, educational needs, and moral needs. One can't pray the Lord's Prayer without becoming fully human — body, spirit, and soul.

It is interesting that as the disciples spent time with Jesus they began to see exactly who God is and, by sheer contrast, who they were. The result was that they asked, "Lord, teach us to pray" (Luke 11:1).

There is no record of their asking the Lord to teach them to heal or work a miracle, to laugh or cry, die, be single, get rich, or perform a liturgy. "Lord," they pleaded, "teach us to pray." It's as if they recognized Christ's prayer life as the source of all he was. This brings us to the third part of the Lord's prayer.

What Prayer Is

The Lord's Prayer defines prayer as a lap talk between a papa and his little child. Rosalind Rinker rightly defines prayer as "A conversation between two people who love each other — God and the Christian." Prayer is the dialog between God who is a Father, hallowed, eager servant, and any person who realizes his creatureliness and needs and is willing to crawl up into God's lap and ask for physical, spiritual, emotional, willful, and social provision.

With this in mind, why isn't God's lap full? Why is it we do not pray more?

I have heard every excuse and have even made most of them myself. "I don't know how." "I'm afraid." "I can't find the words." "I don't have time." "I don't have the faith. After all, isn't the Lord like the little old lady who lives in a shoe? He's got so many children he doesn't know what to do?"

All of these are excuses we give for not talking to God. The real *reason* that underlies it all is feeling no need to pray due to a sense of independence.

Look at it this way: In 1776, American colonists rebelled and declared their independence from England. They told King George to get lost, said they weren't going to pay his taxes any longer, and said they were willing to fight to prove it.

Genesis 3, contains man's declaration of independence from God. There we turned from God to self and Satan in a foolish quest not to die, to have our eyes opened, and to be like God.

When the Lord walked in the cool of the evening searching for us, calling us to account, he found us afraid of him, hiding, and filled with disbelief, disobedience, and deceit.

We've been like that ever since.

Some years ago I was walking with my two-year-old at Monticello in Virginia. Coming to a steep hill, I instinctively stuck out my hand to help my child. But nothing doing! Refusing to take my hand, she said with all the swaggering petulance of a two-year-old, "I do it by myself!" Four steps later, she fell and rolled to the bottom of the hill. There she cried out hysterically and threw out her hand to me!

That's exactly how it is with us and God. Before we will begin to pray two things must happen. One: I must recognize my creatureliness and needs. Two: I must recognize God's nature as a hallowed papa eager to serve my needs that I might be whole.

What is prayer? Childlike dependence upon God.

Are you there yet? Have you come to Jesus and asked, "Lord, teach me to pray!"

It's all so refreshingly simple, isn't it? Yet learning to pray can be a difficult and bewildering experience. A clue to making it easier is found in Luke 11:1. The disciples did not say, "Lord, teach *me* to pray," but, "Lord teach *us* to pray." They simply realized that most anything one wants to accomplish in life is easiest done in a group.

Here in church we come together as a covenant group to learn who God is, who we are, and the conversation that flows between us that is known as prayer. You are invited to come make your declaration of dependence upon God with us.

Suggested Prayer

Lord, teach me to pray! Amen.

It's Called Forgiveness ...
And It's On Your Exam!

And forgive us our debts, as we also have forgiven our debtors. — Matthew 6:12

For if you forgive men their trespasses, your heavenly Father also will forgive you; but if you do not forgive men their trespasses, neither will your Father forgive your trespasses. — Matthew 6:14

Shakespeare's timeless play, *The Merchant of Venice*, is about a businessman who borrows from a Jewish banker to fund a risky import trade. The collateral is a pound of his own flesh, something of a tradition in those days. When the merchant's ships sink and he cannot repay his indebtedness, Shylock, the banker, comes calling to collect his due, a pound of flesh.

Victimized by a lifetime of prejudice, Shylock seeks revenge on his Gentile tormentors. He will have his pound of flesh. He will cut the merchant's heart out!

Townspeople beg the old Jew for mercy. But he who has been shown none, offers none. He bitterly sharpens his knife as the merchant bares his chest.

That's when a lawyer intervenes to utter the immortal words, "The quality of mercy is not strained. It droppeth as the gentle rain from heaven."

See here? Four hundred years ago people were struggling with forgiveness. Even 2,000 years ago it was the same, for in Christ's Sermon on the Mount, the Lord mentions forgiveness eight times. In Matthew 6:14-15, Jesus pauses to reemphasize one thing from the Lord's Prayer. He highlights forgiveness.

Over the years, I've come to see forgiveness as one of our biggest needs. To forgive is a quiet miracle. One does it alone, silently, invisibly, freely. It is a choice, hidden at first. It is a willingness to make something creative and good out of something ugly and destructive.

Forgiveness is a process. It happens slowly, over time. It is often three steps forward and two steps back. Forgiveness is definitely love's toughest work.

Mercy is God's intervention. It is his means of coming to terms with a world that has sin in it. And it is an uncommon grace God wills to share in us.

In this chapter I desire to be very practical, to move beyond theory. I do not want to lambaste you with "how to." I want to get down and dirty, to provide analysis and practical steps.

Hurt

The first stage of forgiveness starts with some sort of pain. The hurt can be one of three varieties.

There is *personal hurt*. Examples of this are not being invited to the party, ridiculed, or victimized by gossip.

There is the hurt of *unfairness*. Some pain we deserve, and there is healing in it if we are willing to learn. For example, if I lose $50 in a sporting bet, it teaches me a lesson! But if I am mugged and robbed of $50, I suffer the pain of unfairness. Life is like this. It is full of indiscriminate hurts.

Some hurt us unfairly because they think we deserve it. John Wilkes Booth shot Lincoln because he thought he deserved it.

Others hurt us unfairly because they are compulsive hurters. For instance, an alcoholic father who can't control himself, verbally and emotionally wounds his children.

Unfair hurts can also result from the spillover from other people's problems. As in a schoolchild caught in the crossfire of busing and racial hatred.

Unfair hurts can also come from people of good intentions. How often I've seen a choleric, willful in-law trample the feelings of an entire wedding party by insisting things be done her way. Thus, a day of joy becomes a day of remorse.

Then there is the unfairness of mistakes. I remember lovely Cathy, a co-ed at Elon College. She was paralyzed in one arm and limped on one leg. She told me that during a routine surgery a drunken doctor had accidentally clipped a nerve.

Indeed, there are *personal hurts*, even a multiplicity of *unfair hurts*. But there can also be *deep hurts*. These are not mere annoyances, slights, or disappointments, but disloyalty, betrayal, and brutality. These type of hurts can wound one more deeply than all others combined.

Disloyalty — when Peter, in Christ's hour of need, denied even knowing him. Haven't we all reached for a friend in a time of great trial and they withdrew from us?

Betrayal — as when Judas sold Jesus out to the Pharisees for a mere thirty pieces of silver. Can anything hurt so badly as a trusted employee who learns your business, steals your secrets, then walks off with half your clients to start a rival business down the block?

Brutality — the soldiers crowned Jesus with thorns. They beat him in the head with a stick. We, too, can be brutalized by slander, rape, or a drive-by shooting.

There are a million ways to be hurt in this world — *personal hurts*, *unfairness*, and the *deep hurts* of disloyalty, betrayal, and brutality.

If you skim through the Sermon on the Mount, you'll see that Jesus was all too familiar with hurt. He spoke of slaps on the face, theft, breaking oaths, and divorce.

Hatred

The second stage of forgiveness is hatred. Jesus showed he was aware of this, also. He spoke of anger, an eye for an eye and a tooth for a tooth. He spoke of courts and hating one's enemy.

The typical human response to the hurts people send our way is hatred. I'm not talking about mere anger! Hatred is being more than mad. It is a tiger let loose in our soul.

There are two types of hatred. Passive hatred is when someone hurts you, you smile at them, excuse yourself, go out, and never speak to them again. They simply become a nonperson to you. You freeze them out, never wish them well, avoid, and ignore them.

The second form of hatred is being aggressive. This hatred is active. It retaliates, fights, shoots, jabs, slanders, and sabotages. It is tit for tat, an eye for an eye, and hurting back. An example would be the husband in a divorce who takes out his chain saw and cuts his house in half, along with the television, the sofa, the dining room table, and refrigerator.

In the text, Jesus says this sort of hatred is destructive. It destroys our very ability to commune with God!

Consider what hate does:

- It shows poor values; we hate the person and not the sin.
- It separates us from those to whom we belong, such as an employee at work, a teammate, a church member, or a family member.
- It makes us like the rest of the world. "You're a Christian, but I've watched you. You're really no different than the rest of us."
- It utilizes huge amounts of energy wastefully. We mull the hatred over and over in our minds. We lay awake nights. We refight battles and develop an emotional focus. We suffer mental anguish and are fatigued. We cross the street to avoid others.

Watch the movie *Eleni*. It's about an investigative reporter who tracks down a Nazi war criminal who killed his mother in World War II. You'll see all of the debilitations of hatred hard at work in a man's life.

Hatred poisons the soul. It unleashes dangerous chemicals in the body that stifle and cripple. The Greeks have a saying, "Before you go out for revenge, first dig two graves."

Hatred also destroys one's prayer life. One can't even pray the Lord's Prayer. We choke on the words, "Forgive us our debts as we forgive our debtors." Hatred interrupts the flow of mercy. We can't receive it unless we give it. For how can I ask God to do for me what I'm not willing to share?

Healing

So far we've looked at the *hurts* and the *hatreds* of life. Both of which we're all too familiar!

Now let us look at healing, something that is alien to us. Jesus urges it upon us throughout the Sermon on the Mount when he talks of being merciful, pure, a peacemaker, and suffering persecution. It is even in the text, "Forgive men when they sin against you."

In January 1984, at the Rebibba Prison in Italy, is inmate, Ali Agca. He is notorious as the man who shot the pope. Suddenly the door opens and Pope John Paul II enters Ali's cell to visit and offer his forgiveness to the villain who shot and nearly killed him.

The merciful deed seemed unnatural. Ali Agca was guilty in the first degree. He'd gone beyond the forgiveness zone. Yet John Paul's act of compassion and courage was a thrilling and unforgettable offer of mercy. We all inwardly yearned to be able to do the same with our more or less public grudges.

The question is "How?" How can I forgive?

First, recognize that forgiveness is a process, not an event. "Let's get it over with." "Let's put this behind us once and for all!" No. Forgiving does not work this way. It can't be accomplished in one step, in a day. It takes time.

Spiritual surgery in your soul is just as complicated a process as physical surgery. There has to be a diagnosis, a treatment plan, checking into the hospital, post-op prep, surgery, the closure, and a recovery period. Healing can take weeks, months, even years! It is no less the same with forgiveness.

Second: Confessional prayer is helpful. "God, I hurt ... I'd like to wring his neck!" Get it all out. Be honest to God. It is no good walking around in denial. "I'm fine. I'm not mad. I love everybody!" Hah!

Third: Choose forgiveness. "God, you've forgiven me far worse sins. I choose to forgive them. I will to do this, Lord."

Fourth: Think forgiveness. When Satan brings up hurt, rather than nurse a grudge, take your thoughts captive to obey Christ. Flee to scripture and meditate on Christ's words. "Father, forgive them for they know not what they do." "Forgive your brother seventy times seventy." "Blessed are the merciful...."

Five: Put your emotions in perspective. Don't deny them. Don't repress them. Just don't follow them. A man deeply hurt told me, "If I do what I feel, somebody's going to die!" Pick a healthy outlet for your emotions: swim it off, chop wood, hit a golf ball.

Six: See your foe as God does. Look at how we dehumanize our enemies and reduce them to ogres by calling them slang names. We reduce them to their sin against us. With tunnel vision all we see of them is their crime.

But stop and ponder for two minutes! The deepest truth about them is not what they did but that God made them in his image. They are one of a kind, beloved of God, infinitely redeemable, and we must ask God to give us faith to see them as he does.

Seven: Ask the Holy Spirit to help you. The fact is — I *choose* it and God *empowers* it. It's like sailing. I raise the sail. The wind pushes the ship. I make myself available. God supplies the mercy.

Eight: Pray for them. Jesus said, "You have heard it said, an eye for an eye, a tooth for a tooth. But I say unto you, love your enemies and pray for those who persecute you." Hand your foe over to God for purging, for growth, and for mercy. Let God handle them.

Nine: Look for a time to put action to your thoughts, a time to come together.

This is not always possible, as in a father/son relationship rife with hatred. The father died and the bitterness was unresolved. All the son can do is go through the first eight steps and leave it there.

In an adulterous marriage that ends in divorce, the parties often marry another. The first eight steps can be tread, but it is not possible to go further. The two cannot be husband and wife again, but they can be civil, cooperate with the children, and pass on the street in a friendly manner.

Sometimes forgiveness must end here. We must avoid the all-or-nothing syndrome. It's like climbing a mountain. One might not make it all the way to the top. Yet the view from 90% the way up is magnificent. We should simply climb forgiveness as far as we can.

The key is to establish reunion within the bounds of reality.

When Jesus forgives you and me, he does not say, "I forgive you, but I'll have nothing further to do with you!" Christ's mercy abolishes the moral hindrances in our memory, will, and emotions and reestablishes our relationship with joy.

Often we seek a meeting, our foe is shameless, "I'm not admitting I did anything wrong" or "Aw! Let's just let bygones be bygones and go on!"

You mustn't paint over rust. It's not forget and forgive! It's forgive and forget! True mercy holds respect for the truth, for justice, for the feelings of the victim.

So we must ask for repentance, a confession, an apology. This is not a condition I need. It is a condition he needs. He must take responsibility for his actions, understand what he did to hurt you, feel the pain he has caused. He must be willing to confess, to begin a new relationship built on truth, not denial.

It is important here to recognize that you two will never agree on the details of the hurtful events. At best, a general understanding can be accepted and then move on.

What if they refuse to confess, to repent, to reestablish rapport? Then forgive and go on without the relationship. They won't buy their ticket to ride the grace train with you.

If, however, they do reconcile, accept it with joy, just as Jesus accepted Peter on the beach after the resurrection. Such healing shows the kingdom of God has come upon you! And what a witness to the world!

Conclusion

Novelist William Faulkner wrote, "The past is not dead. It's not even past." It often lives in our very real hurts and severed relationships. But in Jesus we can redeem the past. We can move beyond the hurt and hate to healing. Let all those of faith keep their feet on this path.

Suggested Prayer

Lord, let's get started ... who's first? Amen.

Are You Going To(o) Fast?

> *And when you fast, do not look dismal, like the hypocrites, for they disfigure their faces that their fasting may be seen by men. Truly, I say to you, they have received their reward. But when you fast, anoint your head and wash your face, that your fasting may not be seen by men but by your Father who is in secret; and your Father who sees in secret will reward you.*
> — Matthew 6:16-18

> *Is not this the fast that I choose...?* — Isaiah 58:6

There are many doctrines in the Bible that receive light billing today. Though the Bible is not silent on the matter, the pulpit is strangely mute. Which of you has heard a sermon on sleep? Indeed, we spend one third of our lives in slumber, yet even though the Bible speaks of our nocturnal habits, few ministers preach on the matter. The same goes for other dogmas such as hell, meditation, tongues, and, of course that which the text mentions, fasting!

Today, let us seek to remedy at least one portion of this abysmal situation and open the book on fasting.

What Is Fasting?

Jesus said, "When you fast...." In the Greek, "fasting" is *nesteuo*, meaning, "not to eat."

Three sorts of fasts are taught in scripture.

1. The normal fast — to abstain from food, solid, or liquid, except for water for a set period of time. Matthew 4 describes Christ fasting for forty days in the wilderness.
2. The absolute fast — to abstain from food and drink, including water for three days. In Acts 9:9, Saul, after being blinded on Damascus Road, resorted to a total fast for three days.
3. The partial fast — to restrict one's diet in some manner, such as giving up sweets or meat. It represents self-denial.

Matthew 3:4 explains such habits in John the Baptist's life. Daniel 1:15 says it was a portion of Daniel's life, also.

However one fasts, we must remember Jesus who gave us his own body and blood. Our fasting is a faith response to him. It is the sacrifice of our own flesh to him.

Who Fasts?

Is fasting for you or is it a form of spiritual discipline no longer relevant? Scouring the scriptures, one compiles a list of fasting adherents that reads like a "Who's Who in the Testaments."

Moses is the first recorded person in scripture who fasted (Exodus 34:28).

King David fasted when Saul perished in battle (2 Samuel 1:12).

Others who practiced fasting include the prophet Elijah; Daniel, the seer (Daniel 9:3); Nehemiah, the builder (Nehemiah 1:4); Job, the sufferer; the children of Israel (Judges 20:26); the people of Nineveh (Jonah 3:5-7); Anna, Hannah, Esther (Esther 4:6); and the apostles (Acts 9:9). Jesus even fasted (Luke 4:2). Great stalwarts of the later church such as Luther, Calvin, Knox, and Wesley fasted.

Should Christians Fast Today?

Jesus said in Matthew 6:16, "When you fast...." He did not say "*If* you fast ..." but "*when*." Furthermore, in Matthew 9:15 Jesus explained, "When the bridegroom is taken away, then they will fast." Clearly, Jesus expected fasting to be a part of our spiritual discipline. Here in Matthew 6 Jesus counts fasting as a normal piety right alongside prayer and tithing.

What Happens When One Fasts?

The text mentions the word "reward" twice. Of what possible benefit is fasting? What reward is there?

Our physical bodies are like that of a camel. We can store up food and water in our inner pantry. But when we begin to fast, several things start to occur.

1. The body begins to use up excess fat.
2. The body is purged of toxins. A sort of physical "spring cleaning" goes on.
3. One has an extra three or four hours a day to pursue spiritual matters since one doesn't have to prepare food, stop to eat, or clean up three times.

During a fast, the volume of the physical world is turned down, while the volume of the spiritual world is turned up. This is at least partially because the oxygen and blood normally going to one's stomach to aide digestion goes instead to one's brain, thus aiding clear thinking. Carnality is diminished. Spirituality is increased. Self-control, a fruit of the Holy Spirit is matured (Galatians 5:22), and one enters a period of greater sensitivity to Jesus.

You've, no doubt, heard the saying, "The way to a man's heart is through his stomach." Satan knows it's true. He used food to tempt Adam and Eve. Esau sold his birthright for a mess of porridge. The Hebrew children went to Egypt for food. God warned Israel against eating their fill and forgetting him in their new homeland.

Jesus even predicted eating and drinking to the full would be a sign of his return (Luke 12:45; Matthew 24:37-38). So, Christ warned, "Man shall not live by bread alone, but by every word that proceeds from the mouth of God" (Matthew 4:4).

So, when we fast, we set food aside for a while to focus on God.

This engenders several splendid things!

1. It allows our digestive system to rest. By fasting one day each week, your stomach will have nearly two months of rest a year! And just as we rest our eyes or feet or minds, so we can rest our digestive track.
2. It allows us extra time to seek God.
3. It increases our spiritual sensitivity.
4. It fosters self-control.

When Should One Fast

Let's not become legalistic! The Pharisees fasted regularly for outward show of piety. For them it was rote and devoid of spirit. It was "to be seen by men."

Simply fast when God moves you to do so. It is a matter of individual conscience.

In scripture, here are some examples of when God's people made the choice to fast.

1. For national repentance (Joel 2:12; Jonah 3:5, 10).
2. During a crisis (Jehoshaphat, 2 Chronicles 19; Paul blinded, Acts 9:9).
3. When power to intercess in prayer was needed (Nehemiah 1:1-11; Ezra 8:23).
4. Before big decisions (Acts 13:3; 14:23).
5. To return to the Lord (2 Samuel 12:7-17; Psalm 69:10).
6. For health and healing (1 Samuel 30:11-15; Acts 9:9). There is an interesting 3,700 year old Egyptian papyrus that quotes a physician, saying, "Man eats too much. He lives on only a quarter of what he consumes. The doctors, however, live on the other three-fourths."
7. To seek God's revelation (Daniel 9:2, 3, 21, 22; Acts 10:10).
8. To free the captives (Mark 9:29).

How Do I Get Started Fasting As A Spiritual Discipline In My Life?

Let me make a few trenchant suggestions. Begin with the book, *God's Chosen Fast* by Arthur Wallis. Then go through the scripture references and read each one. Next, pray asking the Lord to show you what he wants from you and begin slowly, partially fast by missing a meal. Graduate to a 24-hour fast, and take it from there. God will show you.

Always, though, as Matthew 6:16-17 warns, keep your fasting a secret. Don't tell anyone. Only Jesus should know.

Conclusion

When one goes to war, he must not forget his weapons. And fasting is a forgotten part of our spiritual arsenal. Let's pick it up. Let's choose what God has chosen.

Suggested Prayer

Lord, show me the place of fasting in my life. Amen.

Is Your Reward Waiting?

> *... they have received their reward.*   — Matthew 6:2
>
> *... your heavenly Father who sees in secret will reward you.*   — Matthew 6:4
>
> *Therefore, my beloved brethren, be steadfast, immovable, always abounding in the work of the Lord, knowing that in the Lord your labor is not in vain.*
>   — 1 Corinthians 15:58

Where I come from we look forward to payday. In fact, my father says you have never lived until you've been a Crotts boy on a Friday night after payday.

Payday means reward. It means provision and extra enjoyment. It brings a sense of accomplishment. And for one and all alike payday is an occasion of importance.

The Bible talks about a payday God has for us who believe in and serve Jesus Christ. The text says that in the Lord our "labor is not in vain." There is reward in serving Jesus! To emphasize this Jesus mentions the word "reward" seven times in Matthew 6:1-18. "Your Father who sees in secret will reward you" (v. 4). So, to a study of that reward we now turn.

Some Paydays Come On Earth

The Bible teaches that some rewards from God are received right here on earth. Consider Deuteronomy 11:13 following where God makes promises.

> *And if you will obey my commandments which I command you this day, to love the Lord your God, and to serve him with all your heart and with all your soul, he will give the rain for your land in its season, the early rain and the later rain, that you may gather in your grain and your wine and your oil. And he will give grass in your fields for your cattle, and you shall eat and be full.*   — Deuteronomy 11:13-15

Galatians 6:7 also has this in it: "Whatever a man sows that he will also reap."

Last Christmas I was shopping in a big department store and had stopped by the escalator to wait for my wife. It was there that I noticed a nine-year-old boy. From the look on his face I knew he was up to something! He just kept staring at that escalator mischievously. I asked him what he was doing and he said, "I'm waiting for my chewing gum to come back to me!" Obviously, the lad was on to something. He'd discovered a very important principle in life: "What you put down comes back to you." "What you sow you reap." If you honor God, he will honor you. And I watched as the lad retrieved his gum and popped it back into his mouth.

However, be careful here! One can carry this point too far! Some preachers have popularized this principle into a "prosperity theology" saying, "If you serve the Lord, if you are faithful and pray, you will be rich, joyously happy, in perfect health, have lots of children, and be famous!" They point out, "What you sow you reap!" While what they say is true, indeed, some rewards are paid us here on earth, but that's not all the truth of the matter there is.

Most Paydays Come In Heaven

The fact is, most rewards aren't received here on earth. They are given out in heaven. The apostle Paul, near the end of his life, wrote in 2 Timothy 4:7-8, "I have fought the good fight, I have finished the race, I have kept the faith. Henceforth, there is laid up for me the crown of righteousness, which the Lord ... will award me on that day...." Did you hear that? "The Lord will...." It hasn't happened yet, but he *will* in the future. "On *that* day ..." not *this* day. Here Paul clearly points out that his reward is in heaven. He certainly hadn't gotten much of it here on earth! No home, constant misunderstanding, ill health, imprisonment, beatings, friends dying, betrayals, shipwrecks, snake bites — you name it, Paul suffered it. What he had sown he had not fully reaped on earth. But he believed he would most certainly reap it on judgment day when God settled accounts once and for all.

Obviously Paul is struggling with this doctrine. Out of one side of his mouth he says, "What you sow you reap." Then in 2 Timothy 4:7-8 he says he hasn't gotten his reward yet. Which is it?

There is a divine balance here known only to the sovereignty of God, and we must temper our expectations by it. On the one hand is the principle of sowing and reaping. If we do right we may expect to be treated right. On the other hand we must understand that this is a sinful world. And not only our personal sins, but the collective sins of others can block our blessings. Job was faithful to God, but because of Satan he lost his children, his home, his health, and his wealth. Stephen preached right and was stoned to death. Peter was a faithful apostle but was crucified upside down. Watchman Nee was a faithful evangelist in China, but he spent the last twenty years of his life in a communist prison.

A missionary was returning home from 27 years of service in Africa. His health was broken. He was all but penniless, and he knew very few people stateside. The passenger ship that brought him home to Norfolk also had a wealthy oil magnate aboard. His berth was first class. The missionary's was beside the boiler room. Everyone aboard tipped their hat to the rich gentleman. No one seemed to notice the broken, old missionary. As the ship made port, a red carpet and brass band greeted the rich merchant. Women offered their arms. Porters scurried. Newsmen's cameras flashed. However, the missionary crept ashore unnoticed. Feeling ever so lonely and forgotten, he prayed, "Lord, no one cares about me. No one is even here to welcome me home," he whimpered. And a voice within him said, "You're not home yet."

"The Lord, the righteous judge, will award to me on *that* day," Paul said (2 Timothy 4:8). Perhaps on *this* day some rewards will indeed come, for what we sow we reap, but not always in this life. Most rewards come on *that* day and not *this* one.

What Are Rewards Based On?

Passing on, let's consider yet another principle that is best gotten at by the question, "On what are our rewards based?" Are they based on the amount of work we do? Number of converts? Fame? Success? No. Rewards are based on our faithfulness to Christ.

Consider that nowhere in scripture does God command you to be rich or famous or popular or overworked or successful. He simply asks, "Be faithful unto death and I will give you the crown of life" (Revelation 2:10).

This brings up the whole question of motives, doesn't it? Why do we serve Jesus? Why do we minister? Is it to be faithful or is it to be seen? Is it to wield power over others? Is it for fame and for fortune? As Jesus said in Matthew 6:1, "Beware of practicing your piety before men in order to be seen by them."

Father of modern psychology, Sigmund Freud, wrote that there are only two motives behind everything we do — either sex or money. Get honest for a moment as you think about that. There's a lot of truth in what he said.

One night I was driving to Duke University to speak to a Christian student gathering. Halfway there the Holy Spirit asked me, "Why are you doing this?" I had to admit I honestly didn't know. I began to examine my motives before the Lord. Am I doing this just to get out of town for a breather or to see the pretty girls? Am I doing it to admire the Gothic cathedral that sits in the middle of the campus or to try to make a clever speech and to try to "wow" the students? I had to admit there was some of all of that in my motives. But deep down there was a motive beyond Freud's sexual and money motives. That was the love of Christ. I decided I was doing this because I loved Jesus, and I wanted to give others some of what he is giving me!

The Bible teaches in 1 Corinthians 3:12 following that all of our works will be tested by fire on judgment day. The impurely motivated works of wood, hay, and stubble will be burned away. But the golden deeds done for the love of God and man will survive as our reward!

A rich man died and went to heaven. Peter met him at the pearly gates, welcomed him in as a Christian, and then offered to escort him to his eternal reward. Down the golden streets they went passing incredible mansions. Finally the two reached a modest cabin by the river. "Here you are," Peter gestured. "I'm shocked," said the gentleman. "I lived in better than this on earth." "True," Peter replied. "But then you didn't give us much to work with here."

Have you ever noticed how the Bible emphasizes humility in our ministry? Don't give in public, Jesus taught. Give secretly! Your heavenly Father who sees in secret will reward you in secret. "Fast in secret." "Minister to the orphan and widow from whom you have no hope of gain." Again and again in scripture, the word tells us to minister for no other motive than to please Jesus. We are to dismiss all pride, all desire to be seen, and do for Jesus and do for him alone.

What is your motive? What *is* your motive? In the end, all that we do, all that we are will be tested by fire. And our reward will be based on the quality of the deed not the quantity.

No Reward Postponed Will Be Forgotten

All of that — how some rewards are received here on earth, how most aren't received until heaven, and how they are based on faithfulness of motive and what you do with what you've got — now, this final word of assurance! No reward that is postponed will be forgotten. God keeps strict and accurate accounts. If you've got it coming to you, then you can be sure you'll get it!

What does the Bible say? "But I said, 'I have labored in vain, I have spent my strength for nothing ... yet surely my right is with the Lord, and my recompense with my God' " (Isaiah 49:4). "For God is not so unjust as to overlook your work and the love which you showed for his sake in serving the saints" (Hebrews 6:10).

Consider the life of Robert E. Lee. As a child he lost his father, a debt-ridden and irresponsible parent who went to Barbados, died at sea, and was buried on Cumberland Island, Georgia. He lost his childhood working and caring for his mother, growing up quickly in his dad's absence. He lost his inheritance, Stratford Hall, when debt collectors foreclosed on it. He was educated at public expense at West Point Academy because his mother couldn't afford to send him any place else. In a way, he lost his wife, Mary, who so early in life became an invalid. His career in the military was lost in slow promotions when after years of duty he was only a colonel serving as an engineer in such forgotten places as Cockspur Island, Georgia, and San Antonio, Texas. He lost a child, his special daughter,

Ann, who died in Warrenton, North Carolina. He lost the opportunity to become Commander-in-Chief of the Union forces when he told General Winfield Scott he could not bear arms against his native land.

He lost his home, the Custis-Lee mansion in Alexandria, Virginia, when Federal troops captured it and turned it into a cemetery. He lost his citizenship as an American, and it was never returned during his lifetime. He lost his friends, A. P. Hill, Jeb Stuart, Stonewall Jackson, and a host of others, all fallen in battle. He lost his health. A heart attack at Fredericksburg lingered and took him to an early grave in his sixties. He lost the war, surrendering to an inferior general with superior resources at Appomattox Court House in 1865, Palm Sunday. The last years of his life were spent as president of the little-known Washington College in Lexington, Virginia, where he began civilian life with little money, ninety students, and four faculty.

At his funeral, Senator Benjamin Hill said, "He was a foe without hate, a friend without treachery, a soldier without cruelty, and victim without murmuring. He was a public officer without vices, a private citizen without wrong, a neighbor without reproach, a Christian without hypocrisy, and a man without guilt. He was Caesar without his ambition, Frederick without his tyranny, Napoleon without his selfishness, and Washington without his reward." You can be sure Bobby Lee has gone on to a well-deserved reward that he never got here!

Take the Christian composer, Amadeus Mozart. He was always poor, plagued with bad health, and forever working for unappreciative employers. His music was recognized little during his lifetime, and he went to an early grave at age 35. On the day of his funeral, he was being carried to a pauper's grave when a thunderstorm broke out. Those in the funeral procession broke and ran for cover. No one was there at his committal except the gravedigger, and he did his work hastily in the mud.

For Lee and Mozart and countless others known but to God, there was precious little payday here. You can be sure, however, that there was for them a payday in heaven! "For God is not so unjust as to overlook your work ..." (Hebrews 6:10).

What Shall We Do With Our Rewards?

It is thrilling to note in scripture that a portion of our reward in heaven will be in new responsibility and authority. Revelation 2:26 says, "He who conquers and who keeps my works until the end, *I will give him power over the nations*." In Luke 19:17, Jesus told a parable about a man who did such a good job here, he was promoted there: "Well done, good servant! Because you have been faithful in a very little, you shall have authority over ten cities." Here, our rewards are seen as the presence and intimacy and affirmation of God that leads to more responsibility.

Most of all, the scriptures speak of our rewards as coming in the form of crowns! There is the "imperishable crown" mentioned in 1 Corinthians 9:24-29 and given out as a reward for not being carnal. There is the "crown of exultation" found in Philippians 4:1 and 1 Thessalonians 2:19-20 and given out for winning souls to know Christ. There is the "crown of life" (James 1:12; Revelation 2:10) given to those who endure persecution, the "crown of righteousness" (2 Timothy 4:7-8) for those who in faithfulness serve God and look for his second coming, and the "crown of glory" found in 1 Peter 5:1-4, the pastor's crown.

What shall we do with these crowns the Lord has given us as a reward? Revelation 4:10-11 says that we shall gather at Christ's throne, sing his praises, and cast our crowns at his feet!

Conclusion

What is the conclusion of all of this? We must end where we began. "Therefore, my beloved brethren, be steadfast, immovable, always abounding in the work of the Lord knowing that in the Lord your labor is not in vain" (1 Corinthians 15:58).

Suggested Prayer

O my Father God, I commit it all to you in Jesus' name. Amen.

What Does The Bible Say About Materialism?

"Do not store up for yourselves treasures on earth, where moth and rust consume and where thieves break in and steal; but store up for yourselves treasures in heaven, where neither moth nor rust consumes and where thieves do not break in and steal. For where your treasure is, there your heart will be also.

"The eye is the lamp of the body. So, if your eye is healthy, your whole body will be full of light; but if your eye is unhealthy, your whole body will be full of darkness. If then the light in you is darkness, how great is the darkness!

"No one can serve two masters; for a slave will either hate the one and love the other, or be devoted to the one and despise the other. You cannot serve God and wealth.

"Therefore I tell you, do not worry about your life, what you will eat or what you will drink, or about your body, what you will wear. Is not life more than food, and the body more than clothing? Look at the birds of the air; they neither sow nor reap nor gather into barns, and yet your heavenly Father feeds them. Are you not of more value than they? And can any of you by worrying add a single hour to your span of life? And why do you worry about clothing? Consider the lilies of the field, how they grow; they neither toil nor spin, yet I tell you, even Solomon in all his glory was not clothed like one of these. But if God so clothes the grass of the field, which is alive today and tomorrow is thrown into the oven, will he not much more clothe you — you of little faith? Therefore do not worry, saying, 'What will we eat?' or 'What will we drink?' or 'What will we wear?' For it is the Gentiles who strive for all these things; and indeed your heavenly Father knows that you need all these things. But strive first for the kingdom of God and his righteousness, and all these things will be given to you as well." — Matthew 6:19-33 (NRSV)

Every now and then I circulate a questionnaire among the Christians in the church parish. I've found that people are a fund of creative ideas! One of the queries I make about sermons is: "How long?" and "About what?"

My all-time favorite response is, "I'd like to hear a sermon about Jesus and about twenty minutes." But another good idea came in this form: "I'd like to hear a sermon titled, 'Too many BMWs in the church parking lot!' " There you have it! What, indeed, does the Bible say about materialism?

Things are important in our culture. Wall Street stockbroker, Ivan Bosky, in 1986, told the UCLA Berkley Business School graduates, "I think greed is healthy. You can be greedy and still feel good about yourself." He got a standing ovation.

Shortly thereafter, Mr. Bosky went to prison for his part in an insider trading scandal. While in prison, I understand he began to take correspondent school classes from a theology school. He is looking for more but not necessarily from the material world.

Here in the US, the unparalleled land of economic opportunity, citizens from both ends of the spectrum are fixated on materialism. The rich are worried about how to keep it, get more, and pass things nicely on to their children. The poor are simply worried about how to get their share in the first place.

The desire to acquire and retain is in all of us. What does the Bible say? Jesus, in fifteen verses of his Sermon on the Mount, explains his views on materialism quite clearly. Let's ask the right questions and take the measure of our lives in the truth of God's word.

What Is Materialism?

The first question is, "What is materialism?"

We live in a material world. Your hair, breakfast, the air you breathe, cars, clothes, houses — all of these are material things and each of us must learn to relate to them.

Over the centuries three very distinct philosophies of materialism have emerged.

One notion is that *materialism is evil.* From this idea two totally opposite philosophies have arisen.

Asceticism is the thinking behind the monastery. If creation is evil, then the smart thing to do is drop out of the world as much as possible. You should become a monk and deny yourself.

In Israel, 26 miles of hard walking up a dry river gorge, is a monastery. There are no women, no automobiles, and no television. One gets up at 4 a.m. to sing God's praises. One eats dry bread and water. There is a plank bed to sleep upon. Ah! The ascetic life!

On the other had, *epicureanism* also believes the material world to be evil. But it comes to the exact opposite conclusion from the ascetic. Epicureans reason that if the world is evil, then nothing matters. If the body is evil, then the best one can do is "live it up." Go ahead and indulge yourself with wine, women, and song!

Both asceticism and epicureanism are blasphemy. The Bible says, "God looked on all he had made and said, 'It is very good' " (Genesis 1:31). God even took shape among us in the flesh of Christ Jesus. He ate, drank, had clothing, and lived a completely sinless life.

Indeed, some believe the material world is evil. But a second philosophy teaches that *the material world is everything*, all there is, and, hence, *it is the greatest good.*

Communism arises from this school of thought. To the Marxist, the material world is all that matters. If you want a religion, they suggest you try science — empiricism — the logical study of how things relate.

Capitalism comes from this same source. "Good news" is in profit, acquiring more goods and more services. A successful person has plenty of "things."

Recently, I shared with a group of junior high students at their Bible club called *The Fellowship of Christian Athletes*. As part of my lesson, I asked each child to write their response to the question, "What would make you happy in life?" Going over the answers later, a distinct pattern appeared. "To make the right grades, so I can get into the right college, so I can get the right job, so I can make the right money, live in the right house, drive the right car, have the right things...." Their parents trained them well, by age thirteen, to be committed capitalists!

Jesus spoke of this second philosophy of materialism. He said, "Take heed! Beware of all covetousness. For a man's life does not consist of the things he has" (Luke 12:15).

According to the Bible, both extremes are wrong: that *things are evil* or that *things are the greatest good.* The truth simply is in the center.

Notice in Matthew 6:19-33 how several key words teach us to relate properly to this material world. Verse 19: "Do not *store up* for yourselves treasures on earth." Verse 22: "The eye is the lamp of the body." We have both *storing* and *seeing.* Verse 24: "No one can *serve* two masters." We now have *serving.* And, verse 33: "*seek* first the kingdom...."

Storing, seeing, serving, and seeking — how much of my priority, time, effort do I spend storing, seeing, serving, and seeking material things? How much of my time is spent concerning what I eat, put on, drink, live in, and the like?

By definition, materialism is an imbalanced lifestyle with too much emphasis on the world at the expense of the spiritual.

What's Wrong With Materialism?

Now that we've considered what materialism is, let's look at what's wrong with it.

First, materialism seeks the wrong satisfactions. The Bible says, "God ... richly furnishes us with everything" (1 Timothy 6:17). The two key words in this passage are "God" and "everything." Which is the most important? The materialist is one who consistently chooses everything over *God.*

I believe God has given me my house, my car, my clothes, my things "richly to enjoy." He does not want me to be ashamed of them, nor to brag about them to others. They are simply to enjoy.

If I give my child a nice bicycle and he is embarrassed by such a gift and locks it away unused in the basement, I'd be upset with him. On the other hand, if he becomes so attached to it he refuses to come to me when I call him for supper, then I, again, would be angry.

The gift should never obscure the giver. A bike should never usurp a father's place, and the things of creation should never take the place of the creator.

This is what God had in mind when he wrote the first commandment against idolatry. "I am the Lord your God. You shall have no other gods before me." The trouble with materialism is that it seeks satisfaction in things, not God. And Jesus said, "Seek ye first the kingdom of God and his righteousness, and all these *things* shall be yours as well."

Second, materialism is unhealthy because it *stores up* the wrong things. In Matthew 6:19 Jesus talks about storing up treasures on earth where moths and rust and thieves get in and diminish.

Here in the United States we've become absolutely overwhelmed with consumerism. Our houses, closets, and garages are so stuffed with things we can't even turn around. We pack money into IRAs, savings, and investments. And all the while we give no thought to "storing up treasures in heaven."

A highlight of the ministry here in church is hosting some of the missionaries who pass through. I highly suggest it for you. You'll find that missionaries are well-traveled, highly intelligent, skilled people who can talk about anything from the Bible to international politics to geography to native tribal dances. Yet, they drive old beat-up cars, dress in clothing long out of style, own no house or furniture, haven't seen the latest movies, and haven't the slightest notion who "Madonna" is.

Jim Eliot, missionary to the Auca Indians in South America, said of the missionary lifestyle, "He is no fool who gives up what he cannot keep in order to gain that which he will never lose." The trouble with materialism is that it stores up that which one cannot keep and forfeits that which one will never lose.

The third trouble with materialism is that it *serves* the wrong master. Jesus said, "You can't serve God and mammon." "Mammon" is to make a god of your own success, self, things, and money.

A middle-aged actress performed in a Broadway play and received a standing ovation. A friend later found her crying softly in her dressing room. "But why these tears? The critics loved you. You should be happy!" The actress replied, "I know. It is a wonderful night. It's just that I'm afraid as I grow older there won't be many more nights like this."

It's easy to serve mammon. Those who do, find themselves living for things that do not last.

Fourth, what's wrong with materialism is that it sees life through the wrong lenses. This is what Jesus meant when he spoke, "The eye is the lamp of the body."

Henry Ford, the great inventor of the automobile, asked a new manager, "What is your goal?" The manager replied, "Why, to make money, of course!" Mr. Ford quietly removed the man's glasses, taped a silver dollar to each lense, put them back on the man's face, and said, "If your goal is to make money then this is all you'll see — not people, not God, not spring flowers, nor even our fine products. And I pity you."

The trouble with materialism is that it's rich in things and poor in God, rich in this life and poor in the eternal life to come. It *serves* the wrong master, *sees* life through the wrong lenses, *seeks* the wrong satisfactions, and *stores* up in the wrong place. It simply is misspent serving, seeing, storing, and seeking.

What Should We Do About Materialism?

In discussing how to relate to the material world around us, Jesus began by saying, "The eye is the lamp of the body." He warned us to take care what we set our eyes upon and what we focus upon.

Use your best vision here. Hold yourself accountable with hard questions. "Where do my interests really lie?" Unless we're honest, we can live in the twilight gloom of denial and self-deception. All the while our foolish materialism is obvious to others, it's not obvious to us. So, "Where do your interests really lie?" In fishing, business, self, sports, society, career, or God?

In taking inventory of your life, the best place to start is your checkbook. Are you giving to Jesus Christ? Is your gift sacrificial or mere tokenism? Do you have plenty of money for golf, pizza, staying warm, and movies, but only a few crumbs to scatter before God? I like the tither's prayer written to be spoken as one places his gift before Jesus, "Dear God, in spite of all I say and do, this is what I think of you."

Next go to your living room and look around. Check out your bookshelves and your magazine rack. If you find *Better Homes and Gardens, Southern Living,* and *The Wall Street Journal,* do you also find *Guideposts, World Magazine* from a Christian perspective, and the Holy Bible?

Go to your calendar. How are you spending your time? Are you remembering the sabbath day or giving in to sports, too many vacations, and work? Does your child never miss a piano lesson but hit and miss youth Bible study?

Be tough with yourself. Show no mercy. See with an honest eye. Does your life reveal a healthy serving, seeking, seeing, and storing of Jesus Christ?

We must learn to recognize materialism — too much seeking, seeing, serving, and storing at the expense of the spiritual.

We must learn to reject materialism. Do you want to go on serving things or Jesus? Which will treat you better in the long run? The rich, young ruler had to choose. When the Lord asked him to give it all up to follow God, the man went away sorrowfully. We, too, must choose.

We must learn to resist materialism. The apostle Paul wrote, "I die daily." I am not a monk, but I find it healthy to say, "No" to my flesh at least once or twice a day. To deny myself a candy bar, to turn the television off, to make a call I find difficult, or to do something that needs doing that I'd rather not do.

Believe me, recognizing, rejecting, and resisting materialism is an ongoing struggle. We can never kill it once and for all. It's like the ocean tide. It cannot be slain. It must be dealt with daily.

There are no simple solutions.

One is to stay single. Paul wrote, "Those who marry will have worldly troubles." Can I get an "Amen"?

At the World Conference on Evangelism, Christians came up with "The Luzanne Statement." In it is the vow, "I will live a simple lifestyle." But what is a simple lifestyle? It's better to say, "I will live a more simple lifestyle." We can all do that.

In the text, Jesus is saying our faith, our theology, our relationship with God should enter in to what we drink, what we wear, what we eat, and it is vital to see how very relative it all is.

I know people to whom money comes quite easily. They think about it very little. Even though they live in a big house, drive a luxury car, and eat nice food, they are still very committed Christians seeing, seeking, storing, and serving Christ. Their shoulder is to the plow in terms of time, talents, and tithes.

Increasingly, I'm seeing poor people for whom money comes hard. They're working three jobs, eighty hours a week, wanting what the rich man has, not resting without it. They think money will make them happy. So, they've no time for God or the Bible or prayer. Their life is absorbed in things.

Which of these is the materialist?

It's in other cultures, too. I was teaching the young pastors on a Caribbean island. There was a rumbling criticism among the students. It seems that a few of the ministers had managed to buy mopeds to get to their churches, while the others had bicycles or went on foot. "Some of us are getting too materialistic," a young pastor said.

Conclusion

If there is a cure for materialism it is in Christian stewardship. Such begins with an awareness that all I have came from God, it is his now, and it's all going back to him.

Stewardship means I receive from God's hand as a trust all that I have. My time, money, and talents I manage for his glory, not my own, knowing I must one day give a full account to him.

Today, as the poet has said, "The world is much with us." We are living in the richest nation in history. Many of us, awash in things, are enslaved to seeking, storing, seeing, and serving creation. Our spirit of enjoyment is stronger than our spirit of sacrifice, worship, and love.

In all this, the church is seriously wavering. Will we serve Christ or our culture, the creator or creation, or will I serve Jesus or self?

In Java they tell the story of a young man who spied a beautiful maiden on the road and followed her. After several miles she turned and rebuked him, demanding, "Why do you follow me?" "Because," he declared fervently, "you are the most beautiful woman I have ever seen, and I have fallen madly in love with you at first sight! Be mine."

"But," the maiden said, "you have only to look behind you to see my younger sister who is ten times more beautiful than I am."

The gallant suitor turned to see as ugly an old woman who ever drew a breath. "What mockery is this? He demanded. You've lied to me!"

"You lied to me, too," the lovely maiden replied. "If you were so madly in love with me, why did you turn around?"

Today, will you fall madly in love with Jesus? Will he be who you see, store, serve, and seek?

Suggested Prayer

O Lord, forgive! I have too much loved the world. Set my affections upon you and help me to recognize, reject, and resist materialism. Amen.

Television: The Plug-In Drug

The eye is the lamp of the body. So, if your eye is sound, your whole body will be full of light; but if your eye is not sound, your whole body will be full of darkness.
— Matthew 6:22-23

Use of mind-altering drugs is epidemic in our nation today. Cocaine, heroin, crystal meth, crack, speed, angel dust, alcohol, marijuana, and the like are swallowed, mainlined, snorted, or smoked from the halls of high school to the executive suite. You may add to that list of drugs the television set. It's the plug-in drug, and, I fear, most of us are addicted.

Statistically, only 9% of American homes had a television set in 1950. Now, over 97% of American homes have a set. It is estimated that there are at least 190 million televisions in this country alone. I can believe it! Within the past few years I visited in a family's home that had five television sets — one in each bedroom, one in the family room, and one on the kitchen table! And have you ever noticed that wherever the television set is, it becomes the focal point of the room? Chairs all face that way!

What shall we make of this plug-in drug? Are we abusing it? Worse still, is it abusing us?

Let's look at some facts and get into the word and see.

A Powerful Influence

First of all, consider the powerful influence of the media.

If you'll study Genesis 3, you'll discover how Satan tempted Eve through her eyes. "She saw the fruit." "It was a delight to the eyes." And one thing led to another and she turned away from God. Do you see how the eyes are the gate of one's life? This is what Jesus means in the text when he points out, "The eye is the lamp of the body." Anything that catches the eye may well catch you! Inasmuch as television gets your eye, it is a powerful force.

I have heard it argued that what one watches on televison has no influence on them whatsoever. I'd like to be able to believe that! Yet, I point out that advertisers of everything from cereals to cosmetics to chewing gum to luxury cars pay out millions in the belief that what one sees on television is a direct influence on one's lifestyle.

With that in mind, turn your television on and watch what happens. In the sitcom *Friends* a tight group of New Yorkers made up morality as they went along. *Survivor* encourages rank voyeurism. The show *Frazier* was about a psychiatrist who divorced, moved to Seattle, and hosted a radio show. Its message is that marriages may come and go, but analysis is forever. Then there's *Who Wants To Be a Millionaire?* It was all about getting rich quick. And be sure not to miss *Charmed*, the story of four beautiful people who cast spells to get their way in life.

A common thread running through all such shows is a humanistic view of life. When people are vexed they don't pray, they have another drink. God is more often than not ignored, institutions like the church or marriage are belittled, while everybody does their own thing and it all comes out right in the end.

Yes, it would be nice to believe that what we see on the screen has no influence upon us. But Jesus said, "The eye is the lamp of the body." Advertisers, aware of this, are willing to spend more than a million dollars for a prime time thirty-second spot just to tell you about their hamburgers, razor blades, or cars.

In a survey of 208 inmates at Michigan's maximum security prison in Marquette, 90% said they improved their criminal talents by watching television. Half of those said they had actually attempted crimes they first saw on television. The "Junk Food Murder" gang in Florida admitted they got the idea for their killing after watching the horror movie, *The Shining*, on cable television that week. A police movie showed a victim soaked in gasoline and then set aflame by a match. After its screening, the same crime was repeated within the month by youngsters in real life — all of whom had watched it on television. A midwestern high school lad, a victim of a hold-up, was made to drink liquid Drano. His assailant got the idea watching a Clint Eastwood movie.

Make no mistake about it. "The eye is the lamp of the body." What gets your eyes, gets you! Television is a powerful influence. It motivates, educates, guides, woos, and wins for good or ill.

Addictive With Bad Side Effects

Yes, television is a powerful influence. Note television's addictiveness, and its bad side effects. In the text, Jesus said, "If your eye is sound, your whole body will be full of light; but if your eye is not sound, your whole body will be full of darkness." Let's focus now on the "darkness" of television addiction.

Ninety-three million households in this country have television sets. That's 97% of all families and 45% of our households have more than one set. Seventy-seven percent of all television sets are color sets. Adult women average thirty hours and 14 minutes a week in viewing time. Children ages two to eleven average 25 hours and 38 minutes. Adult men average 24 hours and 25 minutes. Teenagers twelve to seventeen average 22 hours and 36 minutes. That's addiction.

By age eighteen, a child has watched over 15,000 hours of television. His school has only influenced him 11,000 hours. If that child has been in Sunday school with the ragged attendance record most families present, he will only have put in about 600 hours of Bible study. The eighteen-year-old will have been bombarded with over 350,000 commercials, witnessed some 24,000 sexual encounters, and participated vicariously in 18,000 murders.

Question: What is all of this television doing to us? What are the side effects of this addictiveness?

More and more, television is leading us into a world of fantasy. People believe what they see on television. Years ago, *Marcus Welby*, television's fictitious medical doctor received 250,000 letters requesting medical advice in the four years of its screening. Television presents to such culpable people a world of glamorous people who get into hopeless situations, but always work things out with fast cars, guns, and alcohol within the hour and go on living happily ever after. A cartoon in *New Yorker* magazine shows a father changing a flat tire on the freeway in a downpour. The children are looking out the car window in wonder as the dad yells, "Don't you understand? This isn't television! This is reality! No, we can't change the channel!" Such is television's influence. It blurs our sense of reality. It maims our ability to bear down in the real world.

Another bad side effect of television addiction is the lowering of our self-esteem. Television models are slender. Most of us are not. They have straight teeth, live in fancy homes, and visit exotic places. Not us. Our self-esteem can fall in comparison. Witness the beautiful teenaged angst that was in *Dawson's Creek*'s cast. They were all lovely, all witty, and all fashionably dressed. These are all the things many of us aren't.

Television is also a time thief! The average American doesn't have six hours a week for church training, but he does have 25 or more hours a week for television. Jack Benny, the late comedian said, "TV is called the medium because nothing it ever serves up is well done." Lee Loevinger said, "Television is the literature of the illiterate, the culture of the lowborn, the wealth of the poor, the privilege of the underprivileged, the exclusive club of the excluded masses; television is the golden goose that lays scrambled eggs." And, I might add, it scrambles our values, our lifestyles, and our brains! Television is a time thief because it robs us of the time we could have spent pursuing the best by over-indulging us in the purely mediocre.

Another bad side effect of television addiction is that it kills one's imagination. Americans are turning from a literary society into a verbal video society. Most of us no longer read the book. Instead, we wait for the movie. Reading bores us. Television entertains us. We take the easy way out and lose our imagination in the bargain.

Further, television can infect us with passivity. We no longer initiate things. We're content to sit back and watch things happen. In short, television is turning us from a nation of participants to a nation of spectators. Instead of going out to the game, we watch it on televison. Instead of going out to worship, we simply watch it on television. Instead of going out to the theater, we turn on the tube. Poet T. S. Eliot defined television as "A modern form of entertainment that permits millions of people to listen to the same joke at the same time and yet remain lonely." In a very real sense, television is not bringing us together, it is separating us into little cubicles of lonely sitcoms, documentaries, and soap operas.

Television addiction can also cause aggressive behavior and paranoia. Vernard Eller said it so well, "Surely it marks some sort of perversion when people are entertained by the sight of other people being cut down, chomped up, knocked around, plowed under, and tromped over. Rome, before it fell, had infamous gladiatorial shows. The US has developed a film and electronic technology that enables people to be closer and more intensely involved as spectators of blood and gore than any Roman in the Colosseum ever could have been." According to the *U.S. News and World Report*, "Violence on television does lead to aggressive behavior by children and teenagers who watch the programs. There is an average of five violent acts per hour on primetime and eighteen per hour on children's weekend shows. At all ages, heavy viewers of television are more apt to think the world is violent ... trust other people less, and believe the world is a mean and scary place."

Television also makes it harder for us to learn. Reading and IQ tests show a pattern: The more television viewing, the lower the scores. In one town that only recently began to get television reception, pupils' scores fell off sharply within two years. Look at it this way: Hundreds of hours of preparation and dozens of workers sink their talents into one thirty-minute television show. A pastor working alone is fortunate if he can get twenty hours of preparation into his thirty-minute sermon. Educationally, there is no way a schoolteacher can compete with television's *Sesame Street*. Television simply spoils us. It inhibits our ability to learn from lectures, books, sermons, and charts.

Another bad side effect of television addiction is loss of physical exercise. A child of seven said, "I'd rather stay inside than play outside. In front of the television, it's exciting. Outside there's nothing to do except the same old stuff like skipping rope and swing sets."

Safe Doses!

That is the power of the media and its addictiveness and harmful side effects. Let's consider how we in Jesus Christ's Spirit may take television in safe doses.

The text mentions, "If your eye is *sound*, your whole body will be full of light." How may we keep our eyes sound on television?

A principle here is: Limit the time you spend watching television.

The real danger of television is not so much in behavior it produces as in the behavior it prevents: visits, walks, talks, games, family festivities and arguments through which we learn and through which our character is formed. The harm of television is that it has turned our family circles in semicircles! A cartoon in a family magazine showed a father saying, "I'll tell you what we did with our evenings before television. We gave dinner parties. We went to dinner parties. We read. We worked jigsaw puzzles. We went to plays. We went to concerts. We went to movies. We popped corn. We played cards. We went dancing. We took walks and we bowled. We attended meetings. We took classes. We went...."

Don't allow television to rob your family life. Limit your viewing time. Buy a *TV Guide* and plan to watch only those shows that will be worth trading family time to see.

Another principle to keep your eye sound and your body full of light: If what you have begun to watch is vulgar, change the channel, turn it off, or walk out.

Isn't it wonderful how movies have progressed over the years? First there were silent pictures, then talkies, then color, and now most of them smell. Don't sit there and be smeared with vulgarities. Turn it off! And to see that such programming is cut out, protest by letter to its sponsors.

Another way to keep your eye sound is to learn and practice discrimination. We learn to eat the meat and throw the bone away. We teach our children to walk on the dry patch and stay out of the puddles. Why not teach discretion in film viewing?

Years ago we took our youth group to see the blockbuster film, *Raiders of the Lost Ark*. We all loved it, agreeing that it was one of the most adventuresome films we'd ever seen! Then we began to discern what we saw. Biblical history was distorted, at least nine of the Ten Commandments were broken — so why did we enjoy it? A frank and revealing conversation followed about carnal appetites and personal righteousness and how to eat the meat of a film and throw the bone away. In today's world, such teaching of discretion is a must in every family!

Another principle for a sound eye: Give the Bible equal time. Why not plan one hour of Bible study for every one hour you watch television? That can work some good stewardship of time into your habits, not to mention working in some biblical truth.

A final principle: If you're a television addict and can't get control of your habit, then take your television outside and smash it! Jesus said, "If your right eye causes you to sin, pluck it out and throw it away; it is better that you lose one of your members than your whole body be thrown into hell" (Matthew 5:29).

Conclusion

In Acts 28:26, Paul spoke to the Roman world steeped as we are in their own media. He said, "You shall indeed hear but never understand, and you shall indeed see but never perceive. For this people's heart has grown dull, and their ears are heavy of hearing, and their eyes have closed...." Aren't his words still true of our televison audiences?

Habakkuk, the prophet, chides us so relevantly about our television addiction.

> *What profit is an idol when its maker has shaped it, a metal image, a teacher of lies? For the workman trusts in his own creation when he makes dumb idols! Woe to him who says to a wooden thing, Awake: to a dumb stone, Arise! Can this give revelation? Behold, it is overlaid with gold and silver, and there is no breath at all in it. But the Lord is in his holy temple; let all the earth keep silence before him.* — Habakkuk 2:18-20

Vladimir K. Zuorykin, a Russian immigrant working as an engineer for Westinghouse, patented his first television tube in 1923. In a 1981 interview, the inventor expressed amazement that television has become such a worldwide force. "The technique is wonderful. The color and everything are beyond my expectation," he admitted. But as to programming, Zuorykin said, "It's awful what they're doing with the subject matter. I would never let my children ever come close to this thing." Words to the wise from the inventor of television!

In our text are even wiser words from the inventor of all of life. He asks, "Is your eye on the television set sound and full of light?"

Suggested Prayer

Lord, give me strength to avoid the addicting influences around me. Help me block the negative messages from television and other electronics. Help me set limits and focus more on you. Amen.

How To Worry Like A Christian!

"Therefore I tell you, do not worry about your life, what you will eat or what you will drink, or about your body, what you will wear. Is not life more than food, and the body more than clothing? Look at the birds of the air; they neither sow nor reap nor gather into barns, and yet your heavenly Father feeds them. Are you not of more value than they? And can any of you by worrying add a single hour to your span of life? And why do you worry about clothing? Consider the lilies of the field, how they grow; they neither toil nor spin, yet I tell you, even Solomon in all his glory was not clothed like one of these. But if God so clothes the grass of the field, which is alive today and tomorrow is thrown into the oven, will he not much more clothe you — you of little faith? Therefore do not worry, saying, 'What will we eat?' or 'What will we drink?' or 'What will we wear?' For it is the Gentiles who strive for all these things; and indeed your heavenly Father knows that you need all these things. But strive first for the kingdom of God and his righteousness, and all these things will be given to you as well. So do not worry about tomorrow, for tomorrow will bring worries of its own. Today's trouble is enough for today."   — Matthew 6:25-34 (NRSV)

Have no anxiety about anything, but in everything by prayer and supplication with thanksgiving let your requests be made known to God. And the peace of God, which passes all understanding, will keep your hearts and your minds in Christ Jesus.   — Philippians 4:6-7

Did you hear about the amateur golfer who challenged the local club pro to a match? "Just give me a handicap of two 'gotchas' and we'll be square," said the amateur. Although the pro hadn't the foggiest idea of what a "gotcha" was, he was confident of his ability and agreed to play. On the first hole, just as the pro was about to tee off, the amateur slipped up, grabbed him around the waist and shouted, "Gotcha!" The twosome completed the round without further incident, but the pro played poorly and was beaten. When asked why he'd lost, he murmured, "Have you ever played 18 holes waiting for a second 'gotcha'?"

There's a bit of this story in us all, isn't there? Our lives are made ineffectual by worry. We're sure someone or something is slipping up behind us to get us! So we grow nervous. We cast a worried look about! And for our worries we can't do our best.

The text helps us deal with our worries. It's like a prescription from the great physician, Jesus Christ. And if taken it'll give us health.

Don't Worry!

The first part of the text says, "Don't worry!" Three times in Matthew 6:25-34 Jesus says, "Do not be anxious." In Philippians 4:6-7, it says quite frankly, "Have no anxiety about anything." Now that's in the form of a command, isn't it? "Have no anxiety about anything!"

Yet, my, my! How we fret and stew and worry over everything! We worry about money and bills. We toss and turn over our children. We are anxious about what others think of us. We despair over our jobs and our possessions and health and drinking habits and relatives and it makes us sick.

Worry, quite frankly, is like sitting in a rocking chair. You do a lot of work but you get nowhere! It's what a friend of mine calls, "Shoveling smoke." Our English term "worry" comes from a root word that means "to strangle." That's exactly what anxiety does — it suffocates our faith and strangles our effectiveness. All that brooding, all that anxious staging and restaging of events before they happen really accomplishes but one thing. It makes you a prisoner of fear of what might happen.

Did you hear about the crowded elevator that wouldn't rise because it was overloaded? A tiny woman got off and the elevator rose! The lady explained, "It's not that I weigh all that much, it's just that I have a lot on my mind today!" And isn't it so with us? We spend our lives like a pastor shaking hands at the door of the church building. You know how it is, he's trying to do too much at once. He's shaking hands with the person in front of him but talking to the fellow two people past him! He's not all there because he's busy dealing with what's ahead or what's behind. And don't we live like that? We can't deal with today because we're so busy dealing with tomorrow! The Bible is saying, "Don't worry! Have no anxiety about anything!" I like the way Jesus put it. He always says it so much better than I do! In Matthew 6, Christ said, "I tell you, do not be anxious about your life, what you shall eat or what you shall drink, nor about your body, what you shall put on... Look at the birds of the air: they neither sow nor reap nor gather into barns, and yet your heavenly Father feeds them. Are you not of more value than they? Therefore do not be anxious about tomorrow. Let the day's own trouble be sufficient for the day." So shake hands with today! Let tomorrow get here before you handle it!

Pray About It!

What have we seen so far? The first part of the text is a command not to worry. Now the second part: It too is a command. "Pray about it," the text is saying. "Have no anxiety about anything, but in everything by prayer and supplication with thanksgiving let your requests be made known to God." Jesus also said in Matthew 6:33, "But seek first his kingdom of...." What's the text saying? Two simple commands: Don't worry about it. Instead, pray about it! Seek God.

There's a hosiery mill in Virginia that uses steam in its manufacturing process. The unused portion is simply vented through a chimney in the plant roof. At the same time, the huge plant is heated by an oil-fired furnace. With energy prices like they are now, it didn't take plant engineers long to realize that they could harness the wasted steam energy to heat the plant in winter and thus do away with their oil furnace. I think that's called reclamation of wasted energy sources for productivity. That's what the text is saying. Worry is like wasted steam vented out the ceiling. Anxiety does not lessen tomorrow's sorrows. It only wears out a day before it gets here. It saps today of vital energy. What God is saying to us from the text is to stop wasting energy on worry and spend it on prayer.

Don't you see? It takes the same amount of energy to worry as it does to pray. Which accomplishes more?

In 1685, the colony of Massachusetts was beginning to talk freedom. Resentment was building against the British crown because of taxation without representation. King Charles II became enraged and decided to send in the troops to nip freedom in the bud. The king determined to send Colonel Percy Kirk and 5,000 troops to bring the colony to heel. When word of his decision reached New England there was immediate despair. Colonel Kirk was also known as "Bloody Kirk." As a notorious governor of Tangier, he'd earned his nickname "Bloody" because he stopped at nothing to crush the opposition. His fury was sure to savage the colonists! To say that folks were worried is to understate the facts. People were all but hysterical with worry.

Increase Mather, a prominent pastor, refused to worry. Instead, he prayed. His diary reveals the fact that as soon as he heard the news of the intended invasion, he shut himself in his study and spent the day fasting and praying for the colony. At length, the heaviness he felt in his heart left him, and he found peace in an inner assurance that things would work out. Two months later, word arrived that King Charles had died of apoplexy on the very day the pastor had been praying. Now James was king of England and "Bloody" Kirk would not be coming at all!

Prayer changes things. Worry only makes matters worse. Prayer brings relief. Worry only leads to distress. Prayer brings freedom. Anxiety brings bondage. Prayer is constructive use of energy. Worry is unconstructive waste. George Mueller said, "The beginning of anxiety is the end of faith, and the beginning of true faith is the end of anxiety." That, my friends, is exactly what the doctor orders in the text. Worry destroys faith or faith will destroy worry, so why not resign as general manager of the universe! Don't, through worry, take on all those responsibilities God never intended you to have. Stop fretting about things and pray about it! Let God take charge!

Peace Is Promised

In the text we have two commands. One: Have no anxiety about anything. Two: Let your request be made known to God. Now a third part of the text. It's a promise to all those who obey God's orders. "And the peace of God, which passes all understanding, will keep your hearts and your minds in Christ Jesus." Again, in Matthew 6, Jesus invites us to watch birds and to peruse flowers. They are not adither with worry. They know God's constant care. "Will he not so clothe you?" Jesus asks.

Do you see the healing therapy offered in this snatch of scripture we call our text? Instead of focusing anxiously on our problems we turn our attention to God. We focus on Jesus, the almighty Father, the able, wonderful counselor, the loving, just, healing master, the Prince of Peace! The text says such a refocusing brings tranquility.

Notice how it worked in Christ's ministry. Remember the Bible story of Christ and his disciples crossing the Sea of Galilee in a boat. While Christ slept, a nasty storm arose. Big waves and gale force winds tossed the boat about like a weightless chip. Focusing on the storm and the sinking boat the disciples were terrified! Finally, spotting Jesus asleep in the bow, they roused him and prayed for help, whereupon Christ rebuked the winds and brought calm. Do you see what happens when you get your eyes off your fears and focus them on God in prayer? Things calm down. There is peace.

Ocean explorers say that there are depths of the sea that are never disturbed. A hurricane can be boiling on the ocean surface with 180 miles per hour winds and monstrous waves, and yet below the surface things are calm. That's the kind of peace God gives, a peace that passes all understanding. A peace that no one can take from us. Just before the reformation, when John Hus was burned at the stake for his Christian faith, the hot flames licked up his legs and began to blister his body. Such a storm without! Yet within there was tranquility. John Hus died singing songs of the Christ he loved July 7, 1415. The Bible promises such a peace to you and to me. No, perhaps God won't take you out of the storm, but he will take the storm out of you.

"Have no anxiety about anything, but in everything by prayer and supplication with thanksgiving let your requests be made known to God." That's the command. Now the result, the promise. "And the peace of God, which passes all understanding, will keep your hearts and your minds in Christ Jesus."

Needed For Voyage!

I once watched an admiral's luggage being taken out of a truck and placed aboard his ship. Of the six or eight trunks, fully two thirds of them were clearly labeled, "Not needed during the voyage." I'm told that such pieces are stored in the hold until the next port of call is reached. Much of the baggage of life we carry with us is not needed for the voyage like that. It can be put away and never missed. Certainly your worries are such. They can be put away! Yet prayer must be kept with you for all time. Of its use you will certainly have need!

A doctor once told one of our members, "There are over forty miles of nerves in the human body. In your case that's 211,200 feet of frazzles." She'd become so prone to worry as to have anxiety attacks. Her mind had become a cycle of ineffective thought and emotion whirling around a thick center of fear. Yet there is relief. There is a healing Savior! "Don't worry about anything," the text prescribes. "Pray about it! And God will give you peace."

Worried souls, God is ready when you are. Take him at his word and see!

Suggested Prayer

Lord, I resign as general manager of the universe. You be God and I'll be your child. Teach me to talk to you about my troubles. For Christ's sake. Amen.

Of Logs And Specks ...

Do not judge, so that you may not be judged. For with the judgment you make you will be judged, and the measure you give will be the measure you get. Why do you see the speck in your neighbor's eye, but do not notice the log in your own eye? Or how can you say to your neighbor, "Let me take the speck out of your eye," while the log is in your own eye? You hypocrite, first take the log out of your own eye, and then you will see clearly to take the speck out of your neighbor's eye. Do not give what is holy to dogs; and do not throw your pearls before swine, or they will trample them under foot and turn and maul you.
— Matthew 7:1-6 (NRSV)

These are some of the most frightening verses in the Sermon on the Mount! Why? Because of verses 1-2. "Do not judge, or you will be judged. For in the same way you judge others, you will be judged, and with the measure you use, it will be measured to you." Terrifying scripture, eh?

The word "judge" in the Greek is *krino* meaning "to distinguish, to decide, to condemn, to conclude, or to finalize." It is to consign someone to hell, to damn them, to call someone worthless and confess they'll never amount to anything.

Let's face it! Judgment is God's business, not ours. Christ is warning us that if we usurp this business and start dishing out harsh critical judgments then we'd better be prepared to take it. This is advice the church would do well to heed, for far too many fellowships have dissolved into seething cauldrons of harsh people, bristling with criticisms, self-righteously picking at the sins of others while overlooking their own.

When people wax critically, they foster an atmosphere that's the opposite of grace. A kind of negativity takes over that can make any marriage, family, job, town, or church unbearable. One has but to read Nathaniel Hawthorne's *The Scarlet Letter* to see what Jesus is talking about.

From scripture, I find at least six reasons why I'm not good enough to judge.

The first reason is that I never know all the facts. God has a complete appraisal of the situation. I do not. The obstruction, literally "the log in my own eye," keeps me from complete vision.

I had a gentleman in my church once, a kindly pharmacist by day and an alcoholic by night. I disdained him for how he failed the church and made his family miserable. Then I found out in college he broke his hip playing baseball. It didn't heal properly, and he was in chronic pain. Thus the pharmacist who used his skills to soothe others, was himself hurting and unsoothed. And I had cheapened my own soul by judging him.

A second reason I make a poor judge is because I am prejudiced. Jesus said it is never possible for me to see clearly because so much pain and junk in my own eyes keeps me from being impartial in evaluating others. I am literally swayed by self, others, passion, and hurts such that I can't be objective.

While a freshman in college I was told, "Don't take Dr. Heusel for English!" I got her in a blind class registration, tried to bail out of the class but couldn't, so I made the best of it, and found, to my surprise, a fascinating teacher. Later, I learned her detractor was a poorly disciplined student who'd garnered a "D" in her study.

A third reason I may not judge is my own sinfulness. It's not that I do not know enough, that I am prejudiced. I also am not good enough.

Leo Tolstoy wrote, "I've had more trouble with myself than with any other person on earth." Indeed, I have my hands full dealing with me. I don't have time to fix you!

This should have been the case with the Pharisees. What with logs in their own eyes, they shouldn't have had any time to be digging at the specs in other's eyeballs! But such was not the case.

For instance, Jesus attended a dinner party in the home of a devout Pharisee. No one affectionately welcomed Christ. No one even cleaned his feet. Christ had been invited to supper that he might be probed, dissected, critiqued, challenged. In the midst of this acrimonious evening came a harlot. She somehow slipped in to wash Jesus' feet with her tears of remorse over her own misspent passion. Then, unbraiding her long hair, something only a wife would do privately for her husband, she began to wipe Jesus' feet clean.

The Pharisees were nonplused, "If this man were a prophet he'd know what sort of woman he's let touch him," they sniffed. Yet Jesus, knowing their thoughts, said, "Leave her be. She's done a beautiful thing for me. For he who is forgiven much loves much. But he who is forgiven little loves little."

Clearly, the Pharisees in this instance were so absorbed in Jesus' "sins" and the woman's sins that they missed completely their own. In all their judgment of others they missed Christ. They simply couldn't see him.

But in her repentance and love, the woman found him.

A fourth reason I'm no good at judging is that being conscious of my own sins, I take comfort in the faults of others. Once in high school football practice, the coach chided me for not executing a block properly. "Here! I'll show you!" he said. He crouched down and proceeded to do the block all wrong himself. Getting up, he looked peeved, then growled, "Crotts! You've messed it up so badly no one can do it right!"

Isn't there some of that justification in us all? We're constantly measuring and rating others, looking for flaws, for variances, for failure. When we find it, we gleefully and, I might add, publicly, point it out. Oh, how we love to rub a little luster off the crown of another. "See there?" we inwardly muse. "They're wrong. I feel better about myself."

Yet a fifth reason I'm not to judge is because I am jealous. Shakespeare called jealousy, "The green-eyed monster." In his play, *Othello*, the villain, Iago, admires the beautiful wife of Othello, Desdimona. With great prejudice and malevolence Iago sows falsehood, distrust, and murder that he might destroy what he cannot have himself. Such is in the human heart — yours and mine.

Fail not, my friend! Fail not to at least glimpse here what Christ Jesus is saying. I may not judge because of ignorance, prejudice, sinfulness, jealously, and the distortion in my heart.

Finally, the sixth reason I may not judge is because of love. In Matthew 7, Christ is saying we have no right to pick at the specks in others' eyes.

The apostle Paul elaborated on this in 1 Corinthians 13:4 following. Among other things, Paul made the following observations: "Love is patient. Love is kind. It does not envy. It's not proud. It keeps no record of wrong. Love never fails."

Love, in other words, takes the prickliness out of us. When my three children were little and we took a car trip, the backseat was a constant blather of, "He touched me!" "You get on your side!" "Mom, make him stop it!" As my children matured they came to love one another. Now they are close and do not mind it. They actually seek each other out.

A woman in this parish speaks of "duck oil." "I coat myself with it daily," she remarks. "Then when people slight me or disappoint me as they are want to do in so many ways, the injury just glides off my back like water on a duck's back." Indeed! "Love covers a multitude of sins," wrote Peter (1 Peter 4:8).

God's The Only True Judge

Though Jesus doesn't say it in the text, he infers it throughout his sermon. God is the only true judge. He is our rewarder (Matthew 5:12; 6:4; 6:6 ff). He is your critic, the final arbiter of all things! (Matthew 7:23).

Paul picked up on this truth in 1 Corinthians 4:3-5. He told the church, "But with me it is a very small thing that I should be judged by you or by any human court. I do not even judge myself. I am not aware of anything against myself, but I am not thereby acquitted. It is the Lord who judges me. Therefore do not pronounce judgment before the time, before the Lord comes, who will bring to light the things now hidden in darkness and will disclose the purposes of the heart. Then every man will receive his commendation from God."

Notice Paul mentions three critics here: people, self, and God.

People try to judge us. They criticize us and condemn. While president, Abraham Lincoln said of his critics, "If I had to respond to everyone who is a critic of my administration, this office might as well be closed for business."

Then there is self-criticism. It, too, can cripple us into inactivity. T. S. Eliot's character "Proofrock" is an example. A balding, middle-aged, single man is cowered before a lovely woman because of his constant self-evaluation. It's literally "the paralysis of analysis," and he is frozen in indecision.

The third judge beyond self and others is God. Paul says he is the only one whose judgment counts. Great Britain's Winston Churchill once made a speech. At his conclusion, the audience thundered their appreciation with applause. As the crowd quieted down, a lone heckler in the balcony blew a raspberry. Churchill, without skipping a beat, said, "I know. I agree with you. But what are we among so many?" The point is: Don't be so hard on yourself. God loves you. He applauds you so it's okay to celebrate his grace in you.

There will certainly come a day when the all-knowing, all-seeing, all-righteous, all-loving Lord will cause us each to stand before him. "He will bring to light what is hidden in darkness and will expose the motives of all men." I take it to mean nobody is going to get away with anything. "Therefore judge nothing before the appointed time."

Until then, be humble. Look not at others. Mind yourself, your own eye. And as George Loch wrote, "There is so much good in the worst of us, and so much bad in the best of us, that it behooves any of us to talk about the rest of us."

Concluding Judgment Versus Discernment

Jesus rather enigmatically seems to reverse himself. He preaches, "Do not give dogs what is holy. Do not cast your pearls before swine. If you do, they may trample them under their feet, and then turn and tear you to pieces!" This sure sounds like judging to me! "You dog!" "Pig!" "I'm not wasting the effort on you!"

Indeed! This is a hard saying, part of the tensions to be found in Christ's sermon masterpiece. "Let your light so shine before men, that they may see your good works" (Matthew 5:16). "Beware of practicing your piety before men" (Matthew 6:1). He tells us to pray in the closet secretly (Matthew 6:5-6). Then he proceeds to pray the Lord's Prayer publicly (Matthew 6:9). He tells us not to judge (Matthew 7:1-5). He tells us to judge the nature of men and women before we get involved.

I'm not certain anyone can relax the tensions here. Such sayings are paradoxical and enigmatic. We must live the mystery and walk this tightrope of faith. It is like two sides of a coin. It's impossible to see both sides at once. While describing one side, we still must remember another side is to be seen.

All I can say about not judging and yet understanding the totally depraved dog and piggish nature of humans is this: People don't need Jesus until they need Jesus. Until the Holy Spirit elects to convict them, to call them to faith. Until we can join God in that work, all ministry to such a one is a waste of time.

Jesus is simply saying, "Don't push your faith on unwanting individuals. Share it with the receptive." Such seems to me more the wisdom of discernment than cruel-hearted judging.

Conclusion

It's frightening, isn't it? "Do not judge or you will be judged." Same full measure!

I close with an old poem only partially memorized, the author anonymous. It keeps me in check. The poem is called, "The Critic."

> *A little seed lay in the ground,*
> *and soon began to sprout.*
> *"Now which of all the flowers around,"*
> *it mused, "shall I come out?*
> *The lily's face is fair and proud,*
> *but just a trifle cold.*
> *The rose, I think, is rather loud,*
> *and then, its fashions old.*
> *The violet is all very well,*
> *but not the flower I'd choose.*
> *Nor yet the Canterbury bell —*
> *I never cared for blues."*
> *And so it criticized each flower,*
> *the supercilious seed,*

*until it woke one summer morn,
and found itself — a weed."*

Suggested Prayer

Lord, teach me it is enough for you and for me to fix myself. Amen.

Praying Through

Ask, and it will be given you; seek, and you will find; knock, and it will be opened to you. For every one who asks receives, and he who seeks finds, and to him who knocks, it will be opened. Or what man of you who, if his son asks him for bread, will give him a stone? Or if he asks for a fish, will give him a serpent? If you then, who are evil, know how to give good gifts to your children, how much more will your Father who is in heaven give good things to those who ask him!
— Matthew 7:7-11 (NRSV)

No doubt you have heard about the postal service's "Dead Letter Department." That's the place where mail goes when it is not clearly addressed or has insufficient postage and the sender's identity cannot be determined. There the letter is opened and its contents examined for clues to the sender's identity. If the return address cannot be determined, the letter is destroyed. It never reaches its destination, and any requests made by the writer remain unanswered. How about you? Do you feel like your prayers end up in some kind of dead letter department? Do you feel like your prayers never reach God? If you do, then this text is for you! Here, in Jesus Christ's own words, we are told how to address our prayers to God so that they will be received and answered.

Ask, And It Will Be Given You

First of all, Christ told us to ask in prayer. He said, "And I tell you, ask, and it will be given you."

As one studies the New Testament accounts of Christ's life, it becomes obvious that the Lord was not afraid to ask things of God. He asked for wine at a wedding party. He asked for more bread and fish to feed a crowd. He asked God to heal the blind, the lame, the mute, and the possessed. Jesus asked much of God. He did not feel like he was imposing. And here in the text, Jesus is telling us to do the same. He is assuring us that we can ask much from God.

I know that in my own life I have often been reluctant to ask God for my needs. I used to think perhaps God was too busy to be troubled over my affairs. I didn't want to bother him. After all, I could not be very important to him. Slowly I have begun to realize that I am a child of God. I am not some orphan. I am not a disinherited son. I am the child of the king of the universe. My Father has told me, "Ask, and it will be given you."

Once in graduate school, my wife and I were running very short of money. Inflation had taken a big bite out of our income. We had a new baby. Rent was going up. Gasoline had soared and our electricity bill had more than doubled. For several weeks I worried and schemed and grew irritable. I could see no way out of our financial plight. During those weeks, I am ashamed to say that I never once prayed about things. I guess I sort of figured seminary students were supposed to be poor. My wife watched me quietly as I turned into a tyrant through worry. Finally, she simply said, "Stephen, why don't we pray about it?" I agreed, and together we told God all about it and asked for his help. Things began to happen!

That very afternoon, the landlady stopped me while I was emptying the trash. She said, "Stephen, for some time now I've been wanting to ask you to be the groundskeeper for this apartment complex. You can do the work between your studies. It'll be good exercise for you. And we'll pay you $2.50 an hour." I quickly accepted and right away we had an extra $25 a week for income. I was also getting some much needed exercise.

The next day, Kathryn and I found an anonymous letter in our mailbox. In it was a check for over $200. Someone had sent it just to help us out.

I can assure you that our family was praising the Lord! He had indeed answered our prayers! Then it suddenly dawned on us that the letter was postmarked two days before we had prayed for help, and the landlady had been thinking of offering me that job long before I had decided to pray. We began to doubt. Perhaps this new financial help was not an answer to prayer after all. Maybe it was all just a coincidence. Then it hit me. I remembered a promise of God from Isaiah 65:24. There the Lord says, "Before they call I will answer, while they are yet speaking I will hear." What the

Lord had done was to go ahead and prepare the answer to our prayers, then he had also promoted our asking!

Asking prayer works just this way. The good Lord has something he wants done. He prepares all the resources that will be needed. Then he begins to prompt us mentally so we will ask him to allow us to do the job. Thus our prayers become a simple asking for what God already is eager to do.

As you live the Christian life, you will undoubtedly find God prompting you to ask him for things. It may be talent, wisdom, health, money, help, or many other things. Whatever, do not be afraid to ask God for that which you feel prompted. You won't bother him. He cares about you. You won't impoverish him. The Lord owns the cattle on 1,000 hills. "Ask," Jesus said, "and it will be given you."

Seek, And You Will Find

Christ not only told us to ask in prayer, he also told us to seek. In the text, Jesus said, "Seek, and you will find."

It is true that Christ did a lot of asking in prayer. He asked for bread, wine, healing, and a host of other things. But Christ also prayed prayers of seeking. In the Garden of Gethsemane, the Lord searched for God's will. He said, "Lord, I ask in prayer that this cup pass from me. Let me not go to the cross, suffer, and die. I ask for some other way!" Then Jesus began to seek in prayer. He said, "But, Lord, if this is not your will, if I must die, then your will be done." Here we find an example of Christ searching in prayer. He is looking for God's will. He is trying to find out what the mind of God is so he can obey it.

Jesus told us to pray like this when he said, "Whatever you ask in my name, I will do it" (John 14:13). Now the key to this verse is the phrase, "In my name." Jesus did not say, "Whatever you ask, I will do it." He said, "Whatever you ask *in my name*, I will do it." The Greek word used here for "in my name" means more than just a label. If you called on someone's name in the Greek world, you were calling on his actual presence. So Jesus was saying, "Whatever you ask in my presence, I will do it."

As Christians, we believe in the presence of Christ. We believe Jesus is with us by the power of the Holy Spirit. In fact, we believe that Jesus is present with us so that we can actually take on the mind of Christ. The New Testament scriptures tell us that we should have in us the actual mind of Jesus Christ (Philippians 2:5).

Here is a great secret of prayer. When we pray, we should ask in the mind of Christ. Jesus said, "Whatever you ask in my name or in my presence or rather, in my mind, I will do it." Thus prayer is not overcoming God's reluctance. It is taking hold of his willingness. It is not presenting your arguments in order to make God change his mind. Prayer is searching for the mind of Christ and then praying in it.

When confronted with a need, it is not good to go right out and pray about it by telling God what you want. You may not know the mind of Christ in the matter. You may ask in the flesh and not in the Spirit. First ask the Lord to reveal to you his mind. Say, "Lord, here is a need. Teach me your mind. Teach me how to pray about this."

Do you see how prayer is not getting God to see it your way but getting you to see it God's way? Let's suppose that you're in a rowboat fifteen feet from the shore. You throw an anchor ashore and pull yourself to the dock. What have you done? Did you pull the land to you or did you pull yourself to the land? The land did not budge. You did. You moved to the shore. Seeking prayer works like this as well. You throw out an anchor to God. You seek in prayer, in scripture, in fellowship, in obedience, and you pull yourself to God's mind and ask in it.

Saint Paul knew how to seek in prayer. He said, "God, I am sick. I have this thorn in my flesh." Three times Paul went to God and asked to be healed. And there in God's presence, Paul began to know the mind of Christ. He quit asking to be healed. He started asking for strength to bear the affliction for the glory of God (2 Corinthians 12).

In your own prayer life you, too, will want to learn seeking prayer. You will want to learn to pray in Christ's name, in his presence and mind, and not in your name and in your mind. When you are facing a need, take that problem directly to God. And do not limit God by telling him what to do about it. Just envision the problem in your hands. Then envision God. Think of his presence. Meditate on his marvelous light, his love, and his power. Lift the problem right up into God's presence and leave it there.

A little boy knelt down to say his bedtime prayers. His parents heard him reciting the alphabet in very reverent tones. When asked what he was doing, he replied, "I'm saying my prayers, but I cannot think of the exact words tonight. So, I'm just saying all the letters. God knows what I need, and he'll put all the words together for me." That is not far from a proper way to pray! In seeking prayer, we are looking for Christ's mind. We are not sure quite how to word our prayer, so we ask God to take our words and fit them into the correct prayer. We ask him to edit our prayers by cutting out the unnecessary, making corrections, and adding the necessities. We ask him to take our minds and make them his. We ask the Holy Spirit to pray through us. When we seek in prayer like that, Jesus assures us in the text, we will find.

Knock, And It Will Be Opened!

Moving along from asking and seeking prayers, we come to knocking prayer, Jesus, in the text said, "Knock, and it will be opened to you."

Here we need to know that there is more involved in answering prayer than your will and God's will. There are other such forces as hard hearts and God's decision to give people a free will. You might be praying that God will save your son. But your son's heart is stony toward God. You want him saved. There is nothing God would like better than to save him, but here is a barrier. God has given your son a free will. He will not violate it by forcing himself on anyone. And your son's cold, cold heart has chosen to leave God out.

There is also the barrier of the satanic. The Bible says, "For we are not contending against flesh and blood, but against the principalities, against the powers, against the world rulers of this present darkness, against the spiritual hosts of wickedness in the heavenly places" (Ephesians 6:12). An example of how satanic forces can hinder answers to prayer is found in Daniel 10. There the prophet prayed for more than twenty days without an answer. Finally, an angel visited him and explained the reason for the delay. He said, "O Daniel, man greatly beloved ... from the first day that you set your mind to understand ... your words have been heard, and I have come because of your words. The prince ... withstood me twenty-one days; but Michael ... came to help me ... so I ... came" (Daniel 10:11-14).

Here we are taught that satanic powers hindered an answer to prayer. We must come to scripture with a sense of wonder. There is much about this world that we do not know. Our finite minds are so frail. Things like Satan, evil, and spiritual warfare boggle our minds. We cannot understand them completely. God has revealed some of this in scripture, and we can accept it by faith. By faith, scripture teaches that satanic barriers can hinder prayer.

The book of Job is perhaps the best place in scripture to study knocking prayer. There, righteous Job is devastated. He loses his children, his friends, his property, and his health. Satan has horribly afflicted him. His wife urges him to curse God and die. Instead, Job begins a knocking prayer.

> *Oh, that I knew where I might find him, that I might come even to his seat! I would lay my case before him and fill my mouth with arguments. I would learn what he would answer me.* — Job 23:3-5

Thus Job begins to knock in prayer. He blindly gropes for God. He patiently and sometimes impatiently years for deliverance. Again and again, Job reaches for God in prayer. Though his body is wasting away, though all seems lost, though he cannot understand, Job has faith in God. His heart is filled with hope.

> *For I know that my Redeemer lives, and at last he will stand upon the earth; and after my skin has been thus destroyed, then from my flesh I shall see God.*
> — Job 19:25-26

With hope, faith, and persistence, Job continues to knock in prayer. Finally, God comes to him. Though the Lord does not explain the affliction, he does heal Job. He restores his fortune and gives him more children than ever before. As Jesus promised, it will be opened to those who knock. Job triumphantly says to God, "I know that thou canst do all things, and that no purpose of thine can be thwarted ... I had heard of thee by the hearing of the ear, but now my eye sees thee" (Job 42:2, 5).

Perhaps Jesus was thinking of Job when he told the parable of the friend at midnight.

> *Which of you who has a friend will go to him at midnight and say to him, "Friend, lend me three loaves; for a friend of mine has arrived on a journey, and I have nothing to set before him"; and he will answer from within, "Do not bother me; the door is shut, and my children are with me in bed; I cannot get up and give you anything"? I tell you, though he will not get up and give him anything because he is his friend, yet because of his importunity he will rise and give him whatever he needs.* — Luke 11:5-8

Jesus teaches us the value of persistent prayer. When confronted with closed doors, hard hearts, and satanic barriers, it becomes necessary to knock in prayer. A knock does not mean only one rap on the door. A knock is a loud and repeated rapping sound. Our knocking prayers must be repetitious.

The question might arise in your mind as to why we must occasionally pray repetitiously. Do we do so to beg God into helping us? Do we do so in order to force him into changing his mind? No! Repetitious prayer is better seen as unleashing spiritual power. Have you ever tried to open a rusty water valve? It is frozen still with corrosion. You strain and strain at it, but little progress is made. You rest a while, then try again. With all your might, you grip the handle and twist. It budges a bit. You rest again then return for another try. Slight progress is made and a trickle of water begins to flow. After yet another rest, you have at it again, and there is more progress. You persist until the valve is wide open, and the water is full on. Repetitious prayer works like this as well. To persist in prayer is to open more and more of the spiritual channels through which the power of God can flow. Closed doors, hard hearts, and satanic obstacles give way to the relentless pressure applied by God and the kneeling Christian.

The Bible gives us numerous accounts of knocking prayer. Moses, during a battle, lifted up his hands and prayed continuously until the sun went down and victory was won (Exodus 17:8-16). Daniel engaged in earnest supplication for 21 days (Daniel 10). In Acts we are told that the church prayed all evening for Peter's release from prison (Acts 12). Even now, many people are praying and knocking on God's door for many things. Some of them have been praying for months, years, even lifetimes! Missionary societies have been praying for years that China will reopen for the church. Saints are praying persistently for a real revival to wake up the Western church. Mothers are praying for erring children, and women are knocking for their husbands. In each case, things all but appear hopeless. Hearts seem too cold. Barriers seem too large. But the power will begin to trickle! Who knows if even one more twist will not open things up all the way!

God Character

Now we turn to verses 9-11. Here Jesus deals with the question of "What sort of God is the Father to whom we pray?" To illustrate his point, Jesus gives several examples. Two here in Matthew and a third in the parallel account in Luke 11-12.

If a son asks for bread, does his father give him a stone? If a son asks for a fish (eel), does his dad give him a snake? If a boy asks his papa for an egg, does his daddy give him a scorpion?

The point of all this has to do with the similarities of a loaf of bread and a stone, an eel and a snake, and an egg and a curled-up scorpion. Jesus is telling us that God is not out to mock us, to trick us, or to refuse us.

In Jesus' day, Greek mythology had many stories of gods who answered the prayers of mortals with trickery. For instance, Aurora was the Greek goddess of dawn. She was in love with a man called Tithonus. Zeus, the god king, offered her anything she wanted. She asked Zeus that her lover live forever and Zeus granted it. The trouble is, her lover grew old and never died. She'd forgotten to ask for perpetual youth.

Here, Jesus is saying God is not out to trick us. He always answers in the best way, his way, like a good father.

Day By Day

There is a rock opera called *Godspell*. In this musical, there is a song called "Day By Day," that expresses so well what our attitude and practice in prayer should be. The words encourage us to pray daily for the ability to see, love, and follow the Lord more and more each day.

The music is new, but few realize that the prayer has been around for over 700 years! Richard of Chichester, in the thirteenth century, prayed, "O most beautiful friend, brother, and redeemer; may I know thee more clearly, love thee more dearly, and follow thee more nearly." "Day By Day" is just an old prayer put to new music! In the text for today we have an old saying of Jesus' that needs to be made new and up-to-date in your life. What the world needs now is more Christians who will seek, ask, and knock. Jesus did not say we should sit around and wait for things to fall into our mouths like a ripe grape. He said, "Seek!" He said, "Ask!" He said, "Knock!" And when you seek and keep on seeking, you find. When you ask and keep on asking, you receive, and when you knock and keep on knocking, the door is opened.

All our praying needs to be a day-by-day-by-day experience. It needs to be an asking experience wherein we see God more clearly, a seeking experience in which we love God more dearly, and a knocking experience wherein we follow the Lord more nearly. All this day by day by day and Jesus' promises of prayer come true.

Suggested Prayer

Day by day, dear Lord, three things I pray: to ask of thee more often, to seek thee more faithfully, and to knock on your door more earnestly. These things I pray day by day by day. For Christ's sake. Amen.

The Most Famous Thing Jesus Ever Said!

So, in everything, do unto others as you would have them do unto you, for this sums up the law and the prophets. — Matthew 7:12

Our text is the most famous thing Jesus ever said. I call it, "The Mount Everest of Ethics." Indeed, it is the summit of Christ's Sermon on the Mount. Master this and you've scaled the heights, Jesus said, "For this sums up the law and the prophets."

So far, in his masterpiece message, Jesus has not uttered anything all that new. It's been mostly a rehash of Old Testament ideals. Ah! But this verse, often called the golden rule, is new, and it is without parallel in the scriptures!

To be sure, there are similar teachings in Judaism. There is the story of a young teenager who goes to a rabbi and agrees to convert to the Jewish faith, "If you can teach me the whole law of God while I stand on one foot." Without hesitation, the old rabbi said, "What is hateful to yourself, do to no other."

Rabbi Eliezer once said, "Let the honor of thy friends be as dear unto thee as thine own." To be certain, something very closely akin to the golden rule is found in most religions and world cultures. Confucius said, "What you do not want done to yourself, do not do to others." Buddhism teaches, "Do as one would be done by." The Romans used to say, "Do not do to others the things which make you angry."

You will carefully notice that almost all of the aforesaid axioms are spoken in the negative. Jesus, however, takes it to the next level by couching it in the positive. In doing so, Jesus makes the law more demanding. In the golden rule we find not what we cannot do, but what we must do.

Paul wrote, "... our word to you has not been Yes and No ... but in him it is always Yes" (2 Corinthians 1:18-19). The Christian life is not all about what we *cannot* do, but rather what we *can* do!

Imagine a hot, thirsty day at the beach. You amble over to the cola machine, fish through your purse for some change, deposit it in the coin slot, then push the button for a cold drink. The machine whirrs and buzzes but no drink emerges. It is out of order. Though the cola machine does not hurt you, neither does it help you!

The same with the Christian life. I have sins of commission — things I do wrong. But I am also guilty of sins of omission. That is, things that are right that I refused to do.

I can satisfy the negative form of the golden rule by inaction. "What you do not want done to yourself, do not do to others." I can be a hermit or a miser and by doing nothing fulfill that law. But the positive restatement of the golden rule, "Do unto others as you would have them do unto you," this prods me to action.

I must serve. I must be kind. I must bristle with helpfulness. I must do my best for others.

Let's say I own a car. To follow the golden rule I must seek to drive so as to harm no one. But, equally, I must drive so as to be helpful — giving you a lift. Thus the golden rule means I must treat you not just as the law allows but as love demands. This means I must forgive as I would hope to be myself forgiven. It means I strive to serve as I wish to be served. It means I speak of others as I wish to be spoken of myself.

The golden rule is very much a principle to dominate one's life at home, at church, at work, and at play.

Radio's *Prairie Home Companion* host, Mr. Garrison Keillor, spoke of having a new book released, and he went on a book tour across the nation. At first he flew into airports, rented a car, and drove himself to author parties. As the book climbed the charts of the bestseller lists, he was met at the airport by a limousine, the hotels got nicer and nicer, the restaurants more swank, and he never saw a bill.

After some months on the celebrity travel circuit, he stopped in the Colorado Rockies for a few days of rest. A close friend gave him the use of his half-million dollar chalet on the side of a ski slope. Mr. Keillor went out the door one afternoon to luxuriate in a hot tub, the door shut behind him, locking him out. After thirty minutes in the bubbly heat, Keillor realized he couldn't stay in the hot water any longer. He couldn't get back in the house. Nor could he tolerate the freezing temperatures in a soaking wet bathing suit.

So he yanked down the plastic tarp used to cover the hot tub, wrapped himself in it and began to walk barefoot for help. A group of elite ladies passed him on the road in their Mercedes. He tried to flag them down but they averted their eyes and kept going. He soon found out no one was willing to open their doors to a shivering stranger wrapped in a blue tarp standing on their steps. It was thirty minutes before a reluctant woman, who wouldn't unlock her door to him, agreed to call the owner of his chalet so he could come with the keys.

Garrison Keillor said he learned that day a great lesson. Always be kind to strangers. For you never know when you're going to go yourself from being a best-selling author riding in limos to a stranger wrapped in a tarp and shivering barefooted in the snow.

Conclusion

I have heard people say, "The gold rule is my religion." But it cannot be, for this rule is not a religion, but an expression of a relationship that causes us to act graciously toward others. Notice that the text begins with the word "so" or "therefore." Notice the text is preceded by a section on prayer. It is "therefore" because of our relationship (or conversation) with God that we share a loving relationship with others.

One finds this in the great commandment of Mark 12:28-34. We first love God. Then we love our neighbor as ourselves.

I'm forever explaining to people that the Christian life is not just difficult. It is impossible. Unless you accept by faith God's love expressed by Jesus on the cross, unless you repent of your sinful selfishness, unless you receive the Holy Spirit and are transformed by his love, one can't hope to duplicate the golden rule in his lifestyle.

See that light bulb nearby that is not on? It looks like a light bulb. But on its own it cannot act like one. The switch must be on. The electricity must flow. Then it can do what it was meant to do — light up.

Likewise, I look like a man, but I cannot act like one until I make the connection to Christ and his power lives the life of Christ in me. Then, and only then, do I become a man in full, able to live the golden rule.

Suggested Prayer

Lord, fill me. Live your love in and through me. For Jesus' sake. Amen.

Door Number One Or Door Number Two?

Enter by the narrow gate. For wide is the gate and broad is the path that leads to destruction, and many enter through it. But small is the gate and narrow is the way that leads to life, and only a few find it.
— Matthew 7:13-14 (NIV)

The late Harvey Milton of Drakes Branch, Virginia, was a gentle giant in my life. When I moved to town in 1975, as a young pastor, he ran a feed store, was a deacon in the church, and took me under his care.

For over 35 years he lived in the same house, went to the same church, worked the same job, and loved the same wife and same Lord Jesus. I asked him about his life. He told me about being drafted into the Army and fighting World War II. Said he came home single, bristling with energy, not knowing what to do. "I stood at the crossroads just down the street," he confided. "To the north was the big city with its bright lights and promise of money. To the south was the bar, the girls, and a chance to drown all the horrors of war in pleasure. The other fork of the road led here — church and honest work and a home. This is the fork I took. Can't say as I ever regretted it."

In the Sermon on the Mount, Jesus brings us each to such a crossroad where we must make a choice. As we stand here thinking through our options, Christ offers us some advice. "Enter by the narrow gate. For wide is the gate and broad is the path that leads to destruction, and many enter through it. But small is the gate and narrow is the way that leads to life, and only a few find it."

Discern The Gate

There are three challenges for us here. First, we must discern the gate. There are but two. The "narrow gate," which few find, but it leads to life, and the wide gate many enter that leads to destruction.

I once tried to get into the University of North Carolina library. The night was cold and snowy and I literally circled the building pulling on one locked door after another. Finally, I backed up fifty yards and watched other students coming and going from the library until I discerned the gate, the one great door atop a huge flight of stairs that opened to all with a pull, not a push as I'd been doing. So, how does one come to God? Where is the door? All religions agree on two things: We once had a close relationship with God, and, somehow we lost it. Where religions disagree is on how that relationship is restored.

Two schools of thought come to bear here. Active religions say one must do something to earn God's love. The very word "religion" means "to bind back." *Re* means "again" and *legio* means "to bind." So it is that Judaism, Islam, and Buddhism teach human effort to make things right with God.

Christianity is different. Not an *active* religion, it is *reactive*. The gospel teaches that our relationship with God is so broken we cannot ourselves hope to fix it. Our sinful condition makes us poor in spirit, we mourn, we're meek, and we hunger for God (Matthew 5:3-6). When Jesus appears, offering us healing redemption by his sacrificial death on the cross, we respond with faith.

Thus our salvation comes from God's hand, not our own. We didn't choose Christ. He chose us. We didn't make things right, Jesus did.

"I am the door," Jesus said (John 10:7). He makes the way and we enter through his gate. The reformers of Europe in the 1500s put it succinctly, "Salvation is by grace alone, through Christ alone, by faith alone."

A Path To Decide

There is not only a gate to discern; there is also a path to decide.

The text mentions two paths. One is "broad," crowded, and leads to "destruction." The other is "narrow," sparsely traveled, and leads to life.

It is indeed strange how small things add up. Two gates, two paths — yet a huge difference in the end result. One ends in life, while the other leads to destruction.

High up in the Blue Ridge Mountains is a sign, "Eastern Continental Divide. Elevation 5,114 Feet." What that means is that all the rain water falling on one side of the sign dribbles into a creek, a stream, a river, and finally flows to the Atlantic Ocean. All the water dropping on the other side of the sign will flow into the Mississippi River. Thus does an inch end in miles of difference!

Here, Christ Jesus is teaching two gates side by side leading to two paths that quickly diverge and make all the difference in the end between life and destruction.

Christians are often accused of being narrow-minded. Yet Jesus said his path of life is "narrow," but the path of destruction is wide. Just so, a river has steep banks that narrow its flow in channels. A swamp has no banks, only a wideness that extends over the horizon. The prodigal son hated the narrowness of disciplined farm life at home with his father. He left for the wideness of the big city, life without boundaries, only to end up in the swampy mire of a tyrant's pigsty.

When I jumped into a taxi at the airport at 3 a.m. in Budapest, I gave the driver a very narrow address — a certain suburb, a certain street, a certain house. Not just any house would do. I wanted to go home, where I was expected.

After I discern the gate, I must decide the path, walk it out, as it were. I'm constantly narrowing my lifestyle; I'm constantly asking, "Will this help get me to where I'm wanting to go in life? Alcohol, cigarettes, lying, adultery, cowardice, neglect of church, self before Jesus, materialism — are these things helping me get there? Bible study, love, right behavior, trust, prayer, the Spirit, worship — there's the path!

We've a gate to discern and a path to decide.

Discipleship To Endure

The word "narrow" in the text has to do with the Greek word for tribulation. It means "to press in." As we enter the gospel gate, walk the path of faith, we are conformed, pressured, shaped by Jesus Christ.

In Romans 12:2 Paul wrote, "Do not be conformed to this world but be transformed by the renewal of your mind."

On a youth retreat years back, a junior high lad fell out of bed in the middle of the night. Lights came on and everyone asked, "Hey, Baldwin! Why'd you fall out of bed. You big baby!" He replied rather sheepishly, "I guess I sort of fell asleep too close to the place I got in." Isn't it so in the church! Far too many Christians discern the gate, decide the path, but rather than endure the discipleship, they promptly fall asleep. There is no church, no sacrifice, no prayer, no witness, no love, no service, no Bible study, and no growth. Yet notice in the text how way leads on to way. There is movement! A gate leads to a path that leads to a life. And there is a narrowing, a shaping pressure along the path that conforms us into the image of Jesus.

Conclusion

Jesus said "few" walk this path. But the sure reward of life is had at the close of the journey.

In Lewis Carroll's tale, *Alice in Wonderland*, young Alice stops to ask directions of a wise-looking bystander. "Which road should I take?" she inquires. "That all depends on where you are going," he said. "But I don't know where I am going," she confessed. "Then take any road," he said, "for one will get you there as good as the other."

Indeed! We've a gate to discern, a path to decide, and a discipleship to endure.

The text is both a warning and a promise. Will it be door number one or door number two? Christ beckons one and all with the first word of the text, "Enter!"

Suggested Prayer

Jesus, I want you. Amen.

The Heart Of The Matter

> *Beware of false prophets, who come to you in sheep's clothing but inwardly are ravenous wolves. You will know them by their fruits. Are grapes gathered from thorns, or figs from thistles? In the same way, every good tree bears good fruit, but the bad tree bears bad fruit. A good tree cannot bear evil fruit, nor can a bad tree bear good fruit. Every tree that does not bear good fruit is cut down and thrown into the fire. Thus you will know them by their fruits. Not everyone who says to me, "Lord, Lord," will enter the kingdom of heaven, but only the one who does the will of my Father in heaven. On that day many will say to me, "Lord, Lord, did we not prophesy in your name, and cast out demons in your name, and do many deeds of power in your name?" Then I will declare to them, "I never knew you; go away from me, you evildoers."*
> — Matthew 7:15-23 (NRSV)

Here are verses to give a Christian pause! Jesus is coming near the end of his sermon. And he is getting very serious with his listeners. He actually threatens judgment.

The crux of the text is in the phrase, "He that doeth the will of my Father in heaven." Christ wants his disciples not just to hear him out but to obey. Indeed, there are important verses to cause self-examination. As 1 Corinthians 10:12 warns, "Let every man who thinks he stands take heed to himself lest he fall."

There are three things for us here.

We Are Vulnerable

The text urges us to "watch out," to "beware," to "look out" for wolves in sheep's clothing.

The picture here is of a church being similar to a flock of sheep. Sheep do not see well. They are not swift. They have no fangs or claws or tusks to defend themselves. They must be tended carefully by a shepherd.

A good shepherd bonds with his lambs. He takes on their smell by wearing lamb skins. They memorize the sound of his voice, and they follow him.

Now, sheep have many enemies — snakes, lions, poisonous plants, and especially wolves. Why, it is terrifying to think of a hungry wolf wrapping himself in lambskins and coming among the flock. This, too, is a common fault in every church — appearing to be something we are not. Jesus warns us against such wolfish predators. He calls them "false prophets."

It was Zephaniah who lamented, "Her officials within her are like wolves tearing their prey ..." (Zephaniah 3:3). The apostle Paul warns the Ephesian church, "I know that after I leave, savage wolves will come in among you and will not spare the flock. Even from your own number men will arise and distort the truth in order to draw away disciples after them" (Acts 20:29-30 NRSV).

Indeed! Such wolves are the bane of the church! Have you seen what a lecherous man can do among the females of a singles group? Or what a false teacher in his clerical robe, all smiles and friendship, can do from the pulpit? Or what one slanderer can do with his whispering tongue behind the scenes?

Beware — watch out! There are some who come into the church for an agenda not that of Jesus Christ. They are here for prestige, for their own ideas, for ego, to lord it over others, to take advantage of folks.

Yes, Jesus wants us to know we are vulnerable.

Vigilant

Jesus wants us to be vigilant. In the text Christ points out, "By their fruits you shall know them." The Lord goes on to inquire, "Does one gather grapes from thorns? Do figs come from thistles?" "You will recognize them by their fruit," Jesus said.

As with trees and fruit, so with Christians and their deeds, their character. Galatians 5 tells us what to look for in false prophets and true ministers. The acts of sinful humanity include, "sexual immorality, impurity, debauchery, idolatry, witchcraft, hatred, discord, jealousy, fits of rage, selfish ambition, dissensions, factions, envy, drunkenness, orgies, and the like" (Galatians 5:19-21a). But the fruit of the righteous is "love, joy, peace, patience, kindness, goodness, gentleness, faithfulness, and self-control" (Galatians 5:22-23a).

One can fake words. But it's hard to fake character. One can prop up appearances for awhile, but a life of good deeds is unmistakable.

"Test the spirits," the scripture says in 1 John 4:1.

Do elders and church leaders meet the standards of 1 Timothy 3 in their knowledge of scripture? Do they meet the standards in their marriage or with their children? How do they stand in their business dealings?

Yes, we are vulnerable. Yes, we must be vigilant. All this from Jesus. Now this:

We Are Victorious

Christ said there is a day of judgment coming. On that day, "Not everyone who says to me, 'Lord! Lord!' will enter the kingdom of heaven."

Who will not enter? Who will hear the shaming words, "Depart from me. I never knew you!"?

Jesus said he does not know those who substitute emotional fervor for faithful obedience. Twice in the text he speaks of those who cry out, "Lord! Lord!" You know the sort. Into sensuous Christianity, riding the crest of feel-good experiences, they cry, "Lord, Lord!" on Sunday and then divorce their spouse on Monday. Jesus said, "I don't know you!"

Then there are those who substitute words for obedience, "Lord! Lord, did we not prophesy in your name!" Aye! This is the one who talks a good talk but refuses to walk it out. There is a radical disconnect between his beliefs and his behavior. And Jesus said, "I don't know you."

There is also one who substitutes works, however miraculous, for faithfulness. "Lord, Lord, did we not prophesy in your name? Did we not cast out demons? Did we not perform miracles?" And Jesus said again, "I do not know you! Depart from me!"

Works are never good enough to save us. Never enough feelings or words. Only faithfulness in Christ that leads to "doing the will of my heavenly Father."

Listen carefully, my friend. Bend your ear down really close. Understanding can wait. Obedience cannot. Feelings can wait. Obedience cannot. Fun can wait. Popularity can wait. Words can wait. But obedience cannot. It is the heart of the matter.

In the epistle of James we are told three times that, "Faith without works is dead." In Matthew 25:21 Jesus told the faithful steward, "Well done!" He did not say, "Well said" nor "Well felt" nor "Well thought." He said, "Well done!"

Conclusion

A young divinity school student preached his first sermon. Insecure, he said to the professor, "My sermon will do, won't it?" "Do what?" the teacher asked. "Will it beat them down in guilt? Or will it whip up their emotions? Will it stir their intellect? Or will it lead to faith that honors Christ in obedience?"

A mother with three unruly sons was constantly being told by them how much they loved her. Finally she said to them all, "I just wish you'd stop telling me how much you love me and show it by how you act." Christ's sentiment exactly when he said, "Not everyone who says to me, 'Lord! Lord!' will enter the kingdom of heaven, but only those who do the will of my heavenly Father."

Suggested Prayer

Jesus, I trust you. Let my faith lead to obedience for Christ's sake. Amen.

The Measure Of Success

> *"Everyone then who hears these words of mine and acts on them will be like a wise man who built his house on rock. The rain fell, the floods came, and the winds blew and beat on that house, but it did not fall, because it had been founded on rock. And everyone who hears these words of mine and does not act on them will be like a foolish man who built his house on sand. The rain fell, and the floods came, and the winds blew and beat against that house, and it fell — and great was its fall!" Now when Jesus had finished saying these things, the crowds were astounded at his teaching, for he taught them as one having authority, and not as their scribes.*
> — Matthew 7:24-29 (NRSV)

> *...for, while physical training is of some value, godliness is valuable in every way, holding promise for both the present life and the life to come.*
> — 1 Timothy 4:8 (NRSV)

Erma Bombeck, the very funny news columnist, wrote the following.

> *I can't remember the name of the man who spoke at my high school commencement, but I remember what he said. He told us the future of the world rested on our shoulders and he charged us with finding our destiny and fulfilling it. He went on to say we alone must cure disease, hunger, and poverty throughout the world, and above all, we must find success.*
>
> *I glanced over at Jack, the class deficient who couldn't even find his parents after they parked the car, and I got an uneasy feeling. Not only that, but for those of us who planned to sleep in for a week, the speech was very depressing, as it seemed to call for a lot of work from such a small class.*
>
> *After the speech, the entire group scrambled out of the auditorium in search of success as if it were the*

first item on a scavenger hunt. We had no idea what it was, where to look for it, how much it cost, whether it was in season or what it looked like, but from that day on we got up early in the morning and pursued it till late at night. Sometimes we heard that another classmate had found it, but when we confronted him, he assured us that if he had, he would be happier.

By our tenth reunion no one had found it yet. The men struggled in their jobs and fertilized their lawns on weekends, and the women raised babies and polished the bottoms of their Revere Ware. It seemed we were never rich enough, thin enough, or important enough to qualify for success.

I've spent a lifetime trying to figure out who has success.[1]

What is success?

Is it in the length of life? Like a string — the longer it is the better? Methuselah is the oldest man in the Bible. He lived over 960 years yet that's all we know of him. There is no record of any of his accomplishments. Mozart, Shubert, and Jesus all died in their thirties. Yet each one left us so much!

Peter Marshall wrote, "The measure of a life is not in its duration but its donation."

Is success, then, in the width of one's life? The man of the twentieth century who ruled more real estate than any other was Adolf Hitler. Yet who would want to be like him?

Then there is height, forever measured by popularity, fame, and wealth. Yet many have reached the top of this ladder only to find it leaning against the wrong wall. Witness the life of Marilyn Monroe. She committed suicide, and she seemingly had it all!

If success is not in length or height, what's left? There is depth. Jesus told the parable of the wise and foolish builders. Two men so alike: both had families, were ambitious, were willing to work. Both built wide and high and long, yet one built on sand and without depth. While the other took time to dig a deep foundation upon rock. And when a terrific storm blew in, the one house collapsed while the other stood.

As an example of depth, consider John the Baptist. His little life had no length or width or height. He was single, had a poor wardrobe, and was frugal. He had a strange diet, lived in a desert home, had no book published, and he never built anything. He never held an office; his was a simple message of repentance. At the height of his ministry, his followers abandoned him to follow Jesus! All John said was, "He must increase. I must decrease." Soon John was jailed for criticizing the king's sexual choices. There, in prison, John was beheaded.

He was not what we'd call a success today. He was not the sort of minister who'd be invited to a Washington prayer breakfast, preach on television, or hold sway in some great cathedral. Yet John the Baptist has the unusual distinction of being the only person in scripture twice called "great" by God. At his birth, an angel declared, "He will be great before the Lord" (Luke 1:15). At his death Jesus affirmed, "I say to you, among those born of woman there has risen no one greater than John" (Matthew 11:11).

With all of this in mind, why not take a few moments and think through success from a biblical perspective in the pages of this book?

In 1 Timothy 4:8, the veteran apostle Paul, writing to the young Timothy, observed, "For while bodily training is of some value, godliness is of value in every way, as it holds promise for the present life and also for the life to come." Here success is divided into two categories: First is worldly success that Paul calls physical training. Today we'd refer to it as material success or prosperity. This sort of achievement is judged without reference to Christ or eternity.

The second form of success is spiritual, which Paul called godliness, and "has value in this life and the one to come." Thus it is measured with reference to Christ and eternity.

Worldly Success

At the risk of sounding like a college professor let me hasten to point out that physical training, worldly success, can be divided into two categories: public and private.

Private Success

Consider the man of solid character, who is married, with fine children, and who does work that is challenging and fulfilling. He pays his bills on time, vacations three weeks a year, is respected by his friends and neighbors, loved by his family, enjoys good health, and is proud of his seven grandchildren. He dies at a ripe old age, is decently buried, and is appropriately mourned.

By no means is this person in the majority. With so much divorce, insanity, poverty, ill-health, depression, war, and such, this man ran the gauntlet of life successfully in his own private world.

Publicly, however, the man was a failure! My son and I were walking on the beach. The sand was hard and compacted. My son observed, "Look, Dad! We're not leaving any footprints!" It is possible to go through life like that — to right no wrong, cure no ill, create no art, marshall no army, and to never manage to scratch one's initials on the walls of history.

Such a one's epitaph might read, "Beneath this stone John Anderson lies. Nobody laughs and nobody cries. Where he is going and how he fares, nobody knows, and nobody cares."

Public Success

The other side of private, worldly success is public success. This sort of achievement discounts your personal life. Feelings do not matter. Neither does character or one's marriage, children, or decency.

Public success basically looks for height or length or width in one of three areas: beauty, brains, and brawn. Beauty as with Marilyn Monroe. Brains as with Albert Einstein. Brawn as with Michael Jordan.

What this standard admires is popularity, fame, glamour, power, money, influence. This is the measure of public success! So, you have your Ted Kennedys, your Madonnas, and such.

Unfortunately we are all descendants of Adam and Eve. As such, we've inherited their sinful nature. First John 2:16 calls it the "lust of the flesh, the lust of the eyes, the pride of life." That translates into a life focused on pleasure, power, and prestige. We've built an economy on all of this: "Bigger! Better! More! Now!"

The Bible brings a strong indictment against all of this! In Luke 16:15, Jesus said, "What is highly esteemed among men is an abomination to God." In God's order, the first shall be the last, the greatest shall be a servant, his strength is manifest in our weakness, and humility is better than pride.

If you wish to see this contrasted, read of the worldly Babylon described in Revelation 18:11-13. A list of sinful society's values is made there. Gold is first. Then silver, oil, wheat, and finally people. Next, turn to Revelation 21. There heaven is described. God is on his throne. People are soothed in his lap and gold is used to pave the streets.

Here in Babylon we use people and love things. But in heaven we love God and people and use things.

So worldly success can be both public and private. The hard part is getting the two together.

I've a friend who is an NCAA football coach. For years he has striven mightily to reach the top. A few years ago he took his team to the national championship game and won. Flying home he said, "I really felt like I was somebody. Number one in the nation! I wore the championship ring!" But when he got home late at night he found a note from his wife on the dining room table. It said she couldn't live with him any longer, and she was divorcing him. Today that coach will show you his championship ring and tell you, "I'd rather have my wedding ring than this ring any day!"

A few magnificent souls do manage to achieve both public and private worldly success. In fact, our generation has made a religion out of the pursuit. We call it being a "yuppie." Its motto is "You can have it all!" Yet Jesus issued a one-sentence indictment against such a life: "For what does it profit a man if he gains the whole world and loses or forfeits himself?"

Spiritual Success

The second category of success Paul calls godliness and it "holds promise for this life and the life to come." This achievement is measured with reference to Christ and eternity.

There are but three hallmarks of spiritual success. The first is Christlike love. First Corinthians 13 reminds us that the greatest is love.

A number of years ago I was called to the poor side of town across the tracks. It was a mill house with four rooms and peeling paint. Wilma lived there. Her elderly mother had died. The funeral fell to me.

I knocked on the door and was invited into the living room crowded with about fifteen people. They were having a wake. In this part of the country when you die, they stick you in a box, and your friends gather back at the house to eat fried chicken and chocolate pie.

I could see the fatigue on Wilma's face. I hugged her, assured her I would take care of the funeral service. We prayed. As I was leaving, someone else rapped on the front door. Wilma's face fell. She had that "Oh-no, not-another-hand-to-shake" look of exhaustion. The gentleman at the door came in. He wore khakis and work shoes. He still had lint in his hair from his shift at the textile plant.

He took Wilma's hands, looked her in the eye, and said, "You have my deepest sympathy, but I have not come to visit! I came to polish your shoes. If you'll gather them all, I'll fix them so you and your children will look nice at the church service."

Driving home that night I told the Lord, "I don't want to be a great preacher, to be rich or well-educated, or even famous. I just want to be a good lover like that mill worker who knows how to polish shoes."

The second mark of spiritual success is servanthood. In Matthew 20:25-27, Jesus said, "You know how Gentiles love power and love to lord it over other people. It shall not be so among you. But the greatest among you shall be a servant."

The modern church has such a long way to go here. Have you noticed how we introduce our leaders?

"Doctor So-and-so was educated at ... He is a most sought after speaker ... Last month he attended the Washington prayer breakfast as the keynote speaker ... His honors include...."

We even judge his merits by the sort of car he drives, the number of people who watch his television show, and how big his wife's hairdo is!

Contrast this with how the apostle Paul introduced himself in Romans 1:1. "Paul, a servant of Jesus Christ...."

By definition, a servant is someone who enjoys helping someone else succeed.

Witness the life of Johann Sebastian Bach. A modest man of deep, abiding faith, he held a series of obscure musical posts for unappreciative churches. He never commanded a large salary, and he never traveled outside Germany. He simply wrote music to celebrate Jesus Christ in the next worship service. Songs like "Sleepers Awake! A Voice Is Calling," "Jesu, Joy Of Man's Desiring," "A Mighty Fortress Is Our God," and "Now Before Thy Throne I Come" poured from his heart.

Bach was never aware of the greatness of his work. He died blind and his music was forgotten until Felix Mendelsson revived it years later. Today this quiet servant's music is the source of solace and renewal for millions.

The third hallmark of spiritual success is faithfulness with talents. In Matthew 25:21, Jesus told the parable of the talents, saying, "Work with these until I come." Those who did so were rewarded — "Well done, good and faithful servant!"

Jesus said we are not all equal in talents. Some have ten! Others have five. Some have two. But each of us has at least one! God has given each of us something to do, and we can be faithful in that task.

A friend of mine served in World War II. He was a sailor. When I asked him what he did, he didn't want to tell me. I persisted, and he finally confessed that he was a garbage grinder on an aircraft carrier. Four stories below deck, he received all the trash, sewage, and worn-out clothing. He ground it in a huge machine, mixed it with sea water, and flushed it out the bottom of the boat.

He explained that the German wolfpack submariners would look for trash floating in the sea and follow it to the fleet. So the Navy began to grind its waste so subs couldn't find a trail to follow.

Such an unheroic, smelly, thankless job! How would you like to give that answer to your grandchild's question, "Papa, what did you do in the war?" But I tell you, such a job done faithfully saves ships!

John Calvin said, "There is no work however vile or sordid that does not glisten before God."

What is spiritual success? It is Christlike love, servanthood, and faithfulness with one's talents.

Conclusion

What about you? How do you measure up to success? Some go forth in life and gain fame, wealth, and honors in public life. In private life we may even demonstrate love, peace, and solid character.

All this and it is possible to be a spiritual success as well. There is nothing wrong with trying to be successful in every area of one's being.

Others of us, however, are destined to plod along in anonymity. It is our lot to clap for others as they pass by in parade. It is sadly true that many of us may be little noticed in our passing. Perhaps we will have a two-line obituary in the local newspaper.

But take comfort! For surely God knows.

I'd like to close with a favorite poem called "God's Hall of Fame."

> *Your name may not appear down here in this world's hall of fame.*
> *In fact you may be so unknown that no one knows your name.*
> *The Oscars here may pass you by, and neon lights of blue!*
> *But if you love and serve the Lord then I have news for you.*
> *This hall of fame is only good as long as time shall be.*
> *But keep in mind, God's hall of fame is for eternity.*
> *To have your name inscribed up there is greater yet by far,*

Than all the halls of fame down here and every man-made star.
This crowd on earth may soon forget the heroes of the past.
They cheer like mad until you fall and that's how long you last.
But God, he never does forget and in His hall of fame,
By just believing in His Son inscribed you'll find your name.
I'll tell you, friend, I wouldn't trade my name, however small,
That's written there beyond the stars in that celestial hall,
For any famous name on earth or glory that they share.
I'd rather be an unknown here and have my name up there.

— Author unknown

Suggested Prayer

Father, bring my life to you in Jesus Christ, and teach me how to build on your rock. Amen.

---

1. Erma Bombeck, *If Life Is A Bowl Of Cherries, What Am I Doing In The Pits?* (New York: Fawcett, 1985).

Afterword

Most scholars agree that with the writing of Malachi the prophet the Old Testament canon was closed. This was around 400 BC.

Thus God had delivered the law to his people.

There followed 400 years that we call the intertestamental period, sometimes known as the silent era. God used these centuries to give the world the best of Greek, Jewish, and Roman cultures. The Jews gave the world good religion. The Greeks gave us good thinking and a common language throughout the Mediterranean community of nations. The Romans gave us good government, a postal system, roads, and a prolonged time of peace.

Into the end of this era and all it needed and offered, Jesus Christ was born. The scriptures call it, "The fullness of time" (Galatians 4:4). Indeed, the stage of history was well set for the appearance of Jesus, Messiah.

Image: God has not spoken since Malachi. It's been 400 years! Suddenly Jesus Christ appeared, and the first thing out of his mouth was the Sermon on the Mount.

What Christ uttered in his mountaintop message could not have been more shocking, more stretching, more ... mind-blowing to the apostles. "You have heard it said...." Jesus intoned, "but I say ..." (Matthew 5:21-22, 27, 31). It represented a whole new way of looking at religion.

For the Jews, the law of God was a bar of soap with which they could wash. In Jesus' day the Pharisees especially believed they were justified. Through their own efforts at keeping the law they were made self-righteous before God.

Ah, but Jesus spoke to deprogram his disciples of such an assurance. He pointed out the law as indicative of God's very character. It was in no way a bar of soap with which to cleanse ourselves. Rather it was a mirror in which we peer to see ourselves as sinners.

A mirror has diagnostic powers. It can tell you your face is grimy, but it has no curative powers. It cannot clean your face.

We look into the law to see our sins, and we fall to our knees asking the holy God to show us mercy because we are helpless to be clean.

The self-righteous cannot do this. Only those who know their poverty of spirit, mourn over their sin, are meekly teachable, and are hungry to devour the righteousness of God as offered in Christ. Thus the Beatitudes are the end-all be-all of Christian faith.

Believe me, this struggle to overcome self-righteousness is not over in our day. How many of us come to Christ as sinners, then join a church only to spend the rest of our lives trying to prove we are not sinners?

The word *religion* is a Latin word. The prefix *re* means again. The root word *ligio* means to bind, as in ligaments that bind our bones together. Religion means "to bind back."

All major religions agree on two facts: God is our creator and somehow our fellowship with him is broken. Where religions disagree is on the third point: How can that relationship be restored? Here religions divide into two camps:

1. Active religion says one must do something to earn God's love. For Jews it means keeping the law. For Muslims it means following the five pillars of Islam.
2. Reactive religion has Christianity as its only brand. The gospel of Christ teaches that our relationship with God is so shattered it is hopeless for us to try to repair it.

There is good news! God himself in the death of Christ atones for our sins and fixes our fellowship with him once and for all. What is left for us to do is respond with wonder, awe, and trust. Or, as it were, to react according to the Beatitudes: mournful poverty and hunger for God's provender.

The remainder of the Sermon on the Mount shows the law in all its through-going demands. Not satisfied with appearance management, Jesus brought the law into one's inner life. He spoke not just against murder but also against anger. Not just against adultery but against lust as well. All this to detoxify us from any self-deceiving notion that we can keep the law and satisfy its demands upon us.

What is preached in the Sermon on the Mount is an ethic of pure grace toward others. "Are you prepared to live like this?" Jesus is inquiring, "To forgive? To give away your coat? To go the second mile? To resist not one who is evil? To love your enemy?"

"How badly you need grace!" Christ is saying. "How badly the world is in need of grace, also. Are you prepared to offer it to them by your life whatever the cost?" This is the radical message of Christ's words.

Some try to make the Sermon on the Mount a Bible unto itself. It cannot be so. In this sermon there is no mention of repentance, the cross, the second coming, or even the Holy Spirit. All are doctrines central to Christianity, which find no voice in this message.

Clearly this is a contextual message meant to challenge self-righteousness by crushing our delusions about ourselves under the full weight of the law. As the incarnation of Christ worked itself out in Christ's death on the cross, a radical shift took place between the Old Testament and the New Testament. This shift is between self-efforts at righteousness and God's efforts in our behalf on the cross, as well as between law's demands and grace's provisions. Clearly Jesus left it up to the apostle Paul in his epistles to spell out all this new gospel means in the dynamic shift that occurred at Christ's appearing. Paul would write in Galatians 3:10-11: "For all who rely on works of the law are under a curse; for it is written, 'Cursed be every one who does not abide by all things written in the book of the law, and do them.' Now it is evident that no man is justified before God by the law; for 'he through faith is righteous shall live.' "

In certain South American nations there have been military coups. A radical insurgency toppled the government and got on the radio to proclaim a new regime. Jesus is doing no less in this, his finest sermon. He came to overthrow our smug systems of pride and our self-righteous faith. "The spirit of the Lord is upon me, because he has anointed me to preach good news to the poor ..." (Luke 4:18).

Oh, how I long to be in that number of poor servants of grace!

www.ingramcontent.com/pod-product-compliance
Lightning Source LLC
Chambersburg PA
CBHW071145160426
43196CB00011B/2017